1 Introduction

1.1 What is audit and assurance and how does it fit within the Professional Stage?

Structure

The syllabus has been designed to develop core technical, commercial, and ethical skills and knowledge in a structured and rigorous manner.

The diagram below shows the twelve modules at the Professional Stage, where the focus is on the acquisition and application of technical skills and knowledge, and the Advanced Stage which comprises two technical integration modules and the Case Study.

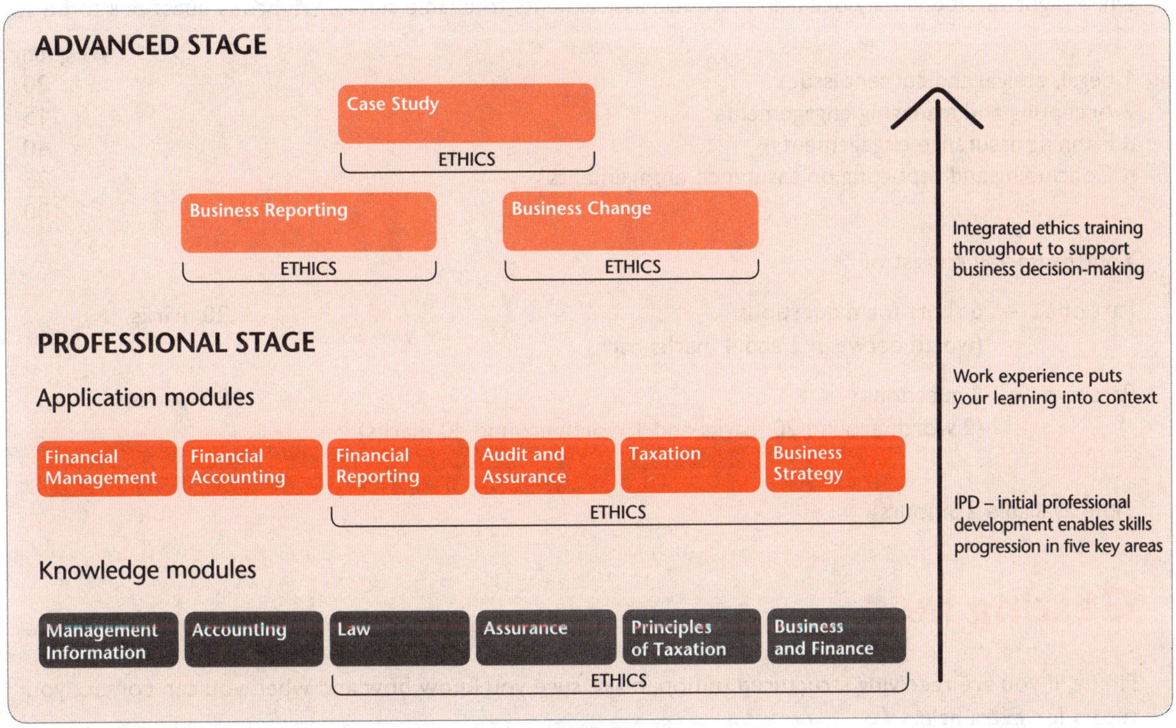

The knowledge base

The aim of the Assurance module is to ensure students understand the assurance process and fundamental principles of ethics and are able to contribute to the assessment of internal controls and gathering of evidence on an assurance engagement.

Progression to application level

The knowledge base put into place at Assurance is taken further in the application level module, where the aim will be to enable students to understand the critical aspects of managing an assurance engagement. This includes acceptance, planning, managing, concluding and reporting.

Progression to advanced stage

The advanced level papers – Business reporting (BR) and Business change (BC) – then take things further again. The aims being that students can apply analysis techniques, technical knowledge and professional skills to resolve real-life assurance issues faced by businesses.

The above illustrates how this paper is an important stepping stone, linking the knowledge and application of assurance to complex real world problems.

2 Audit and Assurance

2.1 Module aim

To develop students' understanding of the critical aspects of managing an assurance engagement (including audit engagements): acceptance, planning, managing, concluding and reporting.

2.2 Specification grid

This grid shows the relative weightings of subjects within this module and should guide the relative study time spent on each. Over time the marks available in the assessment will equate to the weightings below, while slight variations may occur in individual assessments to enable suitably rigorous questions to be set.

	Weighting (%)
1 Legal, ethical and current issues	20
2 Accepting and managing engagements	15
3 Planning assurance engagements	40
4 Concluding and reporting on assurance engagements	25
	100

Your exam will consist of

Part one	–	6 short form questions (worth between 2 and 4 marks each)	20 marks
Part two	–	3 questions (2 worth around 20 marks and 1 worth around 40 marks)	80 marks

Time available 2.5 hours

3 Getting help

Firstly, if you are receiving structured tuition, make sure you know how and when you can contact your tutors for extra help.

Identify a work colleague who is qualified, or has at least passed the paper you are studying for, who is willing to help if you have questions.

Form a group with a small number of other students. You can help each other and study together, providing informal support.

Go to www.icaew.com/students and look under student societies, to find your local society and find out what additional support they offer.

If you need further information on studying, please refer to the Study Guide for each subject. This includes information on planning your studies. These can be found at www.icaew.com/students

Call +44 (0) 1908 248040 or email studentsupport@icaew.com with non-technical queries.

Watch the ICAEW website for future support initiatives.

The Institute of Chartered Accountants in England and Wales

AUDIT AND ASSURANCE

Professional Stage Application Level

For exams in 2010

Study Manual

THE INSTITUTE OF CHARTERED ACCOUNTANTS IN ENGLAND AND WALES

www.icaew.com

Audit and Assurance
The Institute of Chartered Accountants in England and Wales Professional Stage

ISBN: 978-1-84152-688-1
First edition 2007
Second edition 2008
Third edition 2009

British Library Cataloguing-in-Publication Data
A catalogue record for this book has been applied for from the British Library

Printed in Great Britain

Your learning materials are printed on paper sourced from sustainable, managed forests.

Welcome to the ICAEW

Welcome to The Institute of Chartered Accountants in England and Wales (ICAEW).

In addition to the ACA, the ICAEW offers a Certificate in Finance, Accounting, and Business (CFAB), a certificate in International Financial Reporting Standards, the first global Corporate Finance qualification, a Business Sustainability training programme and Diplomas in Charity Accounting and Financial Strategy.

I'd like to remind you that the ICAEW is much more than just the body that awards you your ACA or CFAB qualification – we can be useful to you in many ways, throughout your career.

As a world-leading professional accountancy body, we provide leadership and practical support to over 148,000 members and students in more than 160 countries. We work with governments, regulators and industry to ensure the highest professional standards are maintained, and the skills of our members are constantly developed, recognised and valued.

If you are studying for the ACA, you will develop your professional skills through the initial professional development (IPD) programme. Once you are qualified, you will enhance these skills through continuing professional development (CPD), which ensures that you keep up-to-date in your relevant field.

The ICAEW is recognised as a thought leader, and the Institute's technical operations and support services provide technical expertise and the latest knowledge of best practice. The ICAEW provides expert input to governments and policy makers worldwide, working in the public interest to influence both policy and legislation. See page xx for more details, or visit www.icaew.com and click on 'Technical & Business Topics'.

The ICAEW faculties, which include the Audit and Assurance Faculty, provide additional specialised support to their members in key areas and invaluable networking opportunities. The ICAEW special interest groups further extend the building of sector-specific knowledge within the profession. The groups provide support, conferences, information and representation for members working in – or working for clients in – specific sectors. As a student of the ICAEW you can take advantage of free membership of a faculty or special interest group for one year during your training – choose the faculty that best suits your career needs and see how it can help you.

At the start of your career, our Young Professionals network is a vital resource to link you directly with peers and colleagues with similar interests and aspirations. Young Professional members meet regularly to share ideas, and to network.

To help you with the latest information, topics of interest and guidance you can always turn to our free and confidential Ethics Advisory Service, our Institute magazine *Accountancy*, the dedicated student publication *VITAL* and the student support helpline on +44 (0)1908 248 040. The dedicated student area of the website gives you access to key resources for your exams and work experience requirements – visit www.icaew.com/students. Furthermore, our Library & Information Service, available to all ACA members and students, is always there to guide you to the best sources of information on all subjects, utilising a wide range of online databases, books, journals, and the internet.

You can, of course, find more information about all of the above at www.icaew.com

So make use of your Institute – both before and after you qualify – that's what it's there for.

Good luck!

Michael Izza
Chief Executive
ICAEW

Welcome to the ICAEW

Welcome to the Institute of Chartered Accountants in England and Wales (ICAEW).

In addition to the ACA, the ICAEW offers a Certificate in Finance, Accounting and Business (CFAB), [illegible] Corporate Finance qualification, [illegible] Charity Accounting and Finance [illegible]

[illegible] ICAEW [illegible] ACA [illegible]

As a [illegible] practical support to over [illegible] members [illegible] government, regulators and [illegible] developed, recognised and valued.

If you are studying for the ACA, you will develop your professional skills through [illegible]. Once you are qualified, you will enhance these skills through continuing professional development (CPD) [illegible] keep up to date in your relevant field.

The ICAEW [illegible] technical [illegible] expert input [illegible] government and policy makers [illegible] click on Technical & Business Topics.

The ICAEW faculties, which include the Audit and Assurance Faculty, provide additional specialised support to their members [illegible]. The ICAEW special interest groups [illegible] the profession. The groups provide support [illegible] specific [illegible] special interest group [illegible]. Choose the faculty that best suits your career needs and see how it can help you.

At the start of your career, our Young Professionals network [illegible] colleagues [illegible] Young Professional members [illegible]

To help you [illegible] topics of interest and guidance you can [illegible] ICAEW [illegible] Library [illegible] wide range of online databases, books, journals and the Internet.

You can find more information about all of the above at www.icaew.com

So make [illegible] your membership [illegible] before and after you qualify [illegible]

Michael Izza
Chief Executive
ICAEW

Contents

The sample paper questions for Audit and Assurance appear as self-test questions (STQ) in this study manual as follows:

Sample paper question	Chapter
Q1 Harmony	6 (STQ 9)
Q2 Jay, Finch and Sparrow	7 (STQ 6) and 13 (STQ 11)
Q3 Jog	5 (STQ 9) and 7 (STQ 7)

The sample paper questions for Audit and Assurance appear as self-test questions (STQ) in this study manual as follows:

Q1 Harmony	4 (STQ [illegible])
Q2 Jay Plush and Sons [illegible]	[illegible] (STQ [illegible]) and 13 (STQ [illegible])
Q3 Jog	[illegible] (STQ [illegible]) and [illegible] (STQ 7)

4 Skills assessment guide

4.1 Introduction

As a Chartered Accountant in the business world, you will require the knowledge and skills to interpret financial and other numerical and business data, and communicate the underlying issues to your clients. In a similar way to the required knowledge, the ACA syllabus has been designed to develop your professional skills in a progressive manner. These skills are broadly categorised as:

- Assimilating and using information
- Structuring problems and solutions
- Applying judgement
- Drawing conclusions and making recommendations

4.2 Assessing your professional skills

Set out below is a pictorial representation of the different mix of knowledge and skills that will be assessed in the examinations that comprise the ACA qualification.

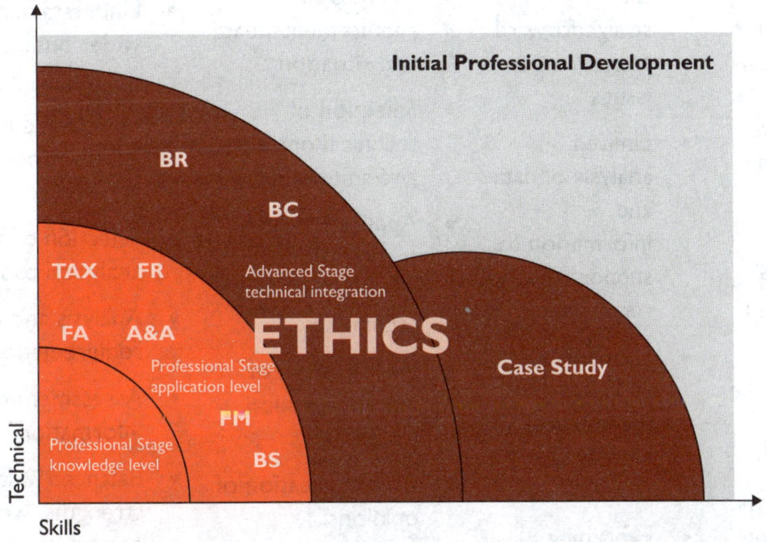

In the six Knowledge Modules of the Professional Stage, you will have experienced a limited amount of skills assessment, generally 'Assimilating and using information'. Most of the questions were set in a context that required you to identify the piece of knowledge that was being assessed. In the Application Modules of the Professional Stage, the context of the examination will be simple business situations, from which you will be required to determine the relevant information to answer the questions.

To be successful in the Audit and Assurance examination, you will need a strong core of subject knowledge and a good understanding of how this knowledge should be applied in simple situations. You will be expected to apply your judgement to determine the relevance and importance of the different information provided and to recommend suitable courses of action.

4.3 Assessment grids

The following pages set out the learning outcomes for Audit and Assurance that are addressed under each of the four skills areas. In addition, for each skills area, there is a description of:

- The specific skills that are assessed
- How these skills are assessed

Using these grids will enable you to determine how the examination paper will be structured and to consider whether your knowledge of Audit and Assurance is sufficiently strong to enable you to apply it in the required manner.

Skills Progression through the ACA Qualification			
Professional Stage		**Advanced Stage**	
Knowledge modules	**Application modules**	**Technical integration modules**	**Case Study**
Core technical knowledge and skills	**Technical knowledge and skills and practical application**	**Technical integration skills applied in complex scenarios**	**Analytical, evaluative and integration skills applied in scenarios of major complexity**
• Understanding the required data or information as given • Recognition of the technical or professional issue based on knowledge learned • Performing the required calculations • Identifying the best explanation • Identifying the best solution or steps	• Understanding the requirement • Understanding the straightforward scenario and issues • Limited analysis of data and information to support the requirement • Drawing upon technical and professional knowledge learned • Explaining, listing, drafting or stating briefly the issues or solution • Preparing, describing, outlining the advice, report, notes required	• Identifying technical issues and business implications • Analysis of requirements, data and situation • Selection of technical options and solutions • Application of technical rules, models and techniques • Identification of risks and ethical issues • Communication of opinions, reservations, advice, recommendations, plans, solutions, options and risks including business implications	• Identification of business and technical issues • Application of technical knowledge to identified issues • Understanding of scenario and wider business issues • Understanding of the relevance of data and information based on learnt, experienced and inferred knowledge • Selection of appropriate analytical tools • Analysis and evaluation of requirements, situation and data • Assessment of quality of information • Balanced judgement of priorities, strengths, weaknesses, opportunities and threats • Consideration of other perspectives, including competitive reaction and internal reaction • Conclusions and recommendations based on evidence, implications, assumptions and information generated
	Communication and articulation skills (applied progressively in more complex situations) • Structure, conciseness and clarity in presentation of data and written work • Integration and positioning of data within and alongside written work • Tact in presentation • Objectivity in presentation • Suitability of format and language		

Audit & Assurance Learning outcomes	Assessed skills	How skills are assessed
Assimilating and using information		
1d Discuss the purpose of laws, standards etc surrounding assurance work 1e Explain the standard-setting process 1f Explain significant current assurance issues 1g and 1h Explain how national legislation affects assurance/audit and appointment/removal of auditors 1i Explain the principles behind, and harmonisation of, auditing requirements in different jurisdictions 1j Describe the principal causes of audit failure 2c Discuss the agreement of the scope and terms of an assurance engagement 2e Discuss the principles and purpose of quality control of assurance engagements 2g Describe how quality can be monitored and controlled through external procedures 2h Discuss how an audit engagement is obtained 2i Discuss the issues and risks regarding accepting an audit engagement 3a Explain the importance of understanding the business when planning an engagement 3h Discuss the benefits and limitations of analytical procedures at the planning stage 3k Outline relevant aspects of employment and social security law 3l and 3m Discuss the differences between the audits of non-specialised profit oriented, specialised profit oriented and not-for-profit entities	• Reading and understanding subject matter • Accessing, evaluating and managing information provided in a few defined sources • Operating to a brief in structured situations • Explaining the nature of ethics and its significance in the business environment • Understanding the public interest and social responsibility • Understanding the importance of contributing to the profession • Appreciating the ethos and culture of the accountancy profession • Understanding the role of the professional accountant within the public interest, practice and business contexts and the regulatory structure of the profession • Understanding the importance of ethical behaviour to a professional and the reasons for the adoption of ethical codes by professions acting in the public interest • Understanding of the pressures on professional ethical behaviour, including the interaction between professional ethics and the law and other value systems	Questions will contain both structured and unstructured detail that candidates have to understand Requirements will include demonstrating an understanding of: • The regulatory, professional and ethical issues relevant to accepting, carrying out and managing assurance engagements • How quality assurance processes mitigate risks

4a Describe the procedures designed to identify subsequent events 4h Explain the elements of the auditor's report issued		
Structuring problems and solutions		
1a Identify professional and ethical issues that may arise during an assurance engagement 2a and 2j Identify the legal etc considerations that must be considered before accepting an assurance or audit engagement 2b Identify the sources of liability arising from an assurance engagement 2f Demonstrate how the assurance function can be monitored through review procedures 3b Identify ways of gaining knowledge and understanding of a client's business 3d Identify the risks relating to a set of business processes and assess their implications 3e Identify the risks arising from error, fraud and non-compliance with law etc 3g and 3k Identify the components of risk 3j Determine an approach appropriate for an engagement for a specified organisation which addresses: • Possible reliance on controls (including those within IT systems) • Possible reliance on the work of internal audit or other experts • Possible reliance on the work of another auditor • Probable extent of tests of control and of substantive procedures, including analytical procedures • Nature and extent of client-generated information • Probable number, timing,	• Understanding data and information given: identifying and understanding issues arising in straight-forward scenarios • Using the data and information given: understanding requirements, analysing data and information to support requirement • Drawing upon technical and professional knowledge learnt to analyse issues • Understanding the workings of, and controls within, an organisational framework • Applying knowledge from different technical areas: analysing problems that combine technical skills in a single disciplinary environment • Using new concepts: evaluating new ideas and concepts • Appreciating the ethical dimensions of situations, problems and proposals • Identifying and selecting appropriate courses of action using an ethical framework • Financial data analysis: performing the required calculations; explaining or stating the issues • Financial statement analysis: performing the required analytical process, explaining or stating the issues • Identifying and explaining the consequence of unethical behaviour • Identifying and using relevant up to date content of International and ICAEW Code of Ethics	Requirements will include planning assurance engagements in accordance with the terms of engagement and appropriate standards, taking account of: • Managing assurance and audit engagements • Reliance on controls • Reliance on the work of internal audit or other experts • Reliance on the work of another auditor • Extent of tests of control and of substantive procedures, including analytical review • Number, timing, staffing and location of assurance visits

staffing and location of assurance visits • the assurance of entities' published sustainability and corporate responsibility reports 3n Specify and explain the steps necessary to plan and perform an audit.	• Recognising ethical issues arising from situations likely to be encountered by trainee chartered accountants; identifying possible courses of action to resolve them	
Applying judgement		
1c Judge when to raise legal and ethical matters with senior colleagues 3c recognize the need on occasion to bring in expertise from other parties 3f Assess significant business risks identified 3h Assess the impact of risk and materiality on the engagement plan, including the nature, timing and extent of assurance procedures, for a given organisation 4f Judge when to refer reporting matters for specialist help	• Applying discrimination: identifying the relevant/reasonable in data and evidence; recognising varying quality in data or evidence • Relating parts and wholes: discerning particular issues as part of wholes • Demonstrating an understanding of different perspectives (eg social, political, economic): analysing and interpreting problems and situations from a given stance • Change management (appreciating the impacts/effects of change): considering and evaluating the effects of a given future scenario • Assessing/applying materiality: understanding the concept of materiality • Applying a sceptical and critical approach in a given straight-forward situation • Appreciating when more expert help is required in a given straight-forward situation • Exercising ethical judgement • Developing arguments, having first appreciated the perspective of all other parties • Conducting critiques: critically reviewing a statement, argument or position	Candidates will be required to identify significant business or audit risks from a given scenario, explain their impact on the financial statements, and finally recommend audit procedures to mitigate the risk of a material error. Requirements will test the ability of candidates to filter those issues which are more relevant than others in a given scenario. Candidates' ability to distinguish the quality of data or evidence will be tested in two potential ways. (i) Candidates will need to distinguish between data generated from within an organisation and that generated by a third party, the latter being less susceptible to management bias; and (ii) candidates will need to appreciate the effect on the quality of evidence that bias caused by specific factors can have e.g. where profits are used to determine a bonus payment to be made to the company's management. Question requirements will include the need to identify the impact of specific economic and political factors on a set of financial statements e.g. in the context of dealing with customers or suppliers from overseas that (i) political instability may cause problems which prevent the customer or supplier from trading, ultimately leading to going concern issues for the client; and (ii)

economic factors may cause exchange rate fluctuations leading to the risk of misstated balances in the financial statements.

Candidates will be expected to evaluate the effect of uncertain future events when describing the procedures to be performed in carrying out a review of a company's financial forecasts.

Question requirements will include the need to assess the materiality of a particular matter (e.g. an unadjusted error) in the context of a set of financial statements. This assessment should then inform the candidate's judgement as to whether or not to modify the opinion given in a statutory audit report.

Candidates are required to exercise ethical judgement in a variety of different scenarios, including:

- Judging the potential independence risks involved in accepting or continuing an audit engagement, and the procedures to mitigate those risks
- Consideration of the required steps upon the discovery of fraud/money laundering

Candidates are expected to display the ability to present a structured argument to a client e.g. in situations where management are questioning the extent of audit work performed

Drawing conclusions and making recommendations		
1a Advise on professional and ethical issues 1b Evaluate the relative merits of different professional and ethical standpoints 2d Formulate the approach suitable for management of an assurance engagement 3o Specify and explain the steps necessary to conclude and report on an audit 4b Evaluate the results and conclusions from assurance tests 4c and 4g Draw conclusions on the ability to report on assurance and audit engagements 4d & 4l Draft suitable extracts for assurance and audit reports 4e Advise on reports to be issued	• Using technical knowledge to support reasoning and conclusions • Decision making: using relevant quantitative approaches in decision analysis • Identifying the best explanation, solution or steps against defined criteria in a given straight-forward situation • Formulating opinions, reservations, advice, recommendations, plans, solutions, options and risks including business implications in a given straight-forward situation • Preparing, describing, outlining the advice, report, notes required in a given straight-forward situation • Presenting a basic or routine memorandum or briefing note in writing in a clear and concise style • Combining cognitive and behavioural skills to communicate to specialists and non-specialists	Requirements will include: • Advising on the regulatory, professional and ethical issues in carrying out an assurance engagement • Concluding and reporting on assurance engagements • Identifying weaknesses in financial information systems, their potential consequences and recommendations for improvement

4.4 Technical knowledge

The tables contained in this section show the technical knowledge covered in the ACA syllabus by module.

The level of knowledge required in the relevant Professional Stage module and at the Advanced Stage is shown.

The knowledge levels are defined as follows:

Level D

An awareness of the scope of the standard.

Level C

A general knowledge with a basic understanding of the subject matter and training in its application sufficient to identify significant issues and evaluate their potential implications or impact.

Level B

A working knowledge with a broad understanding of the subject matter and a level of experience in the application thereof sufficient to apply the subject matter in straightforward circumstances.

Level A

A thorough knowledge with a solid understanding of the subject matter and experience in the application thereof sufficient to exercise reasonable professional judgement in the application of the subject matter in those circumstances generally encountered by Chartered Accountants.

Key to other symbols:

➡ the knowledge level reached is assumed to be continued

Assurance and Audit

Title	Professional stage: Assurance	Professional stage: Audit & assurance	Advanced stage
The International Auditing and Assurance Standards Board			C
The Authority Attaching to Standards Issued by the International Auditing and Assurance Standards Board			A
The Authority Attaching to Practice Statements Issued by the International Auditing and Assurance Standards Board			A
Discussion Papers			C
Working Procedures			C
International Standards on Auditing (ISAs)			
200 Overall Objectives of the Independent Auditor and the Conduct of an Audit in Accordance with International Standards on Auditing	B	A	
210 Agreeing the Terms of Audit Engagements		B	→
220 Quality Control for an Audit of Financial Statements		B	→
230 Audit Documentation		B	A
240 The Auditor's Responsibilities Relating to Fraud in an Audit of Financial Statements		B	A
250 Consideration of Laws and Regulations in an Audit of Financial Statements		B	A
260 Communication with Those Charged with Governance		B	A
265 Communicating Deficiencies in Internal Control to Those Charged with Governance and Management		B	A
300 Planning an Audit of Financial Statements	B	A	→
315 Identifying and Assessing the Risks of Material Misstatement Through Understanding the Entity and its Environment	C	A	→
320 Materiality in Planning and Performing an Audit	C	A	→
330 The Auditor's Responses to Assessed Risks		B	A
402 Audit Considerations Relating to an Entity Using a Service Organisation		C	C
450 Evaluation of Misstatements Identified during the Audit	C	A	
500 Audit Evidence	B	A	→
501 Audit Evidence – Specific Considerations for Selected Items		A	→
505 External Confirmations	B	B	A
510 Initial Audit Engagements – Opening Balances		B	A
520 Analytical Procedures	C	B	A
530 Audit Sampling	C	C	A
540 Auditing Accounting Estimates, Including Fair Value Accounting Estimates and Related Disclosures	C	B	A
550 Related Parties		B	A
560 Subsequent Events		B	A
570 Going Concern		A	→

Title	Professional stage		Advanced stage
	Assurance	Audit & assurance	
580 Written Representations	C	B	A
600 Special Considerations – Audits of Group Financial Statements (including the Work of Component Auditors)		C	A
610 Using the Work of Internal Auditors		C	A
620 Using the Work of an Auditor's Expert		C	A
700 Forming an Opinion and Reporting on Financial Statements	B	A	→
705 Modifications to the Opinion in the Independent Auditor's Report		B	→
706 Emphasis of Matter Paragraphs and Other Matter Paragraphs in the Independent Auditor's Report		A	→
710 Comparative Information – Corresponding Figures and Comparative Financial Statements		B	A
720 The Auditor's Responsibility in Relation to Other Information in Documents Containing Audited Financial Statements		B	A
800 Special Considerations – Audits of Financial Statements prepared in Accordance with Special Purpose Frameworks			B
Special Considerations – Audits of Single Financial Statements and Specific Elements, Accounts or items of a Financial Statement		B	A
810 Engagements to Report on Summary Financial Statements		B	A
International Auditing Practice Statements (IAPSs)			
1000 Inter-bank Confirmation Procedures			D
1004 The Relationship Between Banking Supervisors and Banks' External Auditors			D
1005 The Special Considerations in the Audit of Small Entities			A
1006 Audits of the Financial Statements of Banks			D
1010 The Consideration of Environmental Matters in the Audit of Financial Statements			A
1012 Auditing Derivative Financial Instruments			B
1013 Electronic Commerce: Effect on the Audit of Financial Statements			A
1014 Reporting by Auditors on Compliance with International Financial Reporting Standards			A
International Standards on Review Engagements (ISREs)			
2400 Engagements to Review Financial Statements		C	B
2410 Review of Interim Financial Information Performed by the Independent Auditor of the Entity			B
International Standards on Assurance Engagements (ISAEs)			
3000R Assurance Engagements Other than Audits or Reviews of Historical Financial Information		C	B
3400 The Examination of Prospective Financial Information		C	B

Title	Professional stage: Assurance	Professional stage: Audit & assurance	Advanced stage
International Standards on Related Services (ISRSs)			
4400 Engagements to Perform Agreed-upon Procedures Regarding Financial Information			B
4410 Engagements to Compile Financial Information			B
IFAC Statements			
IPPS1 Assuring the Quality of Professional Services		C	B
ISQC1 Quality Control for Firms that Perform Audits and Reviews of Financial Statements, and Other Assurance and Related Services Engagements		C	B
APB Bulletins			
2009/2 Audit Reports on Financial Statements in the UK		C	B

Students studying for exams in 2010 should be aware that they will be assessed according to pure clarity ISAs in 2010. From 2011 onwards the syllabus will be based on the UK and Ireland auditing standards that will be updated for the new clarity ISAs. The reason for this is because the updated UK and Ireland clarity ISAs will not be available in time for the 2010 syllabus.

5 Faculties and special interest groups (SIGs)

The faculties and SIGs are specialist bodies within the ICAEW which offer members networking opportunities, influence and recognition within clearly defined areas of technical expertise. As well as providing accurate and timely technical analysis, they lead the way in many professional and wider business issues through stimulating debate, shaping policy and encouraging good practice. Their value is endorsed by over 40,000 members of the Institute who currently belong to one or more of the seven faculties:

- Audit and Assurance
- Corporate Finance
- Finance and Management
- Financial Reporting
- Financial Services
- Information Technology
- Tax

For example, the Audit and Assurance Faculty is the focus for chartered accountants working in audit and assurance. It represents the Institute on audit and assurance matters, making representations to the Government and other authorities, and public pronouncements on major audit and assurance issues. It is a free standing body with its own constitution.

The SIGs provide practical support, information and representation for chartered accountants working within a range of industry sectors, including:

- Charity and Voluntary sector
- Entertainment and Media
- Farming and Rural business
- Forensic
- Healthcare
- Interim management
- Non-executive directors
- Public sector
- Solicitors
- Tourism and Hospitality
- Valuation

Students can register for provisional faculty membership of **one** of the seven faculties and **one** SIG free of charge. To register and find out more, visit the student website at www.icaew.com/students and click on student support and services.

6 ICAEW publications for further reading

The ICAEW produces publications and guidance for its students and members on a variety of technical and business topics. This list of publications has been prepared for students who wish to undertake further reading in a particular subject area and is by no means exhaustive. You are not required to study these publications for your exams. For a full list of publications, or to access any of the publications listed below, visit the Technical & Business Topics section of the ICAEW website at www.icaew.com.

The *Members' Handbook* provides essential information and sets out membership obligations for all ICAEW members. It contains regulations and guidance on professional and technical issues, specifically the Code of Ethics and guidance on anti-money laundering. The *Members' Handbook* is available at www.icaew.com/membershandbook.

The TECH series of technical releases are another source of guidance available to members and students. Visit www.icaew.com/technicalreleases for the most up-to-date releases.

Audit and Assurance Faculty – www.icaew.com/aaf

- **Companies Act 2006 supplement** ICAEW, 2009. ISBN: 978-1-84152-639-3

  This updated supplement originally published in December 2006 provides a brief summary of the key sections in the Companies Act 2006 which relate directly to the rights and duties of auditors. It covers the various types of reports issued by auditors and provides a comparison to the requirements and regulations in the Companies Act 1985 and Companies Act 1989. It is designed to be a signposting tool for practitioners and identifies the other pieces of guidance issued by the ICAEW, APB, FRC, POB and others to support implementation of the Act, along with transitional provisions arising from the Act.

- **Auditing in a group context: practical considerations for auditors**, ICAEW 2008. ISBN: 978-1-84152-628-7

  The guide describes special considerations for auditors at each stage of the group audit's cycle. While no decisions have been taken on UK adoption of the IAASB's clarity ISAs, the publication also covers matters in the IAASB's revised and redrafted 'ISA 600 Special Considerations - Audits of Group Financial Statements (Including the Work of Component Auditors)'. The revised publication contains suggestions for both group auditors and component auditors.

- **Quality control in the audit environment,** ICAEW, May 2006, reprinted January 2008. ISBN 978-1-84152-450-4

  A practical guide which identifies seven key actions for firms reviewing their implementation of ISQC (UK and Ireland) 1.

- **Perspectives on assurance: Engaging practitioners**, ICAEW, 2007. ISBN: 978-1-84152-529-7

  Aims to increase awareness amongst practitioners of the nature of external assurance. It explains the key elements of the International Framework for Assurance Engagements, seeks feedback based on practical experience and identifies areas where there may be a need for new guidance.

Corporate Finance Faculty – www.icaew.com/corpfinfac

- **Private equity demystified – an explanatory guide**, (Financing Change initiative) ICAEW, August 2008, John Gilligan and Mike Wright (2008)

  A factual guide to private equity which contains a summary of the findings of academic studies on private equity transactions from around the world. Hard copies of the abstract and full report are free and are also available by download from www.icaew.com/thoughtleadership

Corporate governance – www.icaew.com/corporategovernance

- **Combined Code of Corporate Governance June 2006 and June 2008 version.** The Combined Code was first issued in 1998 and has been updated at regular intervals since. At present two versions are in effect: the 2006 version, which applies to accounting periods beginning on or after 1 November 2006; and the June 2008 version which applies to accounting periods beginning on or after 29 June 2008. Listed companies are required to report on how they have applied the principles of the Combined Code, and either to confirm that they have complied with the Combined Code's provisions or, where they have not, to provide an explanation. In March 2009 the Financial Reporting Council announced a review of the Combined Code.

- **The Turnbull Report Internal Control: Guidance on Internal Control for Directors on the Combined Code was originally published in 1999**. The guidance was revised and updated in October 2005 following a review by the Financial Reporting Council. The updated guidance applies to listed companies for financial years beginning on or after 1 January 2006.

- **The FRC Guidance on Audit Committees** (formerly known as The Smith Guidance) was first published by the Financial Reporting Council in January 2003, and was updated in 2005. It is intended to assist company boards when implementing the sections of the Combined Code dealing with audit committees and to assist directors serving on audit committees in carrying out their role. A new edition of the guidance was issued in October 2008.

Corporate responsibility – www.icaew.com/corporateresponsibility

- **Sustainable Business, January 2009**

  Our new thought leadership prospectus acts as a framework for the work that we do in sustainability/corporate responsibility. In it we argue that any system that is sustainable needs accurate and reliable information to help it learn and adapt, which is where the accounting profession plays an important role. A downloadable pdf is available at www.icaew.com/sustainablebusiness

- **Competitiveness and sustainability: Building the best future for your business**, ICAEW, October 2008, ISBN 978-1-84152-618-8

  Published by the ICAEW and written by David Bent of Forum for the Future this briefing looks at the possible competitive opportunities that sustainable business can offer. Hard copies are free of charge and a downloadable pdf is available at www.icaew.com/corporateresponsibility

- **Environmental issues in annual financial statements**, ICAEW, May 2009, ISBN 978-1-84152-610-2

  This report is a joint initiative with the Environment Agency. It is aimed at business accountants who prepare, use or audit the financial statements in statutory annual reports and accounts, or who advise or sit on the boards of the UK companies and public sector organisations. It offers practical advice on measuring and disclosing environmental performance. A downloadable pdf is available at www.icaew.com/sustainablebusiness

- **ESRC seminar series – When worlds collide: contested paradigms of corporate responsibility**

  The ICAEW, in conjunction with the British Academy of Management, won an Economic and Social Research Council grant to run a seminar series which aims to bring academics and the business community together to tackle some of the big challenges in corporate responsibility. www.icaew.com/corporateresponsibility

- **The Business Sustainability Programme (BSP)**

  In conjunction with the ICAEW's Learning and Professional Development department we have developed a sustainability e-learning package for accountants and business professionals who want to learn about the business case for sustainability.

  The course is spread over five modules taking users from definitions of sustainability and corporate responsibility, through case studies and finally towards developing an individually tailored sustainability strategy for their business. The first two modules are free to everyone. For more information and to download a brochure visit www.icaew.com/bsp

Ethics – www.icaew.com/ethics

- **Code of Ethics** (part of the *Members' Handbook*): overview and latest version are available online at www.icaew.com/ethics
- **Reporting with Integrity**, ICAEW May 2007. ISBN 978-1-84152-455-9

  This publication brings ideas from a variety of disciplines, in order to obtain a more comprehensive understanding of what is meant by integrity, both as a concept and in practice. Moreover, because this report sees reporting with integrity as a joint endeavour of individuals, organisations and professions, including the accounting profession, the concept of integrity is considered in all these contexts.

  Hard copies of the abstract and full report are free and are also available by download from www.icaew.com/ethics
- **Ethical behaviour in business**

  Ethics hits the headlines when things go wrong. Ethical behaviour in business is something that the ICAEW has long considered to be of critical importance as a general issue to maintain confidence in markets. Further detail on the work the Institute undertakes in this area is available at www.icaew.com/ethics.
- **Ethics audio updates**

  A series of ethics related news items and essential information that will help you keep up to date with the current issues are available for download from www.icaew.com/ethics
- **ICAEW P D Leake Lecture 2007**: Meeting the ethics challenge (author Professor Christopher Cowton)
- **Free webcast and CD-ROM May 2007**

  Ethics hits the headlines when things go wrong. However, this lecture is not about the familiar "scandals" of Enron, Worldcom, Parmalat and the like, but focuses on the question of ethics and what it means to be a professional. The lecture considers the professional and practical challenges of promoting credible ethics in the accounting profession and discusses ways for meeting these challenges.
- **Ethics podcasts**

  These are available for download from www.icaew.com/ethics

Finance and Management Faculty – www.icaew.com/fmfac

- **Better Budgeting**, Special report, SR4, July 2004. ISBN 978-1-84152-286-9.

  Is budgeting still relevant? Or have new techniques proved more useful? The Better Budgeting Forum saw a lively debate on this topic, as this 12-page special report summarises.
- **Strategic planning**, Special report, SR3, May 2004. ISBN 978-1-84152-246-3.

  A 48-page special report on making and implementing strategic choices, the role of the finance director and the core elements of corporate strategy.
- **Managing change** SR21 June 2008 ISBN 978-1-84152-5976

  Change can be a stressful process for all involved – from those charged with the demanding job of leading an organisation into uncharted territory, through to those being led, whose roles may change and yet they will have little influence. In this special report we aim to help you understand and therefore manage such projects.
- **Managing teams** SR16, June 2007 ISBN 978-1-84152-504-4

  This special report aims to give you an insight into the theory behind managing finance teams and the changing nature of teams as well as providing you with some practical guidance and tools.

- **Innovation** SR24: March 2009 ISBN 978-1-84152-638-6

  The perceived wisdom during a downturn is to focus on what is core to your business. If something is not necessary then do not do it. But is innovation simply a nice to have? This report provides a practical guide if you have an innovation process that simply needs improving or if you are establishing one for the first time.

Financial Services Faculty – www.icaew.com/fsf

- **Measurement in financial services,** (Inspiring Confidence in Financial Services initiative) ICAEW, March 2008, ISBN 978-1-84152-546-4

  Measurement in financial services, the first issues paper from our better information theme, suggests that more work is required on matching measurement practices in the financial services industry to the needs of different users of financial information, despite the fact that the financial services industry has the greatest concentration of measurement and modelling skills of any industry. A downloadable pdf is available at www.icaew.com/thoughtleadership

- **Webcasts**

  On-demand webcasts are available to view for events and seminars held by the Financial Services Faculty in 2008. For more information see www.icaew.com/fsfwebcasts

- **Skilled Persons' Guidance – Reporting Under s166 Financial Services and Markets Act 2000 (Interim Technical Release FSF 01/08)**

  This interim guidance was issued by the ICAEW in April 2008 as a revision to TECH 20/30 to assist chartered accountants and other professionals who are requested to report under s166 Financial Services and Markets Act 2000. A downloadable pdf is available at www.icaew.com/technicalreleases

Financial Reporting Faculty – www.icaew.com/frfac

- **EU Implementation of IFRS and the Fair Value Directive**.

  ICAEW, October 2007, ISBN 978-1-84152-519-8

  The Faculty undertook a major review of IFRS implementation in 2005 across the EU, published by the European Commission in October 2007

  The Financial Reporting Faculty does not at present publish a newsletter, but makes available to students copies of its highly-regarded factsheets on UK GAAP and IFRS issues at www.icaew.com/frfac

Information Technology Faculty

- **123 Online Accounting Software**

  ICAEW, December 2008, ISBN 978-1-84152-632-4

  The second in the new series of *Chartech* Software Product Guides, focuses on ***Online Accounting Software.*** The guides provide an overview of a particular software area – the business purpose of that kind of software, what there is on the market, points to look out for, pitfalls to avoid – followed by a series of brief, succinct reviews of a selection of specific products in that area.

Tax Faculty

The Tax Faculty runs a Younger Members Tax Club which provides informal presentations, discussions and socialising. All young professionals interested in tax are welcome to attend. See the website for more details www.icaew.com/taxfac

[illegible]

[illegible]

[illegible] in financial services [illegible]

[illegible]

[illegible]

[illegible] Guidance – Reporting Under [illegible] Financial Services and Markets Act 2000 [illegible]

[illegible]

[illegible]

EU Implementation of IFRS and the Fair Value Directive

ICAEW October 2007 [illegible]

The Faculty undertook a major review of IFRS [illegible] across the EU, published by the European Commission in October 2007.

[illegible]

[illegible]

[illegible] Accounting Software

ICAEW December 2007 [illegible]

[illegible]

[illegible]

[illegible]

chapter 1

Reintroduction to audit and assurance

Introduction

Learning objectives

Tick off

- Revise the concept of assurance from Assurance Paper ☐
- Revise the concept of audit from Assurance Paper ☐
- Understand the specific benefits of an audit ☐

Syllabus links

This chapter revises key concepts from your Assurance paper.

Examination context

This chapter is revision of what you have previously been examined on in your Assurance paper. The Audit and Assurance sample paper contained six marks of a written test question on the arguments for and against having an audit.

You will need an understanding of what assurance services are, and in particular, audit, brought forward from your lower level paper to answer any questions at this level.

1 Assurance defined

Section overview

- An assurance engagement is one in which a practitioner expresses a conclusion designed to enhance the degree of confidence of the intended users, other than the responsible party, about the outcome of the evaluation or measurement of a subject matter against criteria.
- Key elements are: three party involvement, subject matter, suitable criteria, sufficient appropriate evidence, written report.
- Different levels of assurance may be given in assurance assignments, reasonable and limited.
- An audit is an example of an assurance engagement giving reasonable assurance.

Definition

Assurance engagement: An **assurance engagement** is one in which a practitioner expresses a conclusion designed to enhance the degree of confidence of the intended users other than the responsible party about the outcome of the evaluation or measurement of a subject matter against criteria.

Assurance engagements include primarily audits but also other services such as reports on internal control and review of a business plan.

In recent years businesses world-wide have been publishing sustainability and corporate responsibility reports, in an attempt to demonstrate accountability for the impact of their activities on society and the environment. Such reports may be the subject of assurance engagements that provide limited assurance to management on reported elements such as key performance indicators, adherence to voluntary codes etc.

1.1 The elements

Any assurance engagement needs:

- A responsible party
- A practitioner
- A user of the report
- A subject matter
- Criteria
- Sufficient appropriate evidence to support the conclusion
- A written report containing a conclusion

The engagement will be governed by its terms of engagement (found in an engagement letter).

The engagement will need to be:

- Planned
- Performed
- Concluded upon
- Reported on

1.2 Levels of assurance

The International Federation of Accountants (IFAC) recognises two types of assurance engagement:

- Reasonable assurance engagements, which result in a positive expression of opinion and where the level of assurance given is deemed to be high, and
- Limited assurance engagements, which result in negative assurance and where the level of assurance given is deemed to be moderate.

Engagements could be either type, and this would need to be specified in the terms of engagement.

So for a report on the effectiveness of management's system of internal control, it might be agreed that the report should read:

'In our opinion management has operated an effective system of internal control' – a positive form of opinion deriving from a reasonable assurance engagement

or

'Nothing has come to our attention that indicates material internal control weakness' – a negative form of assurance deriving from a limited assurance engagement.

No report on an assurance engagement can ever provide absolute assurance, because of the nature of the evidence available.

Assurance type	Assurance level	Opinion/conclusion	Example
Reasonable	High	Positive	Audit of financial information
Limited	Moderate	Negative	Review of financial information

1.3 Benefits of assurance

A key feature of assurance services is that they are provided by independent professionals who therefore give an objective, unbiased opinion. They give the following benefits to users:

- Enhances the credibility of the information being reported on
- Reduces the risk of management bias, error or even fraud in the information being reported on
- Draws the attention of the user to any deficiencies in the information being reported on

Assurance services also give added credibility to the wider share market:

- They ensure that high quality, reliable information circulates in the market
- They give investors added faith in the market
- They improve the reputation of organisations trading in the market

Worked example: Assurance engagement

Predator plc, a large listed company, is considering taking over Target Limited, a small, family owned company.

Predator has asked Talbot and Co, chartered accountants, to carry out due diligence in relation to this prospective purchase. They want them to review the financial statements of the last three years and ensure that they were prepared under generally accepted accounting practice in the UK. They also want them to review the budgets for the coming 12 months and ensure that they are reasonably and internally consistent.

You can see the elements of the assurance service as these:

- Practitioner: Talbot and Co
- Responsible party: Target Ltd management
- Users: Predator plc management
- Subject matter: Financial statements/budgets
- Criteria: UK GAAP/reasonable and internally consistent

Talbot and Co will plan and carry out work to obtain sufficient appropriate evidence to support their assurance opinion, which will be given in a written report.

The benefits of this service to Predator plc are that:

- They are given assurance that the financial statements are in line with UK GAAP and therefore are understandable and comparable with other companies they might be considering for takeover.
- They are given assurance that the budgets are reasonable and internally consistent and therefore can be trusted as an indicator of the company's future operating ability.
- They can therefore make an informed decision about whether to buy Target and for how much.

Interactive question 1: Benefits of assurance [Difficulty level: Exam standard]

During the night of 7 June 20X3 strong gales caused the brick chimney of the factory to crash through the roof of Hancock Ltd's assembly area. Production was severely disrupted for a period of two months.

In addition to claiming from its insurers for the cost of repairing the premises and for the equipment and inventories destroyed in the accident, the company is also including a considerable claim under the loss of profits provision of its policy. The directors have prepared detailed calculations of the loss of profit and have requested the company's auditors to review this claim and provide an assurance report which they will submit with it to the insurers.

What advantages would the directors expect to gain from having this report?

See **Answer** at the end of this chapter.

2 Audit defined

Section overview

- An audit is still a key example of an assurance service in the UK, where many companies are required to have audits by law.
- An audit is an exercise designed to enable an auditor to express an opinion whether the financial statements are prepared, in all material respects, in accordance with an applicable financial reporting framework.
- An auditor usually expresses a conclusion as to whether the financial statements 'give a true and fair view'.
- The 'audit threshold' is the legal qualification for a company to have an audit.
- The benefits of audit are much the same as the benefit of assurance services generally. Users of financial statements subject to an audit are given assurance that the financial statements meet legal requirements as well as accounting ones.

Definition

Audit of financial statements: The objective of an **audit of financial statements** is to enable the auditor to express an opinion as to whether the financial statements are prepared, in all material respects, in accordance with an applicable financial reporting framework. The form the audit conclusion takes is that auditors state whether the financial statements give a true and fair view. This is an expression of reasonable assurance.

Worked example: How audit is an assurance engagement

The key criteria of an assurance engagement can be seen in an audit as follows.

(1) Three party involvement

- The shareholders (users)
- The board of directors (the responsible party)
- The audit firm (the practitioner)

(2) Subject matter

The financial statements

(3) Relevant criteria

Law and accounting standards

(4) Evidence

The auditor is required by international standards on auditing (ISAs) to obtain sufficient and appropriate evidence to support the audit opinion.

(5) Written report in a suitable form

As required by ISA 700 the audit report is a written report issued in a prescribed form.

2.1 The audit threshold

For many years all companies registered in the UK were required to be audited. In the early 1990s certain very small companies were granted exemption from audit and this exemption was later extended to all companies fulfilling the following criteria.

- The company must qualify as a small company under the Companies Act 2006
- The company's turnover must not exceed £6.5m
- The company's gross assets – fixed assets as disclosed at net book value in the balance sheet + current assets – must not exceed £3.26m

The criteria use UK accounting terminology rather than IFRS terminology because they are required by UK law.

In order to qualify as a small company a company must meet at least two out of the following three criteria for the current and previous year:

- The company's turnover must not exceed £6.5m
- The company's gross assets – fixed assets as disclosed at net book value in the balance sheet + current assets – must not exceed £3.26m
- The number of the company's employees must not exceed 50

A company which outgrows these criteria does not lose its small company status until its second year of ceasing to be small. Similarly a former 'big' company has to be small for two years in order to change its status.

So there are companies which qualify as small companies but which might exceed the turnover and/or gross assets thresholds and therefore do not qualify for audit exemption.

A company with turnover less than £6.5m and fewer than 50 employees but assets of more than £3.26m qualifies as small but has to have an audit.

Finally there are companies which, no matter how small they are, are specifically excluded from small company status and therefore must have an audit:

- Companies falling within the ambit of the Financial Services and Markets Act 2000 – broadly banks and financial service providers
- Insurance companies
- Public companies (wherever registered)
- Any company which is a member of a group including one of the above.

As a result of the rise in the audit threshold:

- The majority of owner managed businesses may no longer need to be audited
- Very few companies qualifying to use the Financial Reporting Standard for Smaller Entities (FRSSE) for disclosures in their financial statements will need to be audited
- Very few companies entitled to file small company abbreviated accounts will need to be audited.

2.2 The benefits of being audited

The case for the audit for those companies where it is not required by statute usually revolves around the protection of those who, apart from management, nevertheless have a financial interest in the company.

- Banks and other providers of finance
- Minority shareholders.

In a White Paper, the UK Department of Trade and Industry made the very valid point that if the purpose of the audit was to protect shareholders who are not involved with managing the business and the vast majority of smaller companies were owner managed, what purpose did the audit serve for those companies?

Many would argue (and the auditors of smaller companies have found this to be true) that, in many cases, the audit is valued by management because:

- They value having their business scrutinised by another set of professional eyes
- It provides additional assurance to third parties such as taxation authorities concerning the reliability of the financial statements
- A growing business will one day require an audit
- Audit may have subsidiary benefits, such as the auditors recommending improvements in company systems.

3 Audit and other assurance compared

Section overview

- The earlier sections of this chapter looked at the similarities between audit and other examples of assurance
- All assurance assignments follow the same basic outline with the key difference being the level of assurance given in the final opinion
- This has practical implications at various stages of the assignment

The specific differences relating to agreement of terms and acceptance of appointment are covered in Chapter 6. The differences in the detailed content of reports are covered in Chapter 13.

3.1 Nature of work undertaken

In the Assurance paper you studied in detail the sources of audit evidence and the types of procedure that are generally performed on an audit. For other types of assurance assignment, where lower levels of assurance are being provided, the amount and type of evidence required will be less.

The following table compares the main audit procedures as outlined in ISA 500 with those that would be carried out in an engagement to review financial statements following the guidance of International Standard on Review Engagements (ISRE) 2400, and with those that would be carried out in examining prospective financial information under International Standard on Assurance Engagements (ISAE) 3400:

ISA 500	ISRE 2400	ISAE 3400
• Inspection of documentation • Inspection of assets • Observation • External confirmation • Recalculation • Reperformance • Analytical procedures • Inquiry	• Inquiry • Analytical procedures	• Assessment of assumptions • Recomputation • Written representations

3.2 Quality of evidence

It is clear that far less evidence is obtained during a review assignment, and the evidence is generally less reliable as some of the most reliable sources, such as third party confirmations and evidence generated by the assurance provider are not required.

In some cases, the nature and quality of the evidence that can be obtained is further affected by the nature of the subject matter of the assignment. If the firm is appointed to carry out a review of forecast figures to be presented to potential lenders then again analytical procedures and inquiry will be employed but the reliability of the evidence will be even lower due to the uncertainties involved. The figures being reviewed relate to transactions and events, some or all of which have not yet occurred at the time the opinion is given. The information is based on subjective estimates.

3.3 Reporting

In both of these cases the assurance provider can give only a low level of assurance and in the case of prospective information, such as the forecast figures, may include additional warnings to readers of the assurance opinion about the nature of the information and the assurance that can be given.

Chapter 13 looks at the content of such reports in more detail.

Interactive question 2: Review and audit compared [Difficulty level: Exam standard]

The directors of Connelly Ltd are concerned about the reliability and usefulness of the monthly financial management information that they receive.

As a result, the company's auditors have been engaged to review the system and the information it generates, and to report their conclusions.

Contrast this assignment with the statutory audit of the company's financial statements with regard to the scope of the assignment and to the report issued.

See **Answer** at the end of this chapter.

Interactive question 3: Benefits of an audit [Difficulty level: Easy]

Acrylics Ltd was established in June 20X0 to produce acrylic products which are used as display units in the retail industry. The shares are owned equally by two executive and two non-executive directors.

The company's revenue increased steadily over the first two years of trading. The results for the first year of trading indicated an operating profit margin of 15%, and the management accounts for the second year of trading indicate that this has increased to 18%. The directors are currently negotiating a contract worth £600,000 to supply a major retailer which has over 100 outlets throughout the UK. The company will require an increased overdraft facility to fulfill the order.

The finance director of Acrylics Ltd has prepared a business plan for submission to the company's bankers in support of a request for a larger overdraft facility. The plan includes details of the company's products, management, markets, method of operation and financial information. The financial information includes profit and cash flow forecasts for the six months ending 31 December 20X2, together with details of the assumptions on which the forecasts are based and the accounting policies used in compiling the profit forecast. The company's bankers require this financial information to be reviewed and reported on by independent accountants.

Although the company's revenue was below the threshold for a statutory audit for its first year of trading, the company was required by its bankers to have an audit of its financial statements for the year ended 30 June 20X1. Your firm conducted this audit in accordance with auditing standards and issued an unqualified report.

Requirements

(a) Describe the benefits, in addition to continuance of its overdraft facility, to the company and its directors and shareholders from having an audit of its annual financial statements.

(b) Explain how and why the level of assurance provided by a report on profit and cash flow forecasts differs from the level of assurance provided by an audit report on annual financial statements.

See **Answer** at the end of this chapter.

Summary and Self-test

Summary

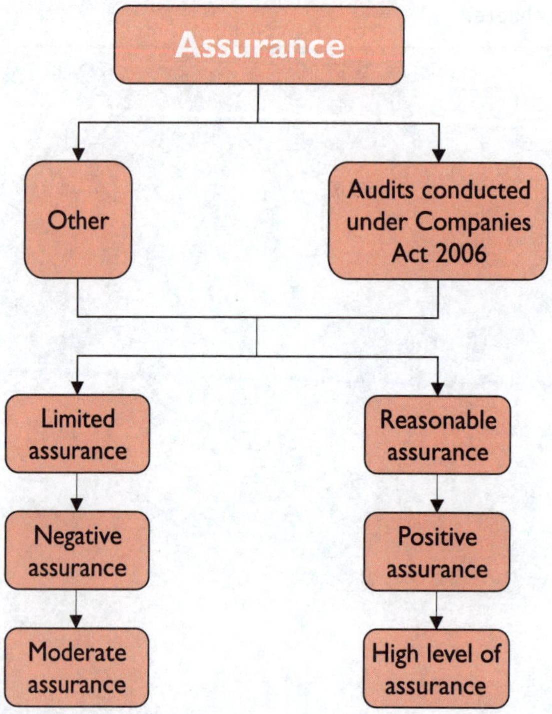

Self-test

Answer the following questions.

1 Define an assurance engagement.

2 Any assurance engagement requires which of the following elements?

A	A user	C	A subject matter
B	A responsible party	D	Criteria

3 In a reasonable assurance engagement, a negative conclusion is drawn.

☐ True ☐ False

4 An audit is a limited assurance engagement.

☐ True ☐ False

5 Tiny Limited has a turnover of £6.7 million. It employs 38 members of staff and has gross assets of £3.26 million. Last year it had a turnover of £5.5 million and gross assets of £3 million. The year before that, it had turnover of £5.3 million and gross assets of £2.6 million. There has been no change in Tiny's staffing arrangements during the last three years. Tiny qualifies as a small company and does not require an audit in the current year.

☐ True ☐ False

6 Which of the following is not a potential benefit of having an audit?

A Management may value having their business scrutinised by a set of professional eyes

B Assurance may be given to parties other than management who have a financial interest in the company

C An audit is likely to be required in the near future by a growing company

D Fraud will be uncovered by the auditors

Exam-style question

7 **Treetops Ltd**

Your firm acts as external auditor for Treetops Ltd, a company whose principal business activity is the manufacture and export of hammocks. Due to recent changes in the statutory audit exemption thresholds, Treetops Ltd is no longer required by law to have an audit of its financial statements for the year ended 28 February 20X5.

The directors of Treetops Ltd have asked you to set out the main advantages of the company continuing to have a statutory audit and also to provide them with examples of some of the other types of assurance work which your firm may be able to carry out for them.

The company's managing director has also requested a meeting with you. He has recently discovered that his purchase ledger clerk has diverted £10,000 of company funds into his own bank account. The managing director wants to know why this was not discovered during the course of your audit for the year ended 29 February 20X4. The company's retained profit for that year was £350,000.

Requirements

(a) Briefly describe the advantages to the directors and shareholders of Treetops Ltd of continuing to have a full audit under the Companies Act 2006 when exempt from the statutory audit. **(4 marks)**

(b) Provide examples of four other types of assurance engagement where the scope of the work is agreed between the assurance firm and the company. For each engagement identified, briefly set out the nature of the assurance given in the accompanying report and, where applicable, identify potential users of the report other than the company's management. **(8 marks)**

Now, go back to the Learning Objectives in the Introduction. If you are satisfied you have achieved these objectives, please tick them off.

Technical reference

1 Assurance defined	**ISA 200.5 (generic reference for audit/assurance engagements)**
2 Audit defined	**ISA 200.11**

Answers to Interactive questions

Answer to Interactive question 1

Advantages of report regarding loss of profits

- Independent opinion from external source
- Enhanced credibility of compilation of claim
- Confirmation that data subjected to review and examination
- Comfort to insurers that risk of inflated claim reduced
- Could accelerate processing of claim

Answer to Interactive question 2

SCOPE	
This assignment	**Statutory audit**
• Agree between parties	• In accordance with Companies Act 2006
• Restricted to instructions	• In accordance with audit regulations
	• In accordance with ISAs

REPORT	
This assignment	**Statutory audit**
• Addressed to board	• Addressed to members
• Format wholly discretionary	• On true and fair view
• Private report	• Format prescribed
	• Report in public domain

Answer to Interactive question 3

(a) Benefits, additional to continuance of overdraft facility, of having an audit:

(i) Shareholders who are not involved in the day-to-day management of the company (non-executives) will have assurance that their interests are protected (ie company assets are not abused).

(ii) Financial information is likely to be more reliable, resulting in more informed decisions.

(iii) An audit improves a company's governance – management benefits from:

- Assurance that they are complying with their statutory responsibilities (including the prevention and detection of fraud, as the audit may act as a deterrent)
- By-products of the audit, such as the identification of weaknesses and recommendations for improvement
- Reducing risks and improving performance.

(iv) An audit imposes financial discipline which is useful for growing companies.

(v) It may be easier to obtain credit, as suppliers and credit rating agencies regard the additional assurance provided by an audit important.

(b) How and why the level of assurance provided by a report on profit and cash flow forecasts differs from the level of assurance provided by an audit report on annual financial statements.

(i) An audit conducted in accordance with auditing standards provides a high level of assurance which is reasonable but not absolute.

(ii) The delay between the balance sheet date and the date of the audit report means that even items such as provisions/estimates can often be substantiated.

(iii) A review of forecasts is only likely to provide a moderate level of assurance.

(iv) This is because financial statements are based on historical information, and forecasts are based on assumptions which are subject to uncertainty.

Answers to Self-test

1 An assurance engagement is one in which a practitioner expresses a conclusion designed to enhance the degree of confidence of the intended users other than the responsible party about the outcome of the evaluation or measurement of a subject matter against criteria.

2 All of the elements listed are required, as well as a practitioner and sufficient and appropriate evidence, leading to a written expression of opinion.

3 False. A positive opinion is given in a reasonable assurance engagement.

4 False. It is a reasonable assurance engagement.

5 False. Tiny exceeds the qualification criteria to be a small company this year. However, it has qualified as a small company in the previous two years and does not lose this status for two years of exceeding the criteria. So, Tiny does qualify as a small company. However, as Tiny has a turnover in excess of £6.5 million, it does require an audit this year.

6 D – although an audit may act as a deterrent to fraud, it does not certify that one has not occurred. We shall look at the responsibilities of auditors in relation to fraud in the next chapter.

Exam-style question

7 **Treetops Ltd**

(a) **Benefits of audit**

(i) The credibility of financial information would be enhanced.

(ii) Enhances the value of accounts for business valuation purposes in the event of a sale.

(iii) Authorities such as HM Revenue & Customs can have more faith in the figures.

(iv) Avoids the future cost of extra work by the auditor when audit exemption limits are exceeded.

(v) Avoids a potential future qualification over the opening inventory figure.

(vi) Makes it easier to raise finance.

(vii) May act as a deterrent to fraud/management abusing assets/reduce risk of management bias.

(viii) More reliable information results in more informed decisions.

(ix) Provides management/shareholders with assurance that the financial statements are true and fair/prepared in accordance with accounting standards.

(x) By-products of the audit such as identification of weaknesses and recommendations should reduce risk and improve performance (management letter).

(xi) Imposes discipline on management and accounts staff if they know that the figures will be subject to third party scrutiny, and therefore encourages best practice.

(xii) Gives management comfort that they are complying with their professional responsibilities/the accounts comply with the Companies Act.

(b) **Four other types of assurance engagement**

Fraud investigation

The conclusion/assurance will be based on the extent of the work carried out.

The report will

(i) Identify likely causes of fraud
(ii) Attempt to quantify the level of fraud.

Potential users would be

(i) Legal experts in a court case
(ii) The Police
(iii) Internal or external auditors.

Working capital reports/reports on inventory and trade receivables recoverability

The report will state whether

(i) Trade receivables are likely to be received
(ii) Inventory can be sold profitably in the near future.

Potential users would be

(i) Potential buyers
(ii) Investors
(iii) Banks
(iv) Internal or external auditors

Internal control reports

Such a report would
(i) Comment on the effectiveness of internal controls and highlight weaknesses
(ii) Make suggestions for the improvement of controls.

Potential users would be

(i) Regulatory bodies
(ii) Shareholders
(iii) Internal or external auditors.

Reports on business plans/cash flow forecasts

The assurance given would be negative/limited/moderate, ie "Nothing has come to our attention".
The report would state whether

(i) The business plan/forecasts have been prepared in line with stated assumptions
(ii) Nothing has come to light to indicate that the assumptions are not a reasonable basis for the plan
(iii) The accounting policies used are consistent with the annual accounts
(iv) The plan is consistent with the past performance of the company.

Potential users would be

(i) Bankers
(ii) Other lenders
(iii) External auditors.

Tutorial note

Additional credit was given for mentioning the following alternative engagements (½ mark for each, up to a maximum of 2 in total for all types of engagement identified).

- Value for money studies
- Environmental audit
- Circulation reports
- Cost/benefit reports
- Due diligence
- Branch audit
- Review of specific business activities
- Internal audit
- Report on website security

chapter 2

Responsibilities

Introduction

Learning objectives

Tick off

- Understand management responsibilities in relation to managing a company ☐
- Understand assurance providers'/auditors' responsibilities, particularly with reference to:
  - Fraud and error ☐
  - Compliance with laws and regulations ☐
  - Related parties ☐
  - Money laundering ☐
- Understand the reasons why audits 'fail' and the nature of the expectations gap ☐

Specific syllabus references for this chapter are: 1a, b, c, d, g, h, j, 3l.

Syllabus links

The issue of responsibilities is usually clarified in an engagement letter, which was introduced in your Assurance paper.

Examination context

Various areas of auditor responsibility are covered regularly in the short form section of the examination paper, including fraud, responsibilities with regard to a review of projected information and compliance with laws and regulations.

In the assessment, candidates may be required to:

- Identify and advise upon the professional and ethical issues that may arise during an assurance engagement.
- Recognise the professional and ethical issues that might arise during an assurance engagement, explain the relevance and importance of these issues and evaluate the relative merits of different standpoints taken in debate.
- Judge when to raise legal and ethical matters arising from assurance work with senior colleagues for review and possible referral to external parties.
- Discuss the purpose of laws, standards and other requirements surrounding assurance work.
- Explain, using appropriate examples, the main ways in which national legislation affects assurance.
- Explain the main ways in which national legislation affects the scope and nature of the audit (including the relationship between the law and auditing standards).
- Describe the principal causes of audit failure and their effects and the gap between outcomes delivered by audit engagements and the expectations of users of audit reports.
- Outline aspects of employment and social security law which are relevant to statutory audit.

1 Management responsibilities

Section overview

- Management is responsible for:
  - Managing the business so as to achieve company objectives
  - Assessing business risks to those objectives being achieved
  - Safeguarding the company's assets
  - Keeping proper accounting records
  - Preparing company financial statements and delivering them to the Registrar
  - Ensuring the company complies with applicable laws and regulations
- It is not the responsibility of the auditors of a company to do any of the above.

The approach adopted in this section is to identify the responsibilities which are either defined by ISAs as being attributable to management, or set out in the UK Companies Act 2006 as being the responsibilities of the company's directors.

It follows, therefore, that these duties cannot belong to the auditor or assurance firm.

1.1 Managing the company

First and foremost it is the directors' job to **manage the business** so that its objectives are achieved. This may mean producing suitable returns for shareholders or the achievement of other targets.

It also means **assessing what business risks face the company** and **devising the necessary strategies to deal with them**.

Clearly it is not the auditor's responsibility to set these strategies. However, the auditor does need to understand the risks facing the business and to understand how it will impact on their approach to the audit or other assurance engagement. We will look at this in more detail in Chapters 9 and 10.

1.2 Directors' responsibilities under the Companies Act 2006

The directors' statutory duties primarily come from the responsibilities laid out in the Companies Act. It is important that the directors of a company fully understand these, as in some cases there are criminal consequences for failing to carry them out correctly. The general duties of directors under the Companies Act are to **act in the way most likely to promote the success of the company** for the benefit of its members as a whole.

Safeguarding assets

It is the directors who have the legal responsibility for safeguarding the assets of the company. It is therefore for them to take reasonable steps for the prevention and detection of fraud and other irregularities.

To carry out this responsibility they need to implement systems and controls to safeguard the company's assets and they then need to ensure that the systems and controls operate effectively. Such procedures may include:

- The safekeeping of documents of title to land and buildings and other assets.
- The setting of authority limits, ie the limitation of what any one individual can do without consulting someone else.
- Implementing other procedures to prevent fraud and reduce the likelihood of error.

We looked at internal control systems in your studies for Assurance.

Books and records of the company

It is also the directors who are legally responsible for keeping proper accounting records which disclose with reasonable accuracy at any time the financial position of the company.

This requires records of:

- The cash payments and receipts
- What the payments and receipts relate to
- The assets (including non-current assets and inventory)
- The liabilities

The nature of the books and records is not laid down by statute and can take many forms, including manual books, loose-leaf folders, computer records or even a shoebox full of invoices with an add listing attached.

Preparation and delivery of company financial statements

Company law also places on the directors the obligation to prepare financial statements for each financial period (usually a year). These statements must give a true and fair view of the affairs of the company at the end of the accounting period and of the profit or loss of the company for that period.

In preparing those financial statements, the directors are required to:

- Select suitable accounting policies and then apply them consistently
- Make judgements and estimates that are reasonable and prudent
- Comply with applicable accounting standards
- Prepare the financial statements on the going concern basis unless it is inappropriate to presume that the company will continue in business.

Once the financial statements have been prepared, it is the directors' responsibility to ensure that they, together with the auditor's report, are laid before the members of the company in general meeting and delivered to Companies House within the specified time.

Interactive question 1: Directors' responsibilities [Difficulty level: Easy]

You are finalising the audit of a company. The audit highlights memorandum indicates that the company has failed to maintain proper books and records. This is because there is no non-current asset register and it was not possible to draw up a register, as some of the invoices were missing. The director is furious that the audit firm says this makes it impossible to give an unqualified audit opinion. He says that the audit firm prepared the accounts and therefore it is simply a matter of the auditors' incompetence.

Explain the directors' responsibilities in relation to the books and records of the company.

See **Answer** at the end of this chapter.

1.3 Compliance with laws and regulations

It is the responsibility of management to ensure that the company complies with the laws and regulations which have an impact on its operations.

This includes laws and regulations concerning

- Money laundering
- Health and safety
- Public liability
- Employer's liability
- PAYE and payroll matters

Background

Following the Enron scandal, the Sarbanes-Oxley Act was rapidly passed into US law in 2002. It introduced a number of measures to attempt to improve the quality of financial reporting, including:

- Having Chief Executive Officers (CEOs) and Chief Finance Officers (CFOs) attest to the veracity of the financial statements
- Much greater disclosure of the amendments made to the financial statements during the audit process

  Companies have had to review systems to ensure that CEOs and CFOs can make such attestations, as there are criminal penalties for making them falsely. This has also affected UK subsidiaries of US companies.

2 Assurance providers' responsibilities

Section overview

- The assurance provider is responsible for:
  - Carrying out the assurance service in accordance with professional and ethical standards
  - Carrying out the assurance service in accordance with the terms of engagement
- In the case of statutory audit, the auditor is, in addition, responsible for:
  - Forming an independent opinion on the truth and fairness of the financial statements
  - Confirming that the financial statements have been properly prepared in accordance with the Companies Act 2006
  - Confirming that the information contained within the directors' report is consistent with the financial statements
- While the assurance provider does not bear the management responsibilities outlined above, many of them will impact strongly on the audit and, in particular, the risk assessment that the assurance provider carries out.

2.1 General

The responsibility of the external provider of assurance services is determined by:

- The requirements of any legislation or regulation under which the engagement is conducted, and/or
- The terms of engagement for the assignment, which will specify the services to be provided, (you learnt about engagement letters in your studies for Assurance)
- Ethical and professional standards
- Quality control standards

2.2 Statutory audit

The legal requirements are now contained in the Companies Act 2006, the provisions of which have gradually replaced the provisions of the Companies Act 1985.

In the case of an audit of financial statements under the Companies Act 2006, it is the external auditor's responsibility to:

- Form an independent opinion on the truth and fairness of the accounts
- Confirm that the accounts have been properly prepared in accordance with the Companies Act 2006
- State in their audit report whether in the opinion the information given in the directors' report is consistent with the financial statements

To achieve these objectives the auditor has to ensure that:

- The audit is planned properly (see Chapters 7, 8, 9 and 10)
- Sufficient appropriate audit evidence is gathered (we covered this in detail in Assurance)
- The evidence is properly reviewed and valid conclusions drawn (see Chapter 13).

In accordance with the law and ethical standards the auditor must maintain independence from the client.

In particular, as stated above, appointment as the Companies Act auditor does not lead to responsibility for the following matters:

- The design and operation of the accounting systems.
- The maintenance of the accounting records.
- The preparation and accuracy of management information.
- The preparation of the financial statements.
- The identification of every error and deficiency in the accounts and the accounting records.
- The prevention of fraud in a company.
- The detection of immaterial fraud in the company.
- Ensuring that the company has complied with the laws and regulations that are relevant to its business (except insofar as it affects the financial statements).

All these remain the responsibility of the management of the company; they have the responsibility to manage and cannot delegate or pass this responsibility on to the external auditor.

Although it is important to know where these responsibilities lie

- Business risks
- Fraud and error
- Non-compliance with laws and regulations
- Accounting policies

all impact on the financial statements to a greater or lesser extent, and

- Systems and controls

impact on the way the auditor conducts the audit.

We shall look at how far auditor responsibilities extend in these areas in the following sections of this chapter.

2.3 Non-assurance services

A firm which is engaged by management to provide additional non-statutory and non-assurance services is only responsible for providing the services specifically negotiated with management. Such engagements do not result in the firm taking responsibility for any aspects of the company's operations or procedures.

For example, a firm may be engaged to perform services additional to the audit such as:

- Assisting the company with the maintenance of its accounting records
- Assisting the company with preparing management information
- Preparing the financial statements of the company
- Preparing the corporation tax return of the company

The key point is that management retains the overall responsibility for all of these matters; the firm is employed as a support to management, providing expert assistance.

The principles and rules concerning the provision of non-audit services by the **audit** firm to its audit clients are set out in the APB's Ethical Standards and are dealt with in Chapter 4.

Background

The Sarbanes-Oxley Act, mentioned above in the context of management responsibilities, also has provisions which relate directly to auditors. In particular:

- There is stricter enforcement of the auditor independence rules as a result of the Act.
- A Public Company Accounting Oversight Board (PCAOB) has been set up to inspect audit files of US listed and other public interest clients.

  PCAOB is entitled to inspect the audit files of major subsidiaries of US listed companies, so US domestic law can impact overseas where the subsidiary is not US based. Auditors of subsidiaries of US listed companies must register (for a fee!) with PCAOB and are liable to inspection.

3 Error

Section overview

- Auditors are responsible for detecting material misstatements in the financial statements, some of which may be caused by error.
- Management are responsible for designing and implementing a system of internal control which is capable of preventing, or detecting and correcting, errors in the financial records.
- Auditors are required to assess the system of internal control as part of their audit in order to determine whether to rely on the system of controls or carry out extended tests of details.
- Auditors are required to report to those charged with governance on material weaknesses in controls which could adversely affect the entity's ability to record, process, summarise and report financial data potentially causing material misstatements in the financial statements.
- Auditors are responsible for giving an opinion whether the financial statements are free from material misstatement caused by error. This means that they should design procedures that are capable of detecting errors.
- As we set out in your Assurance manual, the two types of test generally carried out as part of an audit are tests of control and tests of detail. The more reliance that can be placed on controls (assessed by testing controls), the fewer tests of details may be carried out.

Definition

Internal control: A process designed and effected by those charged with governance, management, and other personnel to provide reasonable assurance about the achievement of the entity's objectives with regard to reliability of financial reporting, effectiveness and efficiency of operations and compliance with applicable laws and regulations. It follows that internal control is designed and implemented to address identified business risks that threaten the achievement of any of these objectives.

Internal controls are designed in part to prevent errors occurring in financial information, or to detect errors and correct them.

Worked example: Computer controls

Katie is the receivables ledger clerk for Happy Limited. She enters sales invoices to the ledger in batches.

The computer has a number of inbuilt controls to ensure that Katie does not make mistakes when she is inputting information.

It has a data range query function so that if Katie enters a figure that exceeds a pre-set limit, it will automatically prompt her to check she is correct.

It has a data type query function so that if Katie enters a figure where she was supposed to enter a letter, it will automatically prompt her to check she is correct.

It has several calculation functions, so that if Katie enters an incorrect amount in relation to VAT or invoice total, or does not enter such a figure, it will automatically prompt her to check she is correct.

It has a batch total calculation, that Katie then compares the total for all the invoices she has entered per her own calculation to the calculation on the computer, to ensure that all the invoices have been entered.

All these controls operate to ensure that Katie does not enter the wrong amounts in respect of each sales invoice, which ultimately helps to ensure that the revenue figure in the financial statements does not contain errors.

We discussed the limitations of systems of internal control in your studies for Assurance.

Interactive question 2: Limitations of internal control **[Difficulty level: Easy]**

What are some limitations of the controls over the receivables ledger at Happy Ltd, outlined above?

See **Answer** at the end of this chapter.

Auditor's assessment of internal controls

As we also outlined in your studies for assurance, the auditor is required to assess the system of internal controls as part of his risk assessment, and determine whether he believes it is capable of preventing or detecting and correcting errors.

If he determines that it is capable of this, it will affect the way that he carries out his audit, as ISA 315 *Identifying and Assessing the Risks of Material Misstatement Through Understanding the Entity and its Environment* requires auditors to:

- Obtain an understanding of controls relevant to the audit
- Evaluate the design of those controls and
- Determine whether they have been implemented

If testing of controls reveals that the system is not only capable of preventing or detecting and correcting errors, but it operates efficiently, the auditor will be able to conclude that the system is strong and the risk of the financial statements containing errors is reduced. This, in turn, will result in a lower level of tests of details being carried out.

ISA 330 *The Auditor's Responses to Assessed Risks* requires the auditor to test controls if:

- The auditor intends to rely on the operating effectiveness of those controls or
- Substantive procedures alone cannot provide sufficient appropriate audit evidence

Reporting on internal control weaknesses

ISA 265 *Communicating Deficiencies in Internal Control to Those Charged with Governance and Management* sets out that auditors should determine whether audit work has identified any deficiencies in internal control. Where, in the auditor's judgement, those deficiencies are significant, they should be communicated in writing on a timely basis.

A significant deficiency in internal control is one that, in the auditor's professional judgement, is important enough to be brought to the attention of those charged with governance.

Summary

In summary then:

- Auditors are responsible for detecting material errors in the financial statements, which they may do by carrying out tests of control or tests of details.
- Management are responsible for internal control systems capable of preventing or detecting error.
- Auditors are responsible for assessing whether that system is capable of preventing or detecting errors.
- If the material weaknesses are found, auditors are responsible for:
  - Reporting these to management
  - Carrying out additional tests of details to uncover any potential errors as a result of the weakness.

4 Fraud

Section overview

- The auditor is responsible for drawing a conclusion as to whether the financial statements are free from material misstatement (which can be caused by fraud).
- The auditor's responsibilities with regard to fraud are set out in ISA 240 *The Auditor's Responsibilities Relating to Fraud in an Audit of Financial Statements* and include:
  - Assessing risks of material misstatement
  - Discussing the susceptibility of the financial statements to material misstatement caused by fraud
- A key issue in relation to discovering material misstatements caused by fraud is professional scepticism.
- When the auditors become aware of possible non-compliance, they should evaluate the possible effect on the financial statements and on other audit evidence obtained and need to make reports to management.

4.1 Definition of fraud

Fraud is a word we normally use to cover a wide range of illegal acts.

For audit purposes, ISA 240, *The Auditor's Responsibilities Relating to Fraud in an Audit of Financial Statements*, identifies two types of risk of misstatement which can arise from fraud:

- Misstatements arising from fraudulent financial reporting
- Misstatements arising from misappropriation of assets

In order to have a reasonable expectation of detecting fraud or error, auditors should follow the procedures in ISA 240.

4.2 Responsibilities regarding fraud

ISA 240 sets out management and auditor responsibilities regarding fraud.

Regarding management, the ISA states that the primary responsibility for the prevention and detection of fraud rests with both those charged with governance of the entity and with management. To fulfil this responsibility, various actions can be taken including:

- Demonstrating that management follow a culture of honesty and ethical behaviour and communicating that they expect all employees to adhere to this culture
- Establishing a sound system of internal control
- From the point of view of those charged with governance, ensuring that management implement policies and procedures to ensure, as far as possible, the orderly and efficient conduct of the company's business.

Regarding the auditor, the ISA states that the auditor must obtain reasonable assurance that the financial statements, taken as a whole, are free from material misstatement, whether caused by fraud or error. The auditor does not therefore offer complete assurance that the financial statements are free from fraud and/or error as audit testing is not designed to provide this assurance.

4.3 Risk assessment

Part of an auditor's work must include assessing the risk of a fraud existing. We will consider risk assessment procedures in more detail in Chapter 9. Appendix 1 to ISA 240 is a very useful document as it gives examples of fraud risk factors.

However, it should not be used as a list to be regurgitated in the examination, as risks are always specific to the client.

ISA 240 sets out that auditors are:

- Entitled to accept representations as truthful and records as genuine, unless there is evidence to the contrary; but also
- Required to bring professional scepticism (as defined) to the work.

Auditors should also carry out a discussion of the susceptibility of the entity's financial statements to fraud. This will usually include a consideration of:

- Where the company's system is weak and how management could perpetrate fraud
- The circumstances that could indicate earnings management which could lead to fraudulent financial reporting
- The known internal and external factors that could be an incentive to fraud being carried out
- Management's involvement in overseeing employees with access to cash or other assets which could be misappropriated
- Any unusual or unexplained changes in behaviour/lifestyle of management or employees
- The need for professional scepticism
- The type of circumstances that could lead to suspicions of fraud
- How unpredictability will be incorporated into the way the audit is carried out
- What audit procedures might be responsive to fraud
- Any allegations of fraud that have been made
- The risk of management override of controls

4.4 Where fraud is suspected

If the auditors identify misstatements which might indicate that fraud has taken place, they should consider the implications of this for other aspects of the audit, particularly management representations which may not be trustworthy if fraud is indicated. This may lead to a limitation in the scope of the audit.

4.5 Management representations

Auditors are required to obtain particular written representations from management that management acknowledges its responsibility to design and implement internal controls to prevent and detect fraud and that management has disclosed any known or suspected frauds by management, employees with a significant role in internal control, or any other frauds which might have a material impact on the financial statements to the auditor.

In addition, management confirm in writing that it has disclosed the results of its own assessment of whether the financial statements may be materially affected by fraud.

4.6 Reporting frauds or suspected frauds

The ISA requires that the auditors should discuss suspected or actual fraud with management and those charged with governance and make the appropriate reports, as set out below:

MANAGEMENT	If they actually discover fraud If they suspect fraud
THOSE CHARGED WITH GOVERNANCE	Unless all of those charged with governance are involved in managing the entity and the auditor has identified or suspects fraud involving management

THIRD PARTIES eg regulatory and enforcement authorities	The auditor shall determine whether there is a responsibility to report the occurrence or suspicion to a party outside the entity

If fraud or error causes the financial statements to not give a true and fair view or there is a fundamental uncertainty, it should be included in the audit report in the usual way, **thereby notifying the shareholders.**

Interactive question 3: Fraud [Difficulty level: Exam standard]

During the course of your audit of Slipstream Ltd the credit controller asks for a private interview with you. During this interview she makes it known that she suspects the chief accountant of misappropriating company funds received from debtors and altering the books.

What steps would you take to enable you to assess whether the credit controller's suspicions are reasonable?

See **Answer** at the end of this chapter.

Interactive question 4: Reporting fraud [Difficulty level: Exam standard]

During the course of the audit you discover that the wages clerk has been defrauding the client through not deleting leavers from the payroll until two months after departure, and was pocketing the money herself.

What should you do with regard to:

(a) Informing the client?
(b) The audit report?

See **Answer** at the end of this chapter.

4.7 Concluding on fraud

Fraud is a major cost for business and the statutory audit is not designed to identify every fraud in an audit, merely those with a material effect. However, many users of accounts expect that the audit process should uncover all instances of fraud in a company. This is a feature of the expectations gap (discussed below in section 8).

From time to time, the issue of whether auditors' duties should be extended in relation to fraud is discussed. It can be argued that the auditors have closer contact with an organisation than any other external advisers and therefore they are in a position to gain a detailed understanding of the organisation and its systems which should lead to an ability to discover all frauds at an organisation.

However, this argument ignores the inherent limitations of the audit process, which you are aware of from your earlier studies in Assurance, and also opens up the possibility that audit becomes seen simply as a fraud investigation and the wider objective of reporting on the financial statements is lost.

Another key issue is the cost to businesses that this would represent, as the level of testing in a fraud investigation would be far more detailed than the sample based testing required for the purpose of an audit, which most businesses would find prohibitive.

It must be concluded that attempts to make auditors more responsible for discovering fraud also miss the point that management ultimately is responsible for everything within the company, including the prevention and detection of fraud. Management should not be able to hide behind the auditors when fraud is eventually discovered or blame the auditors for not discovering the fraud earlier. Implementing and reporting on the principles of corporate governance is one way to enhance the performance of management in establishing effective systems, managing the risks to the security of the organisation's assets and promoting high standards of conduct by all those within the organisation.

Lastly it must be emphasised that this expectation gap with relation to fraud is generally associated with the statutory audit. If an assurance firm is engaged to carry out a different assurance engagement, or a non-statutory audit, then the terms of that engagement will be set out between the parties and all parties should be very clear what the role of the assurance providers in relation to discovering fraud, will be on that assignment. Bear in mind that the cost of providing a service to uncover frauds might be high and therefore this might be rare in practice. Of course, in order to close the gap in understanding of what the purpose of a statutory audit is in relation to fraud, the auditors' responsibilities are set out in the audit engagement letter. However, this letter is a private matter between the directors and the firm, and therefore this measure does not tackle the issue that the view is widely held in 'society at large' that auditors should detect frauds.

5 Compliance with laws and regulations

Section overview

- Management is responsible for ensuring that the company complies with laws and regulations.
- Auditors are responsible for concluding that the financial statements are free from material misstatements caused by non-compliance with laws and regulations.
- Auditors are required to have a general understanding of the legal and regulatory framework within which the company operates.

5.1 Non-compliance with laws and regulations

Auditors are interested in two categories of law and regulations:

- Those with a direct impact on the financial statements, for example, the Companies Act
- Those which provide a legal framework within which the company operates

The auditor should obtain an understanding of the legal framework within which the company operates as part of his understanding of the entity and its environment (discussed in Chapter 8).

Areas of law which affect all businesses will be:

- Employment law. (For example, the auditor should note if work on the payroll appears to indicate that the company pays employees less than the minimum wage.)
- Social security law. (For example, the auditor should ensure that the company appears to be paying over the correct amounts to HMRC in respect of PAYE, NI and payments such as maternity pay and paternity pay.)
- Health and safety law. (For example, the auditor might notice if a company did not have clear safety notices on manufacturing premises and did not display clear fire exit and procedures notifications.)

5.2 Risk assessment

As part of their risk assessment procedures, auditors should assess the risk that the company is not complying with any relevant law or regulation. Risk assessment procedures will be considered in more detail in Chapter 9.

5.3 Evidence about compliance

The auditor is required by ISA 250 *Consideration of Laws and Regulations in an Audit of Financial Statements* to obtain evidence about compliance with laws and regulations. It states that the auditors should:

- Make inquiries of management
- Inspect correspondence with relevant licensing or regulatory bodies
- Ask those charged with governance if they are on notice of any non-compliance.

The auditors should obtain written representations that management has disclosed all known instances of actual or possible non-compliance with laws and regulations.

5.4 Non-compliance suspected

When the auditors suspect non-compliance, they should document findings and discuss them with management. If the auditors cannot obtain sufficient appropriate evidence about the suspected non-compliance, this might represent a limitation on the scope of the audit, which will result in the auditors not being able to give an unqualified opinion. (We shall look at reporting in more detail in Chapter 13.)

5.5 Reporting of non-compliance

The ISA requires that the auditors should communicate discovered instances of non-compliance with laws and regulations to those charged with governance (the directors) without delay, and make appropriate reports, as set out below:

THOSE CHARGED WITH GOVERNANCE	If the auditors suspect non-compliance with laws and regulations If the auditor suspects that management or those charged with governance are involved in non-compliance, the auditor shall communicate the matter to the next higher level of authority at the entity, if it exists, such as an audit committee. Where no higher authority exists auditor shall consider the need to obtain legal advice.
SHAREHOLDERS	**Only** if non-compliance causes the financial statements to not give a true and fair view or there is a fundamental uncertainty – in which case it should be included in the audit report in the usual way (see Chapter 13)
THIRD PARTIES eg regulatory and enforcement authorities	The auditor shall determine whether the auditor has a responsibility to report the identified or suspected non-compliance to parties outside the entity.

5.6 Concluding on reporting non-compliance with laws and regulations

Businesses are faced with ever increasing amounts of legislation across all areas of their activities. It is reasonably asked, 'can auditors be expected to become sufficiently expert on every single regulation that exists?'

Many regulations are concerned with matters that are not recorded in accounting systems, for example, issues relating to employment, health and safety and building planning consents. Auditors already face the problem of how to get sufficient and appropriate evidence in relation to their very limited responsibilities, as evidence in this area can be subjective and general. There must be a limit to how much further into the company's total records auditors should be expected to go.

It is possible that it would be better for companies to have a 'regulations audit' carried out by an industry insider who genuinely understands the types of regulations with which the business has to comply and how compliance should occur.

6 Related parties

Section overview

- Accounting standards require that all transactions with related parties are disclosed.
- Auditors need to consider the risk of there being undisclosed related party transactions.
- The auditors should ask the directors for a list of related parties and watch out for transactions with those parties during the course of testing.
- Auditors need to carry out specific tests to seek to identify related parties.
- The auditors need to ensure that appropriate disclosures have been made about related party transactions.
- Written representations about related parties must be obtained from directors.

6.1 The nature of related party transactions

Transactions with related parties may be carried out on terms which may not be the same as in an arm's length transaction with an independent third party. The approach adopted in financial reporting standards is to disclose the relevant amounts and relationships so that the reader of the financial statements can decide for themselves whether such transactions have led to a manipulation of the financial statements.

Related parties are those people or companies that might have, or be expected to have, an undue influence on the company being audited. So as examples (but the full list is much longer), the directors and key management of a company, together with their families, are regarded as related parties of that company, as are other companies controlled by them, other companies in the same group, and so on.

A director might well be in a position to tell an employee to arrange for the company:

- To sell to the director some goods at a cut down price, or
- To buy from another business owned by the director services at above-normal prices.

Because these transactions may not be at the normal market rate, company law and accounting standards require all transactions with related parties, even those conducted at the market rate, to be disclosed. The party that controls the company being audited must also be disclosed in the accounts, even if there are no transactions between them.

ISA 550 *Related Parties* details the audit work required in respect of related party transactions. The work can be split into the three main stages of the audit:

- Planning
- Detailed work
- Review

6.2 The planning stage

The auditor needs to consider the risk of there being undisclosed material related party transactions. This is an extremely difficult area, because the materiality rule for related party transactions is not just the normal one. The normal rule judges materiality by reference to the company being audited, whereas material related party transactions are judged both by that and by reference to the individual related party (which may be much smaller than the company being audited).

6.3 The detailed testing stage

The auditors should ask the directors, who are, after all, responsible for the proper preparation of the financial statements (which will include full disclosure of related party transactions), for a list of related parties and consider if this is complete. The whole audit team should be aware of the list so that they can keep an eye out for those names when carrying out all of the other audit work needed. For example, an entry in the cash book may give an indication of a related party, so it needs to be picked up by the person auditing cash and bank.

ISA 550 sets out specific procedures that should be carried out:

- Detailed tests of transactions and balances (such as would ordinarily be carried out on audits)
- Reviewing minutes of meetings of shareholders and directors to observe if any related parties or transactions with them become apparent
- Reviewing records for large or unusual transactions or balances, particularly those recognised near the end of the reporting period
- Reviewing confirmation of loans receivable and payable and confirmations from banks (which might indicate guarantor relationships)
- Reviewing investment transactions, for example, when the company has invested in another company

Audit evidence in relation to related parties and transactions with them may be limited and restricted to representations from management. Due to this, the auditor should try carry out procedures such as:

- Discussing the purpose of the transactions with management/directors
- Confirming the terms and amount of the transaction with the related party
- Inspecting information in the possession of the related party
- Corroborating the explanation of the transactions with the related party
- Obtaining information from an unrelated third party if possible
- Confirming information with persons associated with the transaction, such as banks, solicitors, guarantors and agents.

Where related party transactions are found the auditor checks that the appropriate disclosures are made in the accounts. Remember that all transactions with related parties need to be disclosed, even if they are at a normal market rate. However, any disclosures should include information that is needed for a proper understanding of the transaction and this would, of course, include whether the transaction was or was not at a market rate.

6.4 The review stage

Written representations should always be requested from directors, who are in the best position to know the identities of related parties. The auditor then reviews the accounts, together with the audit evidence available, in order to reach a conclusion on the appropriate audit opinion.

Interactive question 5: Related party transactions [Difficulty level: Exam standard]

The training partner in your office is aware that you have covered ISA 550 *Related Parties* in your Professional Stage studies. He has asked you to help him prepare for a training session he is about to give.

Requirements

Prepare notes for a training session for junior staff on how to identify related party transactions. Your notes should include

(a) A list of possible features which would lead you to investigate a particular transaction to determine whether it is in fact a related party transaction.

(b) A summary of the general audit procedures you would perform to ensure that all material related party transactions have been identified.

See **Answer** at the end of this chapter.

7 Money laundering

Section overview

- Accountants have substantial responsibilities in respect of suspected or actual money laundering.
- Money laundering is defined as a wide range of activities in relation to criminal property, including using, acquiring, concealing and removing from the UK.
- Accountants are required to report a suspicion of money laundering to the Serious Organised Crime Agency.
- Failure to make a report is a criminal offence.
- There is also an offence called 'tipping off' – making the money launderer aware that a report has been made.

7.1 Background

The auditor's responsibilities in respect of money laundering are substantial. It is not the purpose of these notes to go into all the implications of these responsibilities, but you do need to be aware of the duties laid on your firm and, from your very first day of work as an accountant, on you.

7.2 What is money laundering?

The purpose of money laundering is to:

- Disguise the origins of funds derived from illicit sources, and
- Enable illicit funds to be used by those who control them.

As you know from your law studies, as a result of the Proceeds of Crime Act 2002 the definition of money laundering has been expanded to include:

- Using
- Acquiring
- Retaining
- Controlling
- Concealing
- Disguising
- Converting
- Transferring
- Removing from the UK

Criminal property is also rather widely defined as the *benefits of criminal conduct.*

The definition extends well beyond the 'obvious' examples involving a criminal, say, a drug dealer, passing the takings of his crimes through the books of a 'front' business, such as a restaurant.

Other examples of criminal conduct and criminal property include:

- **Tax evasion**

  This could relate to direct tax such as corporation tax or to indirect tax such as VAT.

- **Offenses that involve saved costs**

  These could result from environmental offences, or from failure to implement health and safety requirements.

- **Offences committed overseas that are criminal offences under UK law**

  These could involve payments that are deemed to be bribes.

7.3 Your responsibilities

The duty to report

The Proceeds of Crime Act and the related Money Laundering Regulations 2007 both single out accountants (along with, among others, banks, lawyers, estate agents and casino operators) as having special responsibilities. If an accountant has **grounds for suspicion** that money laundering is taking place at a client, **that accountant must report it**. The exception to this rule is where the accountant is offering advice to a client on areas such as compliance with taxation legislation and the accountant claims Legal Professional Privilege and may not therefore be required to make a report. Remember that LPP does not apply to audits.

The regulations override the duty of confidentiality (see the discussion of professional ethics in Chapter 4) towards the client and it is important to note the words '**grounds for suspicion**' – if an accountant waits for incontrovertible evidence, it might be too late.

Accountants do not automatically benefit from any professional privilege under the law. Lawyers do, to some extent, but accountants **generally** do not, unless they are providing legal services, and have always had to tread a fine line of discretion between their duty to their client and the public interest.

An accountant's duty to report money laundering includes reporting actual knowledge or reasonable grounds for suspicion of money laundering. Non-reporting is not an option but mere speculation should not be reported.

Auditors are concerned primarily with the risk of material misstatement of the financial statements, and the audit procedures adopted are designed accordingly. It may be, therefore, that an auditor does not become aware of immaterial matters and there is nothing in the auditing standards to compel the auditor to seek them out. However, if an auditor does come across any misstatement, material or otherwise, this must now be considered from a money laundering perspective.

For non-audit engagements, the terms of engagement will determine whether materiality needs to be considered or not. But here again, any misstatement, regardless of its materiality in whatever context, must be considered for its Proceeds of Crime Act implications.

It would seem that there are considerable amounts of money in the economy which derive from criminal activity – drugs, terrorism, organised crime – and these amounts must go somewhere.

There is therefore a clear ethical imperative (as well as a legal one) to report knowledge or reasonable suspicion of such activity.

If a client is doing well and you do not understand where the money has come from, after exhausting all reasonable lines of enquiry then you have grounds for suspicion and a duty to report without 'tipping off' either:

- The client, or
- Anyone who could prejudice an enquiry into the matter

Report to whom?

Accountants must report to the nominated official (Money Laundering Reporting Officer or MLRO) in their assurance firm, which fulfils their responsibility.

The MLRO then has to decide on whether to report the matter to the Serious Organised Crime Agency (SOCA) and, if appropriate, to make the report.

The legislation protects professionals from any claims for breach of confidentiality even where suspicions are later proved to be ill-founded.

7.4 Offences and penalties

Failing to report and to comply with the regulations – including the need to provide suitable training – are offences under the legislation.

There is also an offence called '**tipping off**' designed to avoid the money launderer being able to escape before the forces of law and order catch up with him or her.

The penalties for non-compliance by accountants are potentially quite severe – for some offences a jail term of fourteen years is a possibility.

7.5 A paradox

The auditor's responsibility is to form an opinion as to whether or not the financial statements give a true and fair view. If included in the company's revenue are material amounts resulting from money laundering, it is probable that the financial statements do not, in fact, give a true and fair view. If the auditors qualify the report, however, they could be accused of tipping off.

7.6 Concluding on money laundering

Money laundering issues affect almost all aspects of an accountant's work and, particularly, due to the privileged position of the auditor, carrying out audit work.

A case has been made to the government by both the ICAEW and the Scottish Institute that, due to the professional standards under which their members operate (which we shall look at in the next two chapters) they should be allowed to use their discretion in making reports to SOCA.

The government has said broadly: 'This is the 'trust me I'm an accountant' argument and past experience of submissions of 'suspicious transactions reports' suggest that not many come from accountants. So we're doing something about it. If you wish to argue to the public that you should have specific rights not to report drugs and terrorist money, go ahead, but we don't think the public will be convinced.'

Yet there is an argument that the profession has, over the years, done much to encourage compliance with the tax laws and the introduction of better business practices and that possibly the wide definition of money laundering in the Proceeds of Crime Act 2002 does not provide the best mechanism for resolving the problem.

There is concern that the reporting requirements of the POCA are set too low putting pressure on accountants to carry out "extra" work.

7.7 Money laundering and the audit approach

The introduction of the Proceeds of Crime Act 2002 (POCA) and the Money Laundering Regulations 2007 (MLR) bring added complications to the auditor's work.

This legislation has regulatory and ethical implications which we have dealt with. Another key principle stressed by the authorities dealing with Money Laundering in the UK and worldwide is **KYC - know your client**.

- The firm will need to have checked the client's identity, when they first became a client and will need to keep the evidence on file for six years after they cease to be a client
- Where does the money come from? Auditors should think about the real nature of the business' sales, but also about the source of the start-up capital and any other equity and loans raised
- Remember the money launderer wants to overstate income and loves paying tax on the excess, which goes against the grain of the way most auditors think.

The APB have revised Practice Note 12 Money Laundering Legislation – Interim Guidance for Auditors in the United Kingdom. It does not extend the scope of the audit but rather highlights how normal audit procedures might identify matters that should be reported.

Further guidance is available from the CCAB's Anti Money Laundering Guidance for the Accounting Sector, which sets out some 'prompts' that clearly illustrate how money laundering suspicions could arise during the planning and risk assessment phase of an audit, or even during the detailed evidence gathering phase.

1 What is its purpose in entering into any transaction forming the basis of the proposed engagement or its purpose in seeking services where not related to a specific transaction?

2 What are the entity's main trading and registered office addresses?

3 What are its business activities or purposes and sector?

4 Who controls and manages it (ie, has executive power over the entity – this may be directors, shadow directors or others depending on the circumstances)?

5 If the client is audited, were the accounts qualified and, if so why?

6 Name and check that the person (s) purporting to represent the entity is/are who they say they are.

7 Who owns it – ultimate beneficial owner (s) and steps in between (as a minimum for companies provide details of any ultimate beneficial owners of more than 25% - for trusts, supply details of trustees and settlors and details of either beneficiaries with more than 25% interest, or the classes of beneficiary, and or collective investment funds to other similar arrangements provide details of the general partner and/or investment manager together with details of any person with more than 25% interest)?

8 What is its business model/intended business model (ie, the mechanism by which a business intends to generate revenue and profits and serve its customers – in terms of broad principles)?

9 What are the key sources of:

- Income (eg, trading, investment etc); and
- Capital (eg, public share offer, private investment etc)?

10 The history and current (also forecast if readily available) scale of its entity's:

- Earnings (eg, turnover and profits/losses); and
- Net assets.

11 The entity's geographical connections, so that you are in a position to ask such questions as "Why is it getting so much money from that place?" and "Why is it sending assets to that place?"

12 Has the entity been subject to insolvency proceedings, or is it in course of being dissolved/struck-off, or has it been dissolved/struck-off?

8 Expectations gap

Section overview

- The expectations gap is the gap between the expectations of users of assurance reports and the firm's responsibilities in respect of those reports.
- There are a variety of misunderstandings about the nature of assurance work.
- The expectations gap has been narrowed by:
  - Improving the required audit report
  - Inserting paragraphs relating to directors'/auditors' responsibilities in the engagement letter
  - The role of audit committees, which liaise with auditors

8.1 What is the expectations gap?

This so-called 'gap' is between the expectations of users of assurance reports, particularly of audit reports under the Companies Act, and the firm's legal responsibilities. For example, users of the financial statements may well expect that an assurance engagement involves the checking of every single transaction, while the firm judges that checks on a test basis are sufficient.

This is further compounded by confusion over the meaning of the report that the auditor gives. The misunderstandings made by lay users of financial statements can be summarised as follows:

- Many believe that responsibility for preparing financial statements lies with the auditor, rather than with management.
- It is widely believed by the general public that the auditor's principal duty is to detect fraud, when in fact the duty is to make a report as to whether or not the financial statements are materially misstated, irrespective of whether such misstatement arises as a result of fraud.

- In most cases the users of the financial statements will also have little perception of the concept of materiality and believe that the auditors check all the transactions that the company undertakes.
- The public generally perceives that an audit report attached to the financial statements means that they are 'correct', rather than just meaning that there is reasonable assurance that they give a true and fair view.

8.2 Narrowing the expectations gap

Various steps have been taken to try to reduce the expectations gap.

Expanding the audit report

The content of the Companies Act audit report has been expanded to:

- Set out responsibilities of auditors and directors
- Explain how an audit is conducted:
  - On a test basis, which implies sampling
  - By assessing significant estimates and judgements
  - So as to give reasonable assurance on the financial statements
  - So as to detect material misstatements – in relation to fraud, error or any other irregularity

In the case of listed companies the report has been expanded further to explain to the users of the financial statements that the auditors review statements made by the company about its corporate governance procedures, and consider other information included with the financial statements to ensure it is consistent.

Engagement letter

When the firm issues an engagement letter, the letter includes a paragraph reminding the directors of their responsibilities and setting out the firm's responsibilities. Additional detail on the engagement letter can be found in Chapter 6.

Directors' responsibilities

The reporting requirement was extended by the guidance on the preparation of audit reports, to include a statement of the directors' responsibilities. This serves to make the respective responsibilities of management and auditors clearer to the users of the financial statements.

Audit committees

Various statements on the principles of corporate governance developed for listed companies have recommended that companies should establish an audit committee of the board to liaise with and receive reports from both external and internal auditors. (Internal auditors are people who work for a company and help the directors to ensure that accounts are properly kept and business risks are minimised. 'External auditors' is the phrase used to describe those involved in the independent Companies Act audit.) The existence of an audit committee serves as a reminder of the division of responsibilities between auditors and management. The disclosures made in the company's annual report about its corporate governance practices should include comments about the operations of its audit committee.

8.3 So why do things still go wrong?

Sometimes companies fail. Sometimes people commit fraud. Sometimes people make genuine mistakes when financial statements are being prepared.

These events are never the fault of the auditor – although as we have seen, the expectations gap means that the users of financial statements do not necessarily understand this.

Sometimes – and these tend to be the most difficult cases – events like this occur, the auditors do not detect them, but no audit failure takes place.

How can this be?

If:

- The effect is immaterial, or
- The accounts, in spite of the event taking place, still give a true and fair view, or
- The auditor's procedures were properly planned, executed and documented but the event could not be detected for some reason, perhaps a carefully executed fraud or a sudden, cataclysmic change leading to the company's collapse

the auditors may not be at fault.

Nevertheless, corporate collapses do happen and the auditors are found to have been negligent in some way. Clearly, in these cases, something must have gone wrong in:

- Planning the audit
- Performing the audit
- Drawing conclusions from the work done

These failures can usually be traced to one of four main causes:

- The failure to assess audit risk properly
- The failure to respond appropriately to audit risk
- The failure to recognise and respond to situations where the auditor's objectivity is threatened
- The failure to recognise and respond to situations beyond the auditor's area of competence

Summary and Self-test

Summary

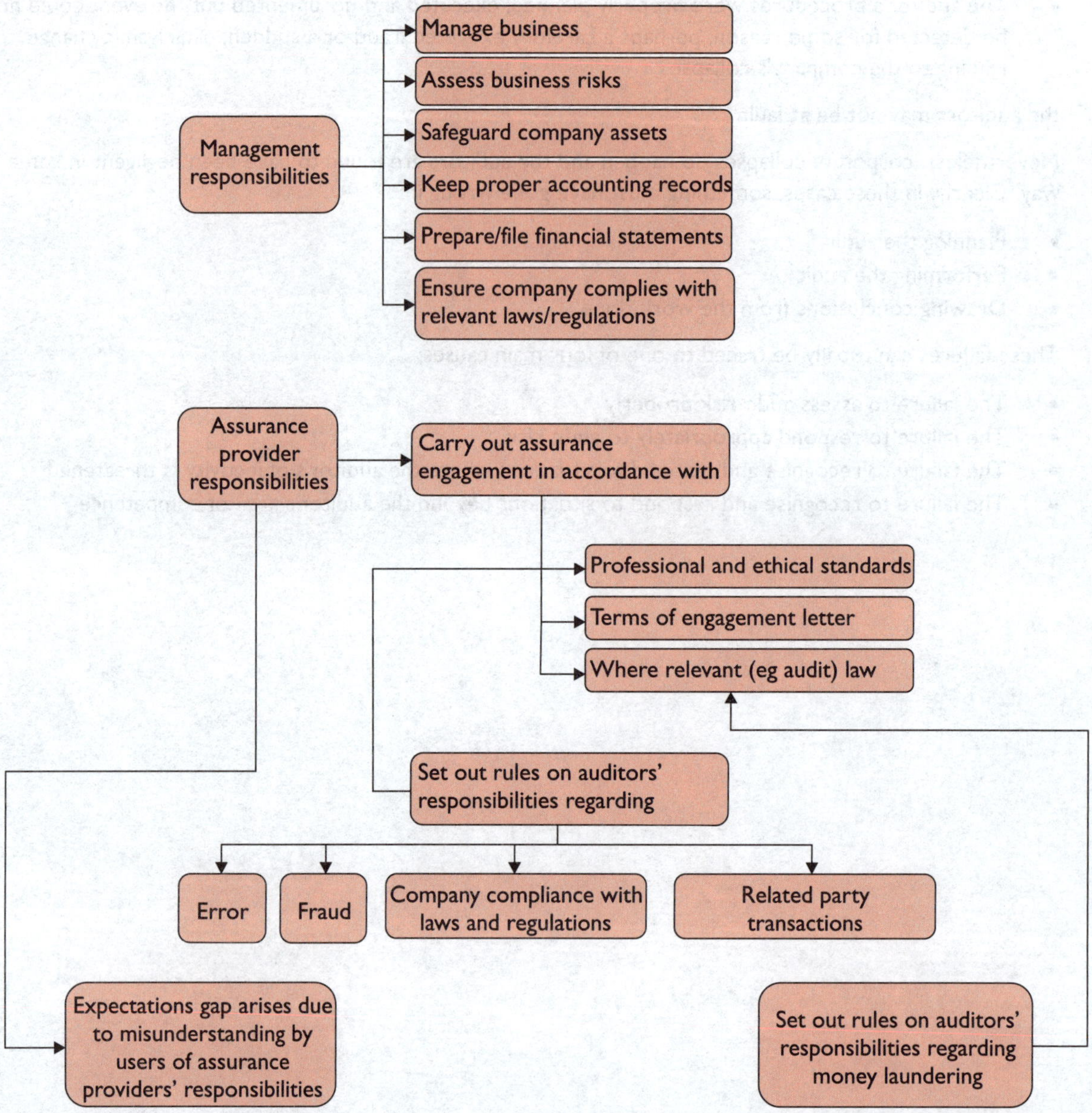

Self-test

Answer the following questions.

1 Which one is management not responsible for?

- ☐ The safeguarding of company assets
- ☐ Keeping proper accounting records
- ☐ Preparing financial statements
- ☐ Auditing financial statements

2 Auditors have a duty to detect frauds which have a material impact on the financial statements.

- ☐ True
- ☐ False

3 The Sarbanes-Oxley Act requires CEOs to certify that the accounts are true.

- ☐ True
- ☐ False

4 Which two of the following are auditors not necessarily required to do?

A Assess the risk of fraud causing material misstatement in the financial statements
B Discuss the risk of fraud causing material misstatement in the financial statements
C Detect instances where fraud has caused a material misstatement in the financial statements
D Report material misstatements caused by fraud to the police

5 Auditors may be required to report instances of non-compliance with laws and regulations to which of the following?

- ☐ Shareholders
- ☐ Directors
- ☐ Regulatory authorities

6 Management are responsible for making appropriate disclosures concerning related parties in the financial statements.

- ☐ True
- ☐ False

7 An auditor fulfils his duty to report a suspicious transaction in relation to money laundering if he makes a report to the MLRO in his firm.

- ☐ True
- ☐ False

8 Which of the following is not a measure designed to close the expectations gap?

A Auditors required to attend company board meetings
B More detailed engagement letter sent to audit clients
C Audit report format revised and extended
D Statement of directors' responsibilities included in the financial statements

Exam-style questions

9 During the course of the audit of Gamma Ltd ('Gamma') an employee of the company informed you that a substantial cash deposit was paid into the company's bank account and a month later, the same amount was paid by direct transfer into a bank account in the name of Epsilon, a company based overseas. The employee also informed you that the managing director of Gamma had instructed him not to record the transaction in the accounting records as it had nothing to do with Gamma's business.

State, with reasons, what further action you should take in relation to this matter. **(3 marks)**

10 Your firm is the auditor of Alpha Ltd ('Alpha'). The managing director of Alpha discovered that the assistant accountant had used company cheques and bank transfers fraudulently to pay his own personal expenses. The expenditure was reported as company expenses in the income statement. Although the amounts involved are immaterial in the context of the financial statements, it transpired that this had been going on for several years. The managing director has expressed concern that your firm did not discover this fraud and has requested a meeting to discuss this matter.

Using Alpha's fraud as an example, compare and contrast the responsibilities of the auditors in respect of fraud with the expectation of the managing director of Alpha. **(3 marks)**

11 If brought to their attention, auditors should consider the implications of any breaches by their clients of employment and social security legislation.

Outline the consequences of not considering the implications and provide examples of such breaches. **(4 marks)**

12 You are the auditor of a company with numerous branches spread throughout the United Kingdom. Revenue for the year ended 31 December 20X1 was £25 million, profit before tax was £1,500,000 and net assets were £9,500,000. Your audit report was signed in March 20X2 without qualification. Your report to management after the audit pointed out that internal controls were weak at the branches due to the small number of staff.

You have been telephoned by the finance director, Ray Gosling, and told that the sales ledger clerk at the Goose Green branch had been caught 'teeming and lading'. His investigations so far show that during the year to 31 December 20X1 the sales ledger clerk had diverted £50,000 of receipts from customers to his own bank account. Ray has asked you to attend a meeting with him to discuss the matter. He is particularly concerned as to why the fraud was not discovered during the course of the audit and what the effect on the accounts might be.

At 31 December 20X1 the Goose Green branch had net assets of £400,000. For the year ended on that date the branch had revenue of £1,000,000 and made a small loss.

Your re-examination of your audit working papers shows that your staff had visited the Goose Green branch, that no grounds for suspicion arose during the audit and that appropriate audit procedures were carried out.

Requirements

(a) Prepare notes to guide you in your discussions with the finance director. **(6 marks)**

(b) Following the meeting the finance director has asked you to carry out additional assurance work to establish the extent of the fraud. Outline the main areas to which you would direct your attention in order to establish the extent of the fraud and the loss to the company and state why you would consider those areas. **(6 marks)**

(12 marks)

Now, go back to the Learning Objectives in the Introduction. If you are satisfied you have achieved these objectives, please tick them off.

Technical reference

1 Management responsibilities	Companies Act 2006 s. 386 and ss. 170-181
2 Assurance provider's responsibilities	Companies Act 2006 s.495
3 Error	IAASB Glossary of Terms
4 Fraud	ISA 240.3, 11, A1 (main references)
5 Compliance with laws and regulations	ISA 250.11
6 Related parties	ISA 550.10
7 Money laundering	Proceeds of Crime Act 2002 s. 330
8 Expectations gap	n/a

b) Area — Why consider

- external confirmation of sales
- why did mgt not detect
- how long was the clerk working at the branch
- other branches

- reduce risk of further errors
- possible further weaknesses in internal control.
- potential fraud from previous years

SoD

CHAPTER 2

Answers to Interactive questions

Answer to Interactive question 1

Directors are responsible for:

- Keeping proper accounting records
- Disclosing with reasonable accuracy at any time the financial position of the company
- Ensuring that the financial statements comply with the Companies Act 2006

Answer to Interactive question 2

The key limitation is that Katie may not carry out the checks that she is in control of (for example, the batch comparison) or that she may try and override the existing query controls.

Another limitation is that sometimes there may be unusual transactions which are outside the parameters set for the controls, in which case it will be necessary to override the controls.

Answer to Interactive question 3

- Review and obtain photocopies of documents which have aroused her suspicions
- Enquire into reasons for altered pages in books/documents etc
- Investigate any apparent override/circumvention of company procedure, eg cancelling a sales invoice instead of raising a credit note
- Review previous management letters for any weaknesses facilitating misappropriations
- Consider credit controller's motives for putting chief accountant under suspicion, eg working relationship/job threat
- Take note of chief accountant's standard of living; appropriate to his status?
- Consider whether past dealings with chief accountant have ever cast doubt on his integrity
- Increase analytical procedures on revenue and receivables, eg monthly revenue/receipts of major customers/extend circularisation if trade receivables collection period has increased
- Discuss with engagement partner, who may wish to discuss with client (eg board of directors)

Answer to Interactive question 4

(a) Informing the client

(i) Report to appropriate level of management

(ii) If believe that management or employees with significant roles in internal control are involved or fraud results in material misstatement in financial statements report to those charged with governance (eg audit committee)

(iv) If integrity/honesty of management or those charged with governance is in doubt, seek legal advice

(b) Audit report

(i) If error is corrected, no need to qualify

(ii) If correction is made, then report should be appropriately qualified

(iii) If outcome of fraud is uncertain then a significant uncertainty paragraph should be included

(iv) If outcome can be determined and amount is not adjusted in the financial statement except for/disagreement

Answer to Interactive question 5

Notes for a training session for junior staff on how to identify related party transactions

Purpose of the training

To assist junior staff in the application of IAS 24 *Related Party Disclosures* and ISA 550 *Related Parties,* and specifically on how to identify related party transactions.

Related parties

IAS 24 defines related parties as individuals or entities (eg companies) with more than a simple business relationship with the client. This would be because they are directors, owners or major investors of the client and can include family and close friends of the directors or owners.

At the start of each audit you will be provided with an up-to-date list of known related parties. It is important that if you come across any transactions involving these parties during the audit you should record them on the audit file.

The directors should provide us with a complete list of these related party transactions. However, we need to be certain that their list is complete, and by comparing the transactions you find with the list from the directors we can obtain evidence as to its reliability.

General audit procedures

Unless we determine that the risk of non-disclosure of related party transactions is high, we gain a significant amount of evidence needed from general audit procedures. These are listed in (b) below.

Additionally, they may intentionally or otherwise leave out certain transactions from the list they provide and you therefore need to be aware of indicators of potential undisclosed related party transactions. These are given in (a) below.

If you notice any such transactions, record them on the audit file. If there is a significant number of such transactions, immediately ask the manager for specific guidance on what action to take.

(a) List of possible features which would lead you to investigate a particular transaction to determine whether it is a related party transaction.

   (i) Transactions which have unusual terms of trade, eg unusual prices, interest rates, guarantees and repayment terms.

   (ii) Transactions which appear to lack a logical business reason for their occurrence.

   (iii) Transactions which are overly complex.

   (iv) Transactions which involve previously unidentified related parties.

   (v) Transactions which are processed in an unusual manner.

(b) Summary of the general audit procedures you would perform to ensure that all material related party transactions have been identified.

   (i) Obtain a list of current known related parties, eg directors, other companies with common directors, family members of directors, significant private company investments of directors, associate or joint venture companies, key personnel and significant investors (>20%).

   (ii) Ensure that the permanent file is updated for related parties.

   (iii) If it is the first year of the audit perform company search; otherwise review statutory records to confirm directorships, other directorships and significant investors.

   (iv) Discuss the list of related parties as disclosed by the directors as to its accuracy and completeness.

   (v) Enquire of directors as to whether there have been any material transactions with the related party, eg loans, purchase or sale of assets, consultancy fees.

   (vi) List all transactions disclosed by the directors.

   (vii) Review the accounting records before and after the year end for any large or round sum amounts; investigate and analyse with reasons.

(viii) Analyse all loans receivable or payable, and seek confirmation of identity of lender or borrower.

(ix) Review board minutes and enquire as to whether the company has provided any guarantees.

(x) Analyse the details of guarantees given and review the terms.

(xi) Include confirmation of all related party transactions or lack of them within the letter of representation.

(xii) Check the accuracy of disclosure within the context of IAS 24.

Answers to Self-test

1 Auditing financial statements.

2 True, as auditors are giving an opinion whether the financial statements are free from material misstatements, they should plan and perform procedures designed to discover material misstatements even if they result from a fraud.

3 True.

4 C – detect fraud causing a material misstatement – auditors are required to plan in a manner that tries to uncover material misstatement caused by fraud, but as fraud is by its nature concealed, they might not necessarily uncover it. D – report fraud to the police. They are required to report to directors, but may be precluded from reporting outside the entity by their duty of professional confidence.

5 All of them, although again, in the case of reporting outside of the organisation, the auditor must take care not to breach his duty of professional confidence.

6 True.

7 True.

8 A – and in fact, this could be a breach of the auditor's professional duties if the auditor attended in a management capacity for example.

Exam-style questions

9 **Actions**

- Check bank statement to confirm employee's assertion
- Report to nominated officer/ money laundering officer in firm
- Avoid tipping off

Reasons

- Represents proceeds of crime under Proceeds of Crime Act 2002/money laundering
- Criminal offence if auditor does not report suspicions of money laundering

10 **Auditor's responsibilities**

- To identify material misstatements in the financial statements
- Plan, perform and evaluate work in order to have a reasonable expectation of detecting material misstatement in the financial statements
- No obligation to prevent fraud although it may act as a deterrent

MD's perception

- Auditor responsible for ALL fraud
- Lacks an understanding of materiality
- Directors often rely on auditors for monitoring they should undertake themselves

Alpha

- Fraud was not material to Alpha financial statements and consequently not auditor's responsibility

11 Failure to comply may result in penalties/fines requiring provision or disclosure

Serious breaches may have going concern implications (closure, inability to pay fines)

May be indicative of poor control environment

Examples

Minimum wage and working time directives
Health and safety at work regulations
PAYE & NI compliance
Pension scheme requirement

12 (a) **Notes for meeting re fraud**

Before meeting

(i) Check terms of engagement letter. Were there any special duties agreed with client (specifically, any extra work on branch audits)?

(ii) Schedule responses to this letter from the client.

(iii) Check that the letter contained the usual paragraph re purpose of audit procedures.

Why fraud not discovered

(i) Remind Ray that the prevention and detection of errors and fraud are primarily the responsibility of management.

(ii) The purpose of audit procedures is not to discover errors and fraud, but to enable the auditor to form his opinion on the financial statements: reasonable expectation of discovering error and fraud.

(iii) Weaknesses were pointed out in the last management letter, covering all branches of similar size, together with suggestions for improvement.

(iv) Discuss management's response – reasons why suggestions not implemented.

(v) Audit working papers give details of the work done at Goose Green, which was in accordance with ISAs.

Effect on the accounts

(i) Amount material in context of branch – particularly as it may have turned a profit into a loss – but probably not in the general context of the company (3.3% of profit before tax). 20X1 accounts do not need adjustment unless fraud found to be more extensive.

(ii) Potential effect of control weaknesses not considered material enough to warrant a qualification in 20X1 accounts, but this matter is reviewed each year.

(iii) Qualification possible this year if there is significant breakdown in controls and/or an actual fraud (has the Goose Green fraud continued into 20X2?).

(b) **Areas to consider to establish extent of fraud/loss and why**

Area	Why consider
• How long the particular clerk has worked at the Goose Green (GG) branch. • Relationships between staff at the GG branch. • Other branches with poor control environments (all?). • Relationships between staff at the GG branch (especially the sales ledger clerk) and staff at other branches. • Whether the GG branch manager runs other branches. • How the fraud was discovered (chance or management control). • Recoverability of the amount from the clerk. • Likelihood of false claims from credit customers (ie having heard of the fraud, customers claim to have settled their accounts). • Adequacy of fidelity insurance.	• To establish how long the fraud is likely to have gone on. • Possibility of collusion. • To establish general likelihood of fraud at other branches. • Could the fraud have been 'sold' to staff at other branches? • Could indicate other branches where fraud might be undetected. • If by management control, then provides some comfort that other frauds would be detected and therefore, generally, fraud less widespread. • To establish actual monetary loss. • To establish any knock-on monetary loss. • Is the loss recoverable?

chapter 3

Professional standards

Introduction

Learning objectives

Tick off

- Understand the sources of professional standards on assurance and audit ☐
- Explain significant current assurance issues ☐

Specific syllabus references for this chapter are: 1d, e, f, i.

Syllabus links

Some auditing standards were introduced in your lower level Assurance paper. In this paper, you will both build on the knowledge you have gained at the lower level, and be introduced to more standards. As this is an open book exam, you should also have a copy of ISAs to refer to when reading through this Study Manual. The Technical reference pages will direct you to the exact places in the standards where the requirements discussed in the chapter can be found.

Examination context

While the content of auditing standards will impact on your exam, the details of who issues them and how they are issued are likely to be of less importance, hence the fact that there are few interactive and other questions in this chapter. Ethics, which are covered in the next chapter, are likely to be far more heavily examined in the context of professional standards.

In the assessment, candidates may be required to:

- Discuss the purpose of laws, standards and other requirements surrounding assurance work
- Explain the standard-setting process used by national and international (IAASB) bodies and the authority of the national and international standards
- Explain, in non-technical language, significant current assurance issues being dealt with by the national standard-setting body and by the IAASB
- Explain the principles behind different auditing requirements in different jurisdictions and describe how national and international bodies are working to harmonise auditing requirements, including the requirements to report on internal controls (Sarbanes-Oxley)

1 The need for professional standards

Section overview

- Professional standards are in the public interest as they add to the quality of assurance services.
- Regulation of audit promotes comparability in the marketplace as all financial statements are audited to common standards.

The benefits of assurance were revised in Chapter 1. A fundamental feature of assurance is that it is provided by independent professionals to particular standards. Users expect assurance providers to be independent and objective (which we shall consider in the next chapter) and competent. They expect an appropriate amount of work to be done to support the conclusion being given. Assurance services are carried out in the public interest. It is important that they are carried out within a context of professional and ethical standards.

In relation to audit, readers **want assurance** when making comparisons of financial statements that **the reliability of the financial statements does not vary from company to company**. This assurance will be obtained not just from knowing each set of financial statements has been audited, but knowing that each set of financial statements has been audited to **common standards**.

Hence there is a need for audits to be **regulated** so that auditors follow the same standards. Auditors have to follow rules issued by a variety of bodies. Some obligations are imposed by governments in law, or statute. Some obligations are imposed by the professional bodies to which auditors are required (by law) to belong.

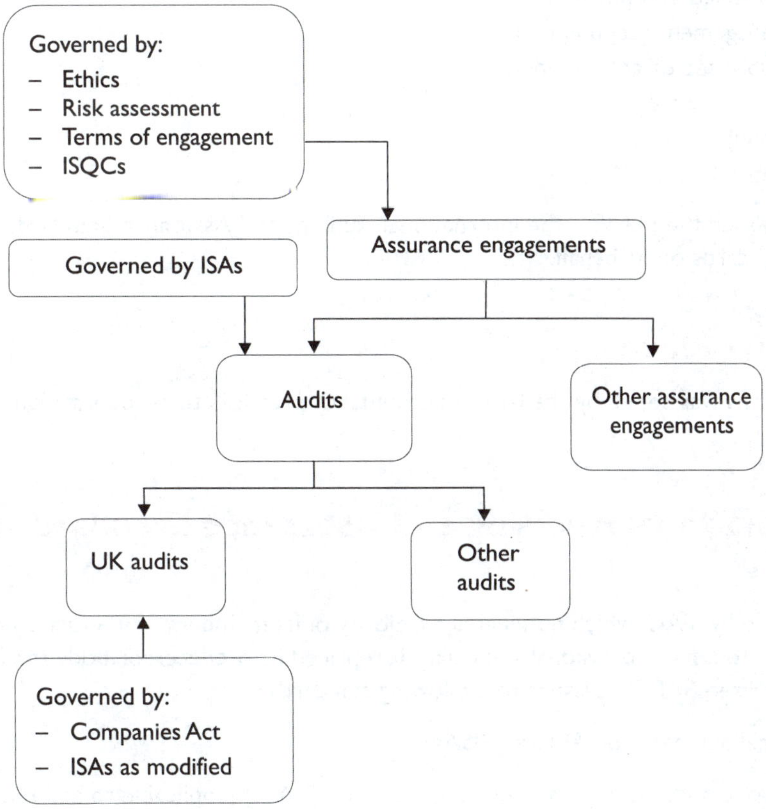

Figure 3.1: Auditing rules

2 The International Auditing and Assurance Standards Board (IAASB)

Section overview

- International standards are developed by IAASB, a subsidiary of the International Federation of Accountants.
- International standards are designed to provide services of a consistently high quality, but they do not override local regulations – although countries are encouraged to develop local systems to comply with these international standards.
- A sub-committee of IAASB works on a particular area and develops an exposure draft which is publicised.
- The exposure draft is revised as a result of comments made by interested parties and sometimes re-exposed.
- When the amendments have been finalised, an international standard is published.

2.1 The International Federation of Accountants (IFAC)

IFAC was set up by the professional bodies representing accountants from around the world. It has 163 member organisations from 119 countries. Members from the UK are:

- ACCA (Certified accountants)
- CIMA (Management accountants)
- CIPFA (Public sector accountants)
- ICAEW
- ICAI (Ireland)
- ICAS (Scotland)

IFAC has established the IAASB – the International Auditing and Assurance Standards Board – to issue professional standards on its behalf.

2.2 The forum of firms

The forum of firms was set up by the largest accountancy practices to co-operate on standard setting and other matters.

2.3 The International Auditing and Assurance Standards Board (IAASB)

IAASB was set up by IFAC, which nominates a majority of its members – others are nominated by the forum of firms – to issue professional standards. It replaced its predecessor body the International Auditing Practices Committee (IAPC). It issues the following standards:

- International Standards on Auditing (ISAs)
- International Standards on Assurance Engagements (ISAEs) (applicable to assurance engagements dealing with matters other than historical financial information)
- International Standards on Review Engagements (ISREs) (applicable to the review of historical financial information)
- International Standards on Related Services (ISRSs) (applicable to other, non-assurance engagements)
- International Standards on Quality Control (ISQCs) (applicable to all engagements carried out under any of the IAASB's standards).

IAASB also issues practice statements which are designed to help practitioners with interpretation and implementation of the standards. (IPPS 1 International Professional Practice Statement 1))

An explanation of the workings of the IAASB, the authority of the ISAs and so on are laid out in the *Preface to the International Standards on Quality Control, Auditing, Review, Other Assurance and Related Services*.

The *Preface* restates the mission of IFAC as set out in its constitution: 'The development and enhancement of an accountancy profession with harmonised standards able to provide services of consistently high quality in the public interest'.

In working toward this mission, the Council of IFAC established the International Auditing Practices Committee, precursor to IAASB, to develop and issue, on behalf of the Council, standards and statements on auditing and related services. Such standards and statements improve the degree of uniformity of auditing practices and related services throughout the world.

Within each country, local regulations govern, to a greater or lesser degree, the practices followed in the auditing of financial or other information. Such regulations may be either of a statutory nature, or in the form of statements issued by the regulatory or professional bodies in the countries concerned.

National standards on auditing and related services published in many countries differ in form and content. The IAASB takes account of such documents and differences and, in the light of such knowledge, issues ISAs which are intended for international acceptance.

The *Preface* also lays out the authority attached to ISAs in general.

Authority of International Standards on Auditing

International Standards on Auditing (ISAs) are to be applied in the audit of historical financial information.

The IAASB's Standards contain basic principles and essential procedures (identified in bold type, black lettering) together with related guidance in the form of explanatory and other material, including appendices. The basic principles and essential procedures are to be understood and applied in the context of the explanatory and other material that provide guidance for their application. It is therefore necessary to consider the whole text of a standard to understand and apply the basic principles and essential procedures. ISAs have recently been revised and or redrafted as part of the IAASB's Clarity Project, which aimed to enhance the understandability of the ISAs.

In exceptional circumstances, an auditor may judge it necessary to depart from an ISA in order to more effectively achieve the objective of an audit. When such a situation arises, the auditor should be prepared to justify the departure.

Any **limitation** of the applicability of a specific ISA is made clear in the standard, for example, it might contain a passage such as the following:

Application to public sector

Considerations Specific to Public Sector Entities are set out at the relevant points in the text of the ISA. Where there are no specific public sector considerations, the ISA is applicable in all material respects to the public sector.

ISAs do **not** override the local regulations referred to above governing the audit of financial or other information in a particular country.

- To the extent that ISAs **conform** with local regulations on a particular subject, the audit of financial or other information in that country in accordance with local regulations will automatically comply with the ISA regarding that subject.

- In the event that the local regulations **differ from**, or conflict with, ISAs on a particular subject, member bodies should comply with the obligations of members set forth in the IFAC Constitution as regards these ISAs (ie **encourage changes** in local regulations to comply with ISAs).

2.4 Working procedures of the IAASB

The working procedure of the IAASB is to select subjects for detailed study by a **subcommittee** established for that purpose. The IAASB delegates to the subcommittee the initial responsibility for the preparation and drafting of accounting standards and statements.

As a result of that study, an **exposure draft** is prepared for consideration by the IAASB. If approved, the exposure draft is widely distributed for comment by member bodies of IFAC, and to such international organisations that have an interest in auditing standards as appropriate.

The comments and suggestions received as a result of this exposure are then considered by the IAASB and the exposure draft is **revised** as appropriate. Provided that the revised draft is approved it is issued as a definitive **International Standard** and becomes operative.

3 Harmonisation

Section overview

- In recent years, international harmonisation of the ethical, financial reporting and auditing standards has become a big issue.
- This is due to the increase in genuinely global companies, harmonisation within the EU, and the scandals of major business failures, particularly Enron.
- The EU has adopted international accounting standards and international auditing standards for listed companies.
- The UK has adopted international auditing standards (augmented for UK issues).

The world of those who set the professional standards affecting accountants, whilst not exactly in chaos, is certainly experiencing a period of great upheaval.

The main force behind these changes is known as 'convergence' or the increasingly close alignment of standards which affect accountants across the world in the areas of:

- Ethics
- Financial reporting
- Auditing

Whilst there have been International Accounting Standards and International Standards on Auditing for some time they seem to have been always regarded as something which, although good in theory, would never have very much impact in any individual jurisdiction.

There was also the problem that Generally Accepted Accounting Practice (GAAP) was markedly different in the US, the UK and Europe and there appeared to be little appetite for compromise.

However there are a number of drivers which have caused attitudes to change:

- Global companies are now truly global, and will move their operations at will
- The EU is increasingly harmonising the rules and regulations affecting business across its member states
- The euro
- The Enron affair

The Enron affair was important in that as Enron was a US company and its auditor Andersen was primarily a US based firm, the regulators in the US were forced to look again at their own standards, and so it probably did as much as anything to enable compromises to be made. However just in case we, over this side of the Atlantic, became too smug, the Parmalat scandal reminded us that such events can happen anywhere.

3.1 So where are we now?

International Accounting Standards (IAS) should have been adopted by all EU listed companies for accounting periods commencing on or after 1 January 2005.

International Standards on Auditing (ISAs) should have been adopted for the audit of all EU financial statements for periods starting on or after 1 January 2005. In the UK the Auditing Practices Board (APB) decided to replace all its own standards – Statements of Auditing Standards (SASs) – with the equivalent ISAs for audits of financial statements covering accounting periods beginning on or after 15 December 2004.

There are some areas where the APB feels that, because of particular circumstances in the UK, it is necessary for the standards as issued in the UK to be supplemented by some additional paragraphs. The APB has issued exposure drafts of the IAASB's clarified ISAs; following the period of comment these ISAs will apply to audits of financial statements for periods ending on or after 15 December 2010.

The APB has not adopted ISA 700 *Forming an Opinion and Reporting on Financial Statements* but has instead issued Bulletin 2009/2 *Auditor's Reports on Financial Statements in the United Kingdom*. The effect of this on auditors' reports in the UK and Ireland will be discussed in Chapter 13.

The system in the UK will work as follows:

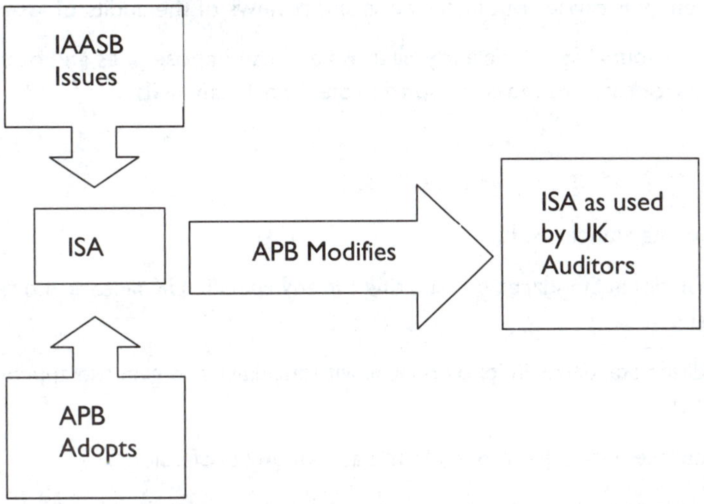

Figure 3.2: UK system for auditing standards

4 The Auditing Practices Board (APB)

Section overview

- Supervision of accountancy related issues in the UK is provided by the Financial Reporting Council.
- The APB, which issues auditing standards in the UK, is a subsidiary of the FRC.
- The APB has adopted International Standards on Auditing, which have been augmented for UK issues and are styled ISAs (UK and Ireland).
- The APB has not adopted other assurance standards issued by the IAASB.

4.1 The Financial Reporting Council (FRC)

The FRC was established in 1990 to promote good financial reporting in the UK through the setting of accounting standards (by the Accounting Standards Board) and the review of published financial statements (by the Financial Reporting Review Panel).

The government has now added regulatory functions to its remit so that it has responsibility for:

- Issuing Auditing Standards – through the Auditing Practices Board (APB)
- Oversight of the accountancy profession – through the Professional Oversight Board for Accountancy (POBA)

- Investigation and discipline – through the Accountancy Investigation and Discipline Board (AIDB)

The structure is shown in Figure 3.3

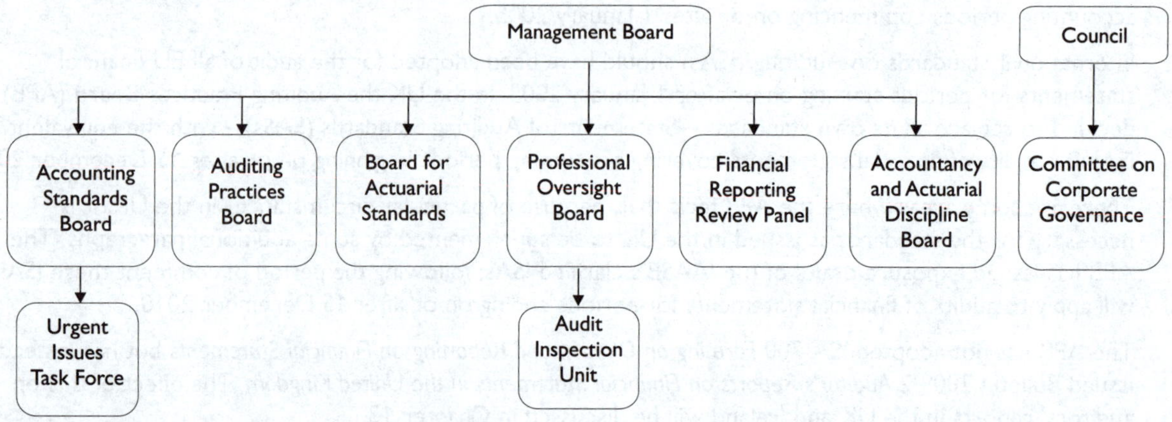

Figure 3.3: Structure of Financial Reporting Council

The Audit Inspection Unit carries out inspections and reviews of the audits of listed companies.

The AADB acts as a tribunal for disciplinary hearings and can impose fines and other sanctions against accountants whose work fails to measure up to professional standards.

4.2 The APB and auditing standards

The APB issues auditing standards. It:

- Amends International Standards on Auditing for any specific UK factors and then issues these as ISA (UK and Ireland)
- Can issue auditing standards in its own right without having to gain the approval of all the professional accounting bodies
- Has strong representation from outside the accounting profession
- Has a commitment to openness, with agenda papers being circulated to interested parties and an annual report being published

The APB makes three categories of pronouncement:

- Auditing standards (quality control, engagement and ethical)
- Practice notes
- Bulletins

We are primarily concerned with the auditing standards. The scope of these is as follows: 'APB quality control and engagement standards contain basic principles and essential procedures (identified in bold type lettering) together with related guidance in the form of explanatory and other material, including appendices. The basic principles and essential procedures are to be understood and applied in the context of the explanatory and other material that provide guidance for their application. It is therefore necessary to consider the whole text of a Standard to understand and apply the basic principles and essential procedures.'

At the time of writing the APB has yet to adopt the IAASB's Clarified ISAs although they have been issued as Exposure Drafts for consultation and comment. This Study Text refers to the IAASB's Clarified ISAs, which are applicable for the audits of financial statements for periods beginning on or after 15 December 2009.

Interactive question: The Financial Reporting Council [Difficulty level: Easy]

What are the main functions of the Financial Reporting Council and by what bodies are those functions carried out?

See **Answer** at the end of this chapter.

5 Internal controls

Section overview

- Internal control is an important issue given prominence by the UK Turnbull Report and the US Sarbanes-Oxley Act.
- The issue of providing assurance on internal control is important, particularly as little assurance is given on the effectiveness of internal control by the audit.
- The APB issued a briefing paper on providing assurance on internal control in 2001, which sets out the key issues.
- Knowledge of the business will be an important factor in providing assurance on internal controls.
- Assurance may be provided on the different stages of the process: identifying the risks, the design of the system, the operation of the system.
- Reports providing assurance on the effectiveness of internal controls should mention the inherent limitations of internal control systems to avoid an expectations gap arising in relation to this issue.

Internal control is an important issue in business. It has been given particular prominence in the UK by the investigations into corporate governance in the 1990s, notably the Turnbull Report which concentrated on the risks facing companies and the need for directors to manage those risks.

In addition, it has been given prominence by the Sarbanes-Oxley Act in the US, and the requirements that places on chief executive officers to give more certification that the financial statements produced are true, by implication, that the systems supporting them are strong and capable of preventing error.

The auditors' responsibilities with regard to internal control were discussed in the previous chapter and in your earlier studies in relation to Assurance. Due to the limitations of the assurance given in relation to internal control as part of an audit, provision of additional or alternative assurances in respect of internal control has become an important issue.

In July 2001, the APB issued a Briefing Paper on the issue of providing assurance in the effectiveness of internal control. Briefing Papers are not directly examinable, but we shall look at the issues raised in that Briefing Paper as a way at looking at this important issue.

5.1 Providing assurance on internal control

The APB draws a clear distinction between two areas of assurance:

- Assurance on the **design** of internal control systems
- Assurance on the **operation** of the internal control system, in accordance with the design

These are two very distinct issues, and the two assignments should be approached very differently.

5.2 Process of internal control

The APB recognises the following process in relation to internal controls:

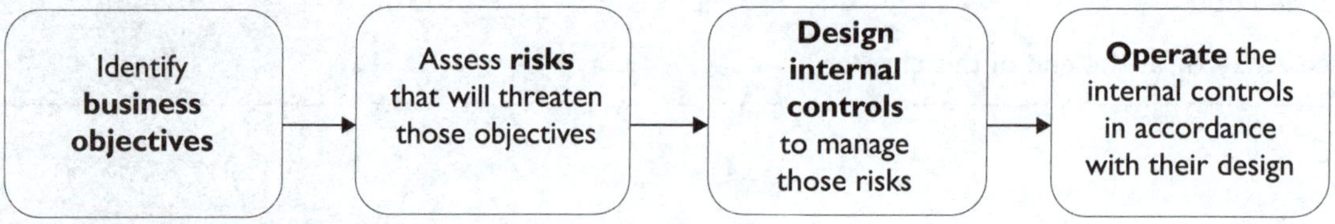
Identify **business objectives**
Assess **risks** that will threaten those objectives
Design internal controls to manage those risks
Operate the internal controls in accordance with their design

Figure 3.4: Internal control

Figure 3.4 also illustrates the points of the process where assurance services can be given:

- Risk identification
- Design of system
- Operation of system

In order to carry out an engagement in relation to the internal controls, the practitioners will require sufficient **knowledge of the business** that they can **identify and understand** the events, transactions and practices which will impact on the system of internal control.

5.3 Providing assurance on the operation of the system

The practitioner should establish whether the engagement relates to a period of time or a point of time. The practitioner will only be able to provide a **high level of assurance** on this point if the entity has a detailed description of the design of their system of internal control.

The **report** arising from such an assignment need not be extensive, but is likely to be narrative. This is because practitioners are likely to include such issues as:

- Isolated control failures
- Observation about the abilities of staff involved in operating the system of control
- Potential weaknesses observed which were not contemplated within the design

5.4 Providing assurance on the design and operation of the system

In such an engagement practitioners will consider two issues:

- The design of the system in addressing a set of identified risks
- The operation of the system (discussed above)

Such an engagement will involve significant **discussions with management** at the outset, to establish matters such as:

- The desired balance between prevention and detection controls
- The balance between costs and benefits
- The importance of specific control objectives

The outcome of these discussions will necessarily be included in the assurance **report**, to provide a context for their conclusions. The following things will also be included in the report:

- The applicable risks
- Any framework for design used by either the directors or the practitioners
- A description of the design of the system of internal control.

The **level of assurance** given by the practitioners will **depend on several factors**, including the nature of the entity, the knowledge of the business the practitioner possesses and the scope of the engagement. It is likely that the report in this instance would be quite long.

5.5 Providing assurance on the applicable risks and the design and operation of the system

This engagement would include consideration of all three stages of the internal controls process identified above. The identification of risks is likely to involve a **high degree of judgement** as there are no universally recognised criteria suitable for evaluating the effectiveness of an entity's risk evaluation. This means that practitioners are **unlikely to be** able to provide a **high level of assurance** in this area.

The starting point for the practitioner would be the entity's business objectives. The key considerations will include:

- The completeness of the applicable identified risks
- The probability of a risk crystallising
- The materiality of the likely impact of the risk
- The time period over which crystallisation is anticipated

In their **report**, the practitioners would have to outline the business objectives of the entity, a description of the risk identification process and the applicable risks.

5.6 Inherent limitations

Internal control systems have inherent limitations, a key one of which is the chance of staff colluding in fraud to override the system. **Any assurance report on internal control** systems should **include a mention of these inherent limitations**, in order to prevent an unnecessary expectations gap.

5.7 Reports

The nature of the individual reports has been touched on above. The discussion paper also includes an example report. However, as the APB make the key point that it is difficult to issue a standard report for assurance services, which are largely dependent on the scope and nature of the individual assignment, this has not been reproduced here.

6 Current issues

Section overview

- The key current issue for UK standard setters is harmonisation, particularly with European-wide requirements in relation to audit on the horizon.
- In 2009 the IAASB completed a clarity project which led to the updating and reissuing of ISAs.

6.1 Harmonisation

The APB Work Programme highlights the need for the APB to be at the forefront of international developments by contributing to IAASB work projects and, in particular, the development of European-wide auditing standards following recent amendments to the 8th EC Directive, which will result in EU statutory auditors being required to carry out audits in accordance with international standards on auditing. Of course, the UK has already adopted ISAs. The completion of the IAASB clarity project (see next section) has resulted in the issue of ISAs (UK and Ireland) exposure drafts for comment prior to finalisation.

6.2 Clarity project

IAASB has completed a clarity project, during which they reissued existing ISAs, redrafted so as to make the requirements within them clearer.

Some of the purposes of the project were:

- Eliminating ambiguity in ISAs
- Improving the overall readability of ISAs

When the APB first issued the ISAs (UK and Ireland) in December 2004, these standards were based on the IAASB ISAs in issue at that time. Since then the IAASB have made changes to all of the standards in line with their Clarity Project. These standards will be effective for audit of financial statements for periods beginning on or after 15 December 2009.

The APB has contributed to the project but has not yet adopted the resulting standards in their current 'international' form. This means that for the time being there is a 'gap' between the ISAs currently issued by the IAASB and those adopted by the APB for use in the UK and Ireland.

The ISAs listed in the technical knowledge grid in the introduction to this Study Manual are those issued by the IAASB.

Summary and Self-test

Summary

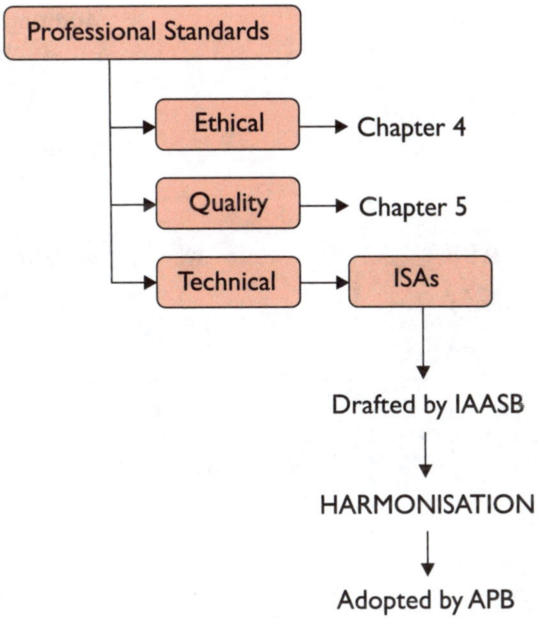

Self-test

Answer the following questions.

1 Auditing is regulated by the government in the UK.

☐ True

☐ False

2 The Auditing Practices Board issues auditing standards which auditors are required to follow.

☐ True

☐ False

3 Why are professional standards important?

4 Which of the following is a UK auditor required to follow?

☐ International Standards on Auditing

☐ International Standards on Auditing (UK and Ireland)

☐ The APB's Ethical Standards

Exam-style question

5 Discuss the advantages and disadvantages of accounting and auditing standards to auditors and the consequences of such standards being enforceable by statute. **(4 marks)**

Now, go back to the Learning Objectives in the Introduction. If you are satisfied you have achieved these objectives, please tick them off.

Technical reference

1 The need for professional standards	
2 The International Auditing and Assurance Standards Board (IAASB)	**Auditing Practices Board – Scope and Authority of Pronouncements** **IPPS 1**
3 Harmonisation	**Auditing Practices Board – Scope and Authority of Pronouncements**
4 Auditing Practices Board (APB)	**Auditing Practices Board – Scope and Authority of Pronouncements**
5 Internal controls	**ISA 315.4(c) and 12**
6 Current issues	**n/a**

Answer to Interactive question

Answer to Interactive question

Functions	Boards
• Sets accounting standards	• Accounting Standards Board (ASB)
• Reviews published FS	• Financial Reporting Review Panel (FRRP)
• Issues auditing standards	• Auditing Practices Board (APB)
• Oversees accountancy profession	• Professional Oversight Board (POB)
• Responsibility for investigation and discipline	• Accountancy and Actuarial Discipline Board (AADB)

CHAPTER 3

Answers to Self-test

1 False. It is regulated by RSBs and the FRC.

2 True. Auditors face discipline by their RSB if they do not.

3 It is in the public interest that assurance services are carried out to professional standards.

4 Auditors in the UK are required to comply with ISAs (UK and Ireland) and the APB's Ethical Standards (which we shall look at in the next chapter).

Exam-style question

5 The major **advantages** of accounting standards and auditing standards can be summarised as follows.

(a) **Accounting standards**

(i) They reduce the areas of uncertainty and subjectivity in accounts.

(ii) They narrow the areas where different accounting policies can be adopted.

(iii) They increase the comparability of financial statements.

(iv) They codify what is considered in most circumstances to be best accounting practice.

(v) They give an indication of the interpretation of the concept 'true and fair' in many circumstances.

(b) **Auditing standards**

(i) They give a framework for all audits around which a particular audit can be developed.

(ii) They help to standardise the approach of all auditors to the common objective of producing an opinion.

(iii) They assist the court in interpretation of the concept of 'due professional care' and may assist auditors when defending their work.

(iv) They increase public awareness of what an audit comprises and the work behind the production of an audit report.

(v) They provide support for auditors in a dispute with clients regarding the audit work necessary.

The possible **disadvantages** include the following.

(a) **Accounting standards**

(i) They are considered to be too rigid in some areas and too general in others, making their application difficult in some circumstances.

(ii) They can be onerous for small companies to adopt.

(iii) Their proliferation could be said to increase proportionately the number of qualified audit reports thereby reducing the impact of such qualifications.

(iv) They can create divisions within the profession of those who agree and those who disagree with a particular standard.

(v) They would be difficult to change once they become statutory as alterations to company law can take years rather than months to enact.

(b) **Auditing standards**

(i) It may appear that they impinge on, rather than assist, professional judgement.

(ii) They are considered by some to stifle initiative and developments of new auditing methods.

(iii) They may create additional and unnecessary work and thus raise fees, particularly on the audit of small companies.

If either type of standard were to be enforceable by statute it would mean that there would be government intervention in areas currently controlled solely by the profession itself. This might ultimately lead to a diminished role in self-regulation. To be enforceable by statute the standards would have to be applicable to all circumstances and thus need to be very general and broad in their instructions. This might reduce their usefulness to the auditors. Auditors might spend unnecessary time ensuring that they have complied with the law rather than considering the quality of their service to their clients.

Finally, it should be considered whether full statutory backing for standards would force auditors into narrow views and approaches which might gradually impair the quality of accounting and auditing practices.

Note: A legal opinion on truth and fairness, accounting standards and the law in the **Foreword to Accounting Standards** strengthens the legal backing for accounting standards and UITF pronouncements.

chapter 4

Professional ethics

Introduction
Examination context
Topic List
1 The need for professional ethics
2 Code of Ethics
3 APB Ethical Standards
4 ICAEW Code of Ethics
Summary and Self-test
Technical reference
Answers to Interactive questions
Answers to Self-test

Introduction

Tick off ☐

Learning objective

- Understand professional and ethical issues relating to assurance work

Specific syllabus references for this chapter are: 1a, b, c, d.

Syllabus links

This topic was covered in detail in Assurance.

Examination context

As this is an important practical area, you can except it to be examined regularly.

In the assessment, candidates may be required to:

- Identify and advise upon the professional and ethical issues that may arise during an assurance engagement
- Recognise the professional and ethical issues that might arise during an assurance engagement, explain the relevance and importance of these issues and evaluate the relative merits of different standpoints taken in debate
- Judge when to raise legal and ethical matters arising from assurance work with senior colleagues for review and possible referral to external parties
- Discuss the purpose of laws, standards and other requirements surrounding assurance work

1 The need for professional ethics

Section overview

- The importance of professional ethics is that in order for accountancy services to be meaningful, the public must trust accountants.
- Trust is built by the knowledge that accountants are bound by a professional code of ethics.
- Independence and objectivity (key features of the Code of Ethics) are fundamental to the provision of assurance services.

The accountancy profession has a paradoxical image. On the one hand accountants are seen as pillars of society, providing reliable financial information in their working lives and acting as treasurer for the PTA or the local church in their spare time.

The other side of the coin is the image of aggressive tax schemes, financial scandals and money laundering.

Yet accountants believe that financial information is important. It is necessary for governments, shareholders, trading partners, management and any number of other stakeholders, that the financial and other reports and information provided by accountants are reliable and can be used by others as they go about their daily lives. So the work that accountants and other assurance providers do has benefit for the public interest.

It follows from this that, if the profession is to survive and thrive, and if its members are to maintain their position there has to be a code of conduct so that the public are able to feel that they can trust accountants.

The profession needs a code of professional ethics.

When a good deal of the profession's income comes from audit and other assurance services, where the users of those services are seeking to gain additional confidence in the reliability of information, it is no exaggeration to say that the profession's income actually depends on accountants' reputation for ethical behaviour.

You have already studied professional ethics in relation to assurance services in your earlier studies for your Assurance paper. The following summary is therefore revision, except in the case of the APB Ethical Standards, which you have not yet looked at in detail.

2 Code of Ethics

Section overview

- IFAC issues a Code of Ethics, with which you should be familiar.
- The IFAC Code has been used as the basis for developing UK codes, in particular, compliance with the ICAEW code ensures compliance with the IFAC Code.

2.1 IFAC code of ethics – fundamental principles

The fundamental principles are:

- **Integrity**. A professional accountant should be straightforward and honest in all professional and business relationships.
- **Objectivity**. A professional accountant should not allow bias, conflict of interest or undue influence of others to override professional or business judgements.

- **Professional competence and due care**. A professional accountant has a continuing duty to maintain professional knowledge and skill at the level required to ensure that a client or employer receives competent professional service based on current developments in practice, legislation and techniques. A professional accountant should act diligently and in accordance with applicable technical and professional standards when providing professional services.
- **Confidentiality**. A professional accountant should respect the confidentiality of information acquired as a result of professional and business relationships and should not disclose any such information to third parties without proper and specific authority unless there is a legal or professional right or duty to disclose. Confidential information acquired as a result of professional and business relationships should not be used for the personal advantage of the professional accountant or third parties.
- **Professional behaviour**. A professional accountant should comply with relevant laws and regulations and should avoid any action that discredits the profession.

2.2 APB code of ethics – threats to objectivity and independence

The IFAC Code of Ethics, the ICAEW Code of Ethics and the APB Ethical Standards all work on the basis that an assurance firm's integrity, objectivity and independence are subject to various threats and that the firm must have safeguards in place to counter these threats.

The APB's approach is to stress that the perceptions of 'a reasonable and informed third party' are more important than the firm's own view.

The APB's list of threats includes the management threat, which is not covered by either the IFAC or ICAEW documents.

The threats are as follows:

- **The self-interest threat**

  All firms face the self-interest threat, simply because the client pays the fee, and to lose a client may be painful.

  The risk is increased for audit engagements, because, although technically the auditor is appointed by and reports to the shareholders, in practice the appointment depends on the client's management. The auditor may be tempted to allow inappropriate accounting treatments in order to keep the client.

- **The self-review threat**

  It may be difficult for the firm to maintain its objectivity if any product or judgement made by the firm needs to be challenged or re-evaluated at a later date.

  Examples might be brand or company valuations or aggressive tax schemes. If the firm has valued a client's new subsidiary at a price which is questioned when it comes to the audit, there may be some embarrassment, or the temptation to gloss over the differences in values.

  Where the auditor also carries out accounting work on behalf of the client, this may seem innocent enough. Indeed there may be perceived ethical advantages, because the accountant should be able to prepare the accounts 'properly'.

  There will be a self-review threat where the accountant prepares financial statements and then acts as auditor, effectively reviewing his own work. The auditor may not want to report mistakes that he, as accountant, had made. Where accounts are prepared by auditing firms, another department always carries out the audit to remove this threat. In some jurisdictions, auditors are not allowed to prepare financial statements for a client, removing this threat completely.

  But consider the position where the use of different accounting policies may give very different results, or where different interpretations can be placed on treatments required by accounting standards.

- **The management threat**

  A management threat arises when the audit firm undertakes work that involves making judgments and taking decisions, which are the responsibility of management.

- **The advocacy threat**

  The advocacy threat occurs where the professional adopts a stance arguing for or against the client's point of view, rather than taking a balanced (objective) position.

The advocacy threat is difficult to deal with because, surely, the professional adviser wants to give the client the best possible support.

In a tax case, for example, is it not the tax consultant's job to win on behalf of the client at all costs?

- **The familiarity or trust threat**

  This recognises that, if the professional gets to know the client too well, objectivity may be threatened because the auditor becomes too trusting of the client and professional scepticism is impaired.

  This is also quite a difficult area. As we shall see in Chapter 8 the auditor needs to understand the client's business well. Changing the engagement partner may or may not enhance objectivity, but if it does, it may open up greater audit risks due to lack of familiarity with the client's business.

- **The intimidation threat**

  This threat may range from the effective hi-jacking of the auditor's professional qualification by clients with criminal tendencies – something which the UK Government is concerned about as demonstrated by the anti-money laundering regime they have introduced – to the bullying behaviour of a dominant personality who insists on getting his (or her) own way. The situation may go as far as threatening the auditor with removal if a qualified audit report is produced.

2.3 APB code of ethics – safeguards against the threats

There are a number of general safeguards against the threats which come from the environment in which the professional accountant operates:

- Training
- ICAEW also offers support systems for its members and students – a local and central counselling service and helpline.

The quality control systems in place at engagement, firm and profession levels including:

- Planning, supervision and review procedures
- Hot and cold file reviews
- Regulatory inspections

Procedures envisaged under the APB Ethical Standards include:

- The overall control environment at the firm which ensures a professional approach towards ethical issues
- The segregation of duties between those engaged on audits and those providing non audit services
- Rotation of engagement partners and staff
- Consulting the ethics partner
- Procedures for evaluating the integrity of potential new clients
- The formal process of reviewing the appropriateness of the firm's continuing in office before its name is allowed to go forward for reappointment
- Staff recruitment procedures
- Regular completion of 'fit and proper' and independence declarations by partners and staff
- Staff training, development and performance appraisal
- Monitoring and evidencing the firm's own systems

Interactive question 1: Fundamental principles [Difficulty level: Easy]

Set out the ethical fundamental principles which should be followed by members of the profession.

See **Answer** at the end of this chapter.

3 APB Ethical Standards

Section overview

- The Auditor's Code highlights nine qualities which should characterise the auditor.
- The APB has also issued five ethical standards and a standard relating to smaller entities.
- ES 1 focuses on independence and objectivity, together with the key indicator of 'what a reasonable and informed third party would think' of a situation.
- ES 2 focuses on relationships between accountants and clients.
- ES 3 focuses on long association between accountants and clients.
- ES 4 focuses on the 'benefits' of the professional relationship, such as fees and remuneration.
- ES 5 focuses on providing other services to audit clients.

3.1 The auditor's code

The nine qualities which the APB believes should characterise the auditor are:

- Accountability
- Integrity
- Objectivity and independence
- Competence
- Rigour
- Judgment
- Clear, complete and effective communication
- Association
- Providing value

You should look these up in the open book text. They are, on the whole, fairly self-explanatory, with the possible exception of 'association' which concerns the inclusion of auditors' reports in documents containing other information which may conflict with the matters covered by the audit report.

3.2 The APB Ethical Standards

- ES 1 *Integrity, Objectivity and Independence*
- ES 2 *Financial, Business, Employment and Personal Relationships*
- ES 3 *Long Association with the Audit Engagement*
- ES 4 *Fees, Remuneration and Evaluation Policies, Litigation, Gifts and Hospitality*
- ES 5 *Non-Audit Services Provided to Audited Entities*
- ES *Provisions Available for Small Entities* (ESPASE)

The APB reviewed the Ethical Standards (ESs) during 2007 and concluded that no major changes were required.

The revised versions of the standards that were issued in April 2008 are included in the open book text. The amendments resulted from

- The revised EU Statutory Audit Directive (implemented in the UK via the Companies Act 2006)
- Changes to keep the ESs in line with expected changes to the IFAC Code
- Clarification of wordings in the existing ESs.

3.2.1 ES 1 *Integrity, Objectivity and Independence*

The definition of integrity and objectivity are dealt with above.

The concept of independence is what is really at the heart of the standards.

Definition

Independence is 'freedom from situations and relationships which make it probable that a **reasonable and informed third party** would conclude that objectivity either is impaired or could be impaired.'

ES1 *Integrity, Objectivity and Independence*

The concept of the 'reasonable and informed third party' is important.

ES1 sets out the requirement for the audit firm to have policies and procedures to deal with the rules in the standards which need to be documented and communicated to all concerned with the engagement.

It deals with:

- The control environment (ie the whole culture and working practices of the firm which should lead to ethical behaviour)
- The engagement team, consisting of:
  - The engagement partner
  - Independent partner
  - Other key partner(s)
  - Audit staff

It sets out requirements for partners and staff to report:

- Family and other personal relationships
- Financial interests in an entity audited by the firm
- Decisions to join an audited entity

which might be perceived as casting doubts about the firm's independence.

It then requires a firm to:

- Monitor compliance
- Have systems to ensure that actual or possible breaches are promptly communicated to the engagement partner
- Evaluate the implications of identified possible or potential breaches
- Report specific circumstances as required by ESs
- Prohibit management decision taking on behalf of the audited entity
- Establish an enforcement mechanism, to ensure that compliance actually happens, through disciplinary procedures etc
- Empower staff to communicate about ethical issues

The ethics partner

ES1 requires all firms except the very smallest to appoint an ethics partner, who will be a senior partner with a good deal of authority within the firm, and who will be available for consultation on ethical matters for engagement partners and other matters of judgement that arise.

The ethics partner should be consulted when judgments are being taken about whether the safeguards in place in the firm are sufficient to counter potential threats.

For firms with three partners or less, this function is expected to be covered by regular discussions between the partners.

Review by independent partner

For listed clients, the firm's compliance with ethical standards should be reviewed by an independent partner.

Conclusion about compliance

Just as the engagement partner should reach and document his technical conclusion about the audit, he or she should similarly reach and document a conclusion about the firm's compliance on ethics matters. This conclusion should be made at the end of the audit process, but before the audit report is signed.

Other auditors

Where other auditors – perhaps where there is a group of companies being audited – are involved with the engagement, the firm has to be satisfied that they too comply with the ethics rules.

Communication with those charged with governance

The audit engagement partner should ensure that those charged with governance of the audited entity are appropriately informed on a timely basis of all significant facts and matters that bear on the auditors' objectivity and independence.

3.2.2 ES 2 *Financial, Business, Employment and Personal Relationships*

This standard can be summarised relatively simply:

- If you are tempted to take a financial interest in an audited entity – do not do it.
- If you are tempted to go into a business venture jointly with an audited entity – do not do it.
- If staff move from the audit firm to the audited entity there should be disclosure during the process.
- If a former director/employee of an audited entity who was in a position to exert significant influence over the preparation of the financial statements joins the audit firm, he should not be assigned to a position where he can influence the conduct/outcome of the audit (eg the audit opinion) or its affiliates for two years following leaving the audit client.

Financial interests

The standard recognises that financial interests can be direct – owning shares in or making loans to an audited entity – or indirect where there is some intermediary like an investment trust, and whilst there are some minor relaxations in the rules where the interest is both indirect and immaterial to both the auditor and the client, nevertheless the prohibition on such interests should be regarded as absolute.

You may wonder what the issue is here, but consider the case of a 'Big 4' firm which audits a major listed company and where the firm's pension scheme has a holding in a unit trust which invests in, among others, the audited entity.

Joint business ventures

You may think that it is common sense not to allow joint ventures with audit clients, but consider the following situations:

Worked example: Joint business ventures

You have an audit client Technofix Ltd which installs computer systems and another audit client Shoppa Ltd which is looking for some new IT equipment.

Consider the following possibilities:

- You simply put Technofix and Shoppa in touch with each other and say you hope that everything will work to mutual advantage.
- Technofix offers your firm a commission if the deal is successful.
- Technofix provides the equipment and your IT arm agrees to install Shoppa's new accounting software on it as a separate exercise.
- Your firm and Technofix jointly agree to supply the complete system including installation, software and implementation.
- Your firm manages the whole contract, although the equipment is supplied and installed by Technofix.

'Recommending' the services of a client tends towards an advocacy threat because the accountant is promoting the client, which could affect objectivity.

Accepting a commission from a client constitutes a self-interest threat. The danger is that the firm will recommend Technofix because of the economic benefit to the firm rather than because it is the best professional advice that they could give Shoppa. Regardless of whether this is the case or not, it might seem to a reasonable third party that the firm had acted in its own interests and therefore independence is threatened.

The more involvement in the deal that the firm has, the more of a self-interest threat is created. If the IT arm of the firm install the equipment, the firm earns additional fee income and the objectivity of the audit might be threatened by the provision of other services and the overall increase in the firm's dependence on Shoppa Ltd for fees. In addition, the IT system will support the financial reporting system which the auditing arm of the firm might be seeking to rely on and will certainly be assessing as part of the audit, so there is also a self-review threat.

Partners, staff or client staff moving between the audit firm and its audit client

The objective of this part of the statement is to prevent the auditor's independence and objectivity being questioned, because former auditors join a client, or former clients join the auditor.

Where a partner – who could be:

- The engagement partner
- The partner who carries out an independent review of the audit files, or
- Another partner involved on the audit (known as a key audit partner or partner in the chain of command)

is appointed a director or takes on some other key management position at the client, within two years of being involved in the audit, the firm shall resign as auditors.

The firm shall not accept re-appointment as auditor until a two-year period, commencing when the former partner ceased to have the ability to influence the conduct and outcome of the audit, has elapsed or the former audit partner ceases employment with the former audited entity, whichever is the sooner.

So the firm needs procedures and rules so that:

- Partners and any other members of the audit team intending to join a client know they must inform the firm of their intentions.
- If someone gives notification, they should be moved off the audit immediately.
- A review shall be carried out on any audit work performed by the resigning team member in the current audit, and, where appropriate, the most recent audit.
- If someone joins the firm from a senior position at the client, they should not be allowed to work on the audit for two years.

Similarly the rules are extended to cover situations where close family members and other people connected with those involved with the audit are employed by, or have financial dealings with, an audit client.

3.2.3 ES 3 *Long Association with the Audit Engagement*

Again there are some relatively straightforward rules so that when an engagement partner or other key people have been involved with an audit engagement for:

- Ten years – engagement partner for non-listed clients
- Five years – engagement partner and engagement quality control reviewer for listed clients
- Seven years – key partners involved in the audit and senior staff for listed clients

they should be moved off that job.

Clearly the firm needs to have procedures in place to ensure that the length of time partners and other senior members of staff are associated with the audited entity can be monitored and appropriate action taken.

For non-listed clients the rule is relaxed a little – the standard talks about giving 'careful consideration to whether a reasonable and informed third party would consider the audit firm's objectivity and independence to be impaired'. The obvious implication is that partners should be 'rotated' after acting for the same client for ten years, but that it might be possible to make a case for them remaining in place.

3.2.4 ES 4 *Fees, Remuneration and Evaluation Policies, Litigation, Gifts and Hospitality*

Again there are some relatively straightforward rules for you to understand:

- 'Contingent' fees for audit work are banned.

Definition

Contingent fees are fees where the amount of the fee is dependent on some event taking place or some other condition being met. An example might be that the audit fee would be increased if the client's bankers agree to extend available borrowing facilities.

- The audit engagement partner shall ensure that sufficient partners and staff are assigned to the audit irrespective of the audit fee to be charged
- Audit fees should not be influenced or determined by the provision of non-audit services to the audited entity
- Fees for audit and non-audit services for a listed client should not exceed 10% of the firm's fee income.
- The limit for non-listed clients is 15%.
- Audit staff should not be assessed, or have their performance appraisal or their pay related to their ability to cross sell the firm's products.
- There should be a firm's policy on the extent to which gifts, hospitality etc may be accepted from audited entities.
- The firm should resign as auditor where there is actual or potential litigation between the firm and the audited entity.

The fee percentages are based on expected regular levels of fee income and relate to the whole firm or unit within the firm where a 'reasonable and informed third party' might consider the firm/partner's objectivity to be impaired.

Where fees amount to 5% – 10% (listed clients) or 10% – 15% (non-listed) the fact needs to be disclosed to the ethics partner and those charged with governance at the client and appropriate safeguards adopted where necessary; for non-listed clients an external hot review needs to be undertaken (listed clients will be hot reviewed anyway).

The standard also recognises that in its early years a new firm may find the fee percentage limits difficult to comply with and gives a two year grace period providing external hot reviews are conducted.

Similar 'reasonable and informed third party' considerations apply to the firm's policy on gifts and hospitality and whether there are overdue fees outstanding.

3.2.5 ES 5 *Non-Audit Services Provided to Audited Entities*

This is the standard which has generated the most controversy.

The reason for this is that for a very long time – probably throughout the history of the accountancy profession in the UK – clients have come to accountants for a range of services. Because, until comparatively recently, all companies required an audit, audit was at the core of the services provided. It also made a good deal of sense for the auditors to provide any assistance needed with accounting matters and to 'do the tax'.

You should bear in mind the following:

- In many jurisdictions, notably France, Germany and the US, tax work tends to be handled by lawyers rather than accountants.
- The range of services offered by accountants in the UK has expanded to include actuarial services, brand valuations, IT services and many others.
- Tax services can include controversial tax 'schemes'.
- The increase in the audit threshold to exempt the vast majority of small companies from audit has meant that those clients who do require an audit may well be of a size to have their own, in-house accounting experts.

ES 5 sets out a clear general approach to non-audit services provided by the auditor based on:

- What a reasonable and informed third party would think about the impact on the firm's objectivity and independence
- The need for the firm to have procedures to monitor and deal with potential threats
- The need for the client to have 'informed management' as defined below, where the audit firm concludes it can provide non audit services
- It is never appropriate for the audit firm to find itself in a position where it undertakes, or is perceived as undertaking, a management role

This approach states that the firm should:

- Consider the impact of the provision of non-audit services
- Establish safeguards to counter any threats (which may include resignation or refusal to accept appointment as auditor or provider of the non-audit services)
- Communicate with 'those charged with governance', and
- Document the rationale for the decisions taken

ES 5 identifies the following non-audit services, although this is clearly not an exhaustive list:

- Internal audit
- IT
- Valuation
- Actuarial valuation
- Tax
- Litigation support
- Legal
- Recruitment and remuneration
- Corporate finance
- Transaction related
- Accounting

Some points concerning these services are highlighted below, but you need to read ES 5 and understand the overall approach which is applied consistently throughout.

Internal audit

The firm should not undertake internal audit work, where its external audit opinion is based on significant reliance on its internal audit role.

IT

The firm should not undertake work on IT systems which would be important to any significant part of the accounting system on which the auditors would place significant reliance.

Valuation and actuarial valuation services

The firm should not undertake valuation services for an unlisted audited entity where the valuation would both:

- Involve a significant degree of subjective judgment, and
- Have a material effect on the financial statements.

For a listed audited entity, valuation services should not be provided where the valuation would

- Have a material effect on the financial statements

Tax

The firm should not undertake tax services which 'would involve acting as an advocate for the audit client before an appeals tribunal or court in the resolution of the issue' where the outcome of the tax work is:

- Material to the financial statements, or
- Dependent on a future or contemporary audit judgement.

CHAPTER 4

Appeals tribunal or court is defined as appearing before the General or Special Commissioners in the UK and any superior tribunals.

This rule, when it was first discussed, was thought to be especially tricky for the smaller firm, and it may prove to be so, but it is important to note that:

- The rule does nothing to prevent the usual discussions on points of detail with inspectors of taxes or the provision of information if the case goes to the commissioners.
- Most tax issues are neither material nor dependent on future or contemporary audit judgments.
- Where the matter progresses to the commissioners, the conditions of the ESPASE may well apply.

For listed companies the audit firm shall not prepare current or deferred tax calculations for the purpose of making accounting entries that are material to the financial statements.

Transaction related services

Transaction related services are 'one-off' engagements such as due diligence work.

Accounting services

The provisions dealing with accounting services were also expected to prove controversial for smaller practitioners, but in the event this seems unlikely due to:

- The increase in the audit threshold
- The acceptability of appropriate safeguards
- The impact of the ESPASE

Nevertheless firms will need to remember:

- Providing accounting services for listed audit clients is banned except in emergencies.
- The auditors must never find themselves undertaking a management role.

3.2.6 *ES Provisions Available for Small Entities*

It is probably true to say that, in a conceptually pure world, the idea of exemption from ethical rules should be simply impossible – you are either ethical in your conduct, or you are not. As a result, when the APB was persuaded that the ethical rules affecting smaller entities needed to be modified in comparison with those dealing with larger clients, it was thought that the only sensible approach was to come up with a document which recognised that in the context of work with smaller entities, there are a number of different safeguards of independence and objectivity in operation.

APB chose to disagree and issued the ESPASE, which relaxes the rules for smaller entities by making use of exemptions and some additional disclosures. It is quite possible that APB took the most practical approach to the problem.

The ESPASE applies where the client qualifies as a small company under the Companies Act 2006 and covers three issues dealt with by the ethical standards:

- Fee dependence
- Non-audit services
- Partners joining an audit client

Fee dependence

Where it is expected that the total fees for audit and other services receivable from small entity will regularly exceed the 10% threshold but will not regularly exceed 15% the ESPASE exempts the audit firm from the requirement in ES 4 for an external independent quality control review. The expectation should be disclosed to the ethics partner and to those charged with governance of the audited entity.

Non-audit services

For small entities the restrictions on the provision of non-audit services are waived, but:

- There needs to be 'informed management'.
- The audit firm needs to extend its cycle of cold reviews.
- The departure needs to be mentioned in the audit report for which suggested wording is provided in the ESPASE.

Partners joining audit client

For small entities the provisions concerning partners joining audit clients are waived provided there is no threat to the audit team's integrity, objectivity and independence and disclosure is made in the audit report.

3.3 Informed management

In the APB's ethical standards, the concept of 'informed management' is regarded as a crucial safeguard where there are potential conflicts of interest posed by the provision of non audit services and where the provisions of the ESPASE apply.

'Informed management' is defined as follows:

- Objective and transparent analyses need to be provided for the client.
- The client must have the genuine opportunity to decide between alternative courses of action.
- There should be a member of management designated to receive the results of non-audit services and make necessary judgments and decisions.
- That member must have the capability to make independent judgments and decisions on the basis of the information provided.

3.4 It is all about timing

Knowing what the threats are is all very well, knowing what you are supposed to do about them is even better, but how are you supposed to detect the threats in the first place?

ES1 has some suggestions.

The impact of any threats needs to be assessed:

- On appointment or reappointment as auditor
- When planning the engagement
- When forming the opinion
- When considering appointment or reappointment for non-audit services
- When potential threats are reported

At all times it is the perceptions of third parties which matter and this means that the consideration of potential problems cannot be restricted to the particular engagement currently under consideration.

The auditor has to ask how the ethics of the situation look in the context of

- Past engagements?
- Other engagements currently on hand?
- Potential future engagements?

Interactive question 2: Fee income [Difficulty level: Exam standard]

Aitken and Waterman have been asked by a long-standing client, Lewis plc (a quoted company) to perform a special assignment. This would take the total fees received by Aitken and Waterman from this client to £55,000. Gross practice income is £500,000.

Requirement

Comment and reach a conclusion on the above situation.

See **Answer** at the end of this chapter.

CHAPTER 4

Interactive question 3: Threats to objectivity [Difficulty level: Exam standard]

Your firm is the auditor of Alpha Ltd and Beta Ltd.

(1) It provides quarterly VAT services to Alpha Ltd, which involves completing the VAT return for submission by management from information extracted from the company's records.

(2) It is also the auditor of Beta Ltd's largest customer.

What potential threats to objectivity do each of these situations pose to your firm, and what safeguards should be in place to address them?

See **Answer** at the end of this chapter.

4 ICAEW Code of Ethics

Section overview

- The ICAEW Code covers independence and objectivity (but we shall look at this in the context of the APB Ethical Standards in the next section).
- Accountants are required to keep information obtained in the course of professional work confidential.

Many of the independence issues covered by the ICAEW Code of Ethics are also covered by the APB Ethical standards in section 4, so we shall concentrate on issues of confidentiality here.

4.1 ICAEW Code of Ethics Section 140 Confidentiality

Due to the nature of their work, Chartered Accountants find themselves in a privileged position in that they gain access to books and records and have access to information and explanations from the directors of the company that they would otherwise not be party to.

This is particularly true of the Companies Act auditor, but does apply to all members. So the Institute's guidance is designed to reinforce to all members that information that comes into their possession as a result of the work they are completing should remain confidential.

Section 140 states that the principle of confidentiality is not only to keep information confidential, but also to take all reasonable steps to preserve confidentiality. The professional accountant should assume that all unpublished information is confidential, however it is gained. The professional accountant should not disclose information received in confidence except in the circumstances set our below and should not use confidential information to their own personal advantage or the advantage of third parties.

Disclosure of information

Section 140 identifies three circumstances where the professional accountant is or may be required to disclose confidential information:

- Where disclosure is permitted by law and is authorised by the client or the employer, for example where the auditor has uncovered a fraud and the client is in agreement that the matter should be referred to the police.
- Where disclosure is required by the law.

  Examples include:

  – Reporting directly to regulators, such as the Financial Services Authority, on regulatory breaches in respect of financial service and investment businesses or the Charity Commission in respect of charities

  – The reporting of suspected money laundering to SOCA

In making such a report, an auditor is not deemed to have broken the confidence of the client. It is normally addressed by setting out the auditor's right to disclose in the engagement letter.

- Where there is a professional duty or right to disclose, when not prohibited by law. In this case the Code of Ethics states that a professional accountant may disclose confidential information to third parties if the disclosure can be justified in 'the public interest'.

Difficult judgements are required by auditors as to whether the 'public interest' overrides the duty of confidentiality. Usually, the auditors should take legal advice on the matter.

ISA 240 *The Auditor's Responsibilities Relating to Fraud in an Audit of Financial Statements* and ISA 250 *Consideration of Laws and Regulations in an Audit of Financial Statements*, also provide guidance on this issue.

ISA 240 and ISA 250

What the ISAs require is that when the auditors become aware of suspected or actual frauds or instances of non-compliance which should be reported to the relevant authority, they should:

- Report to management
- Report to those charged with governance
- Report to regulatory and enforcement authorities, where appropriate

Obviously, if they suspect management of being involved in the non-compliance, etc. they should report the matter directly to those charged with governance or, if appropriate, to a higher authority such as the audit committee.

In addition, professional accountants may also be entitled to disclose confidential information for the purpose of defending themselves.

Improper use of information

A professional accountant acquiring or receiving confidential information in the course of his or her professional work should neither use, nor appear to use, that information for his or her personal advantage or for the advantage of a third party.

Examples of particular circumstances are:

- On a change in employment, professional accountants are entitled to use experience gained in their previous position, but not confidential information acquired there.

- A professional accountant should not deal in the shares of a company in which the member has had a professional association at such a time or in such a manner as might make it seem that information obtained in a professional capacity was being turned to personal advantage ('insider dealing').

- Where a professional accountant has confidential information from Client 1 which affects an assurance report on Client 2 he cannot provide an opinion on Client 2 which he already knows, from whatever source, to be untrue. If he is to continue as auditor to Client 2 the conflict must be resolved. In order to do so normal audit procedures/enquiries should be followed to enable that same information to be obtained from another source. Under no circumstances, however, should there be any disclosure of confidential information outside the firm.

Informants

The majority of confidentiality issues relate to the professional accountant's treatment of confidential information belonging to the client or employer. However, the accountant may also be approached in confidence with information about alleged illegal or improper acts on the part of employees or management of the business for which the informant works. This information must be treated sensitively, particularly as it is likely that the informant has approached the accountant on the basis that he is someone that the informant can trust. In this situation the professional accountant should:

- Advise the informant to pass on the information to his employer in accordance with company procedures.

- Protect the identity of the informant to the extent that this is possible.

- Take care in the way that this information is used, if at all.

4.2 ICAEW Code of Ethics Section 220 Conflict of Interest

Situations are frequently perceived by clients as 'conflicts of interest' where in reality they involve no more than concerns over keeping information confidential. Hence the issues of confidentiality covered above and conflicts of interest are related.

4.2.1 General principles: conflict of interest

Section 220 states that firms should have in place procedures to enable them to identify whether any conflicts of interest exist and to take all reasonable steps to determine whether any conflicts are likely to arise in relation to new assignments involving both new and existing clients.

If there is no conflict of interest, firms may accept the assignment. If there is a conflict of interest, but it is capable of being successfully mitigated by the adoption of suitable safeguards, firms should record those safeguards.

There is nothing improper in a firm having two clients whose interests are in conflict provided that the activities of the firm are managed so as to avoid the work of the firm on behalf of one client adversely affecting that on behalf of another.

Where a firm believes that a conflict can be managed, sufficient disclosure should be made to the clients or potential clients concerned, together with details of any proposed safeguards to preserve confidentiality and manage conflict. If consent is refused by the client then the firm must not continue to act for one of the parties.

Where a conflict cannot be managed even with safeguards, then the firm should not act.

4.2.2 Conflict between the interest of a professional accountant or his firm or a client

A self-interest threat to the objectivity of a professional accountant or his firm will arise where there is or is likely to be a conflict of interest between them and the client, or where confidential information received from the client could be used by them for the firm's or for a third party's benefit.

The test to apply is whether a reasonable and informed observer would perceive that the objectivity of the member or his firm is likely to be impaired. The member or his firm should be able to satisfy themselves and the client that any conflict can be managed with available safeguards.

Safeguards might include:

- Disclosure of the circumstances of the conflict
- Obtaining the informed consent of the client to act
- The use of confidentiality agreements signed by employees
- Establishing information barriers
  - Ensuring that there is no overlap between different teams
  - Physical separation of teams
  - Careful procedures for where information has to be disseminated beyond a barrier and for maintaining proper records where this occurs
- Regular review of the application of safeguards by a senior individual not involved with the relevant client engagement
- Ceasing to act

Interactive question 4: Confidentiality **[Difficulty level: Exam standard]**

You are in the middle of an audit with a tight deadline, the manager is due to visit you at the client tomorrow and you need to be home early to meet the builders at your new flat. You are considering taking the sales ledger and the cash book home with you to finish the trade receivables section ready for the manager to review tomorrow.

What must you consider before you remove any client files from their offices?

See **Answer** at the end of this chapter.

Summary and Self-test

Summary

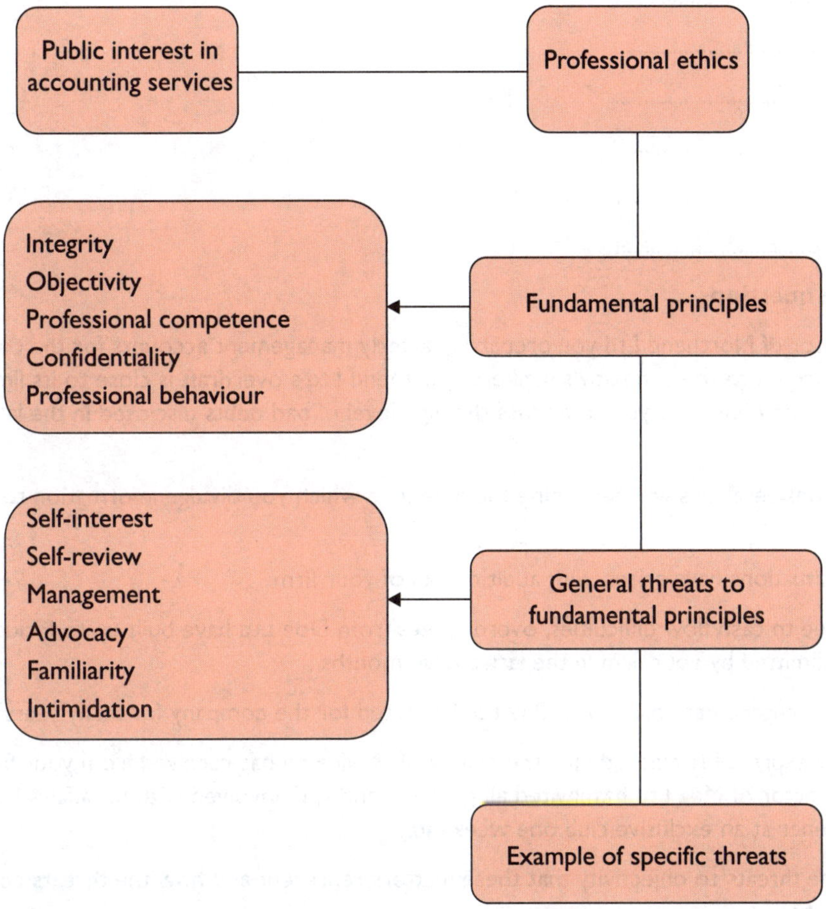

Self-test

Answer the following questions.

1 What are the six general threats to integrity and objectivity?

1 ....

2 ....

3 ....

4 ....

5 ....

6 ....

2 Give three examples of when auditors are entitled to make a disclosure in breach of the duty of confidence.

1 ....

2 ....

3 ....

CHAPTER 4

3 Name the nine qualities which the APB state should characterise an auditor.

1 ....

2 ....

3 ....

4 ....

5 ....

6 ....

7 ....

8 ....

9 ....

Exam-style questions

4 As auditor of Northend Ltd you prepare quarterly management accounts for the company, and these are passed on to the company's bankers. Northend Ltd's overdraft is close to its limit and the bank manager has contacted you to discuss the high level of bad debts disclosed in the latest management accounts.

What considerations will determine the extent to which you divulge information to the bank manager? **(2 marks)**

5 Three situations have arisen with audit clients of your firm.

(1) Due to cash flow difficulties, overdue fees from Doe Ltd have built up to include all bills submitted by your firm in the last twelve months.

(2) The engagement partner of Ray Ltd has acted for the company for many years.

(3) To express his gratitude for the quality of service he has received from your firm, the managing director of Mee Ltd has invited all partners and staff involved with his affairs for a golf day and dinner at an exclusive club one weekend.

State the threats to objectivity that these matters represent and how the threats could influence objectivity. **(4 marks)**

6 Your firm has been invited to tender for the audit of East Ltd. Your firm has not previously acted in any capacity for this company but does act for West Ltd, which is East Ltd's major competitor.

Identify and explain the principal ethical issue relating to this situation, and state the procedures you would implement to address this issue. **(3 marks)**

7 Examples of situations when the auditors' independence may be impaired include the following.

(1) Providing taxation services to the company and its directors.

(2) Providing accountancy services, including preparing periodic management accounts and annual financial statements.

(3) Providing management consultancy, including advice on new computer systems and systems of internal control.

(4) Preparing confidential reports to the company's bank and other lenders on the financial position of the client. The conclusions of these reports are not made available to the audit client.

Requirement

Describe how each of the situations listed above may compromise auditors' independence, and the ways in which an audit firm can minimise the effect which the provision of other services has on independence. **(13 marks)**

8 You have recently come across the following professional issues.

(1) During the audit of a listed company on which you were involved, you overheard the finance director on the telephone to a family friend requesting him to buy shares on his behalf, prior to an announcement about a new product which you know is likely to increase the share price significantly. The finance director is a chartered accountant.

(2) During a night out at the pub following your exams one of your fellow students told you in strictest confidence that he had tampered with his degree certificate on his computer to improve the classification. He explained that he had done this to satisfy the minimum requirements to secure a job at his firm, one of your main rivals. He boasted about how easy it was with new computer technology currently available.

(3) One of the audit clients you recently worked on was so impressed with your courtesy towards his staff members that he wanted to make you a gift of tickets to the World Cup football final, along with an overnight stay in a hotel.

Requirement

Set out the problems inherent in each of the above situations and the action that you should take.

(10 marks)

9 Proper Ltd is a small company which develops specialist software for the insurance and banking sector. Its finance director, Peter Stewart, has recently been on a training course called 'Reducing the Stress of an Audit'. He has returned to the office with a number of concerns which he had not previously known existed. As a result he has written to you as audit partner for clarification on the following issues.

(1) Is it appropriate for your firm to continue as auditors when it also provides other services (most notably preparation of the company's corporation tax computation and dealing with the tax affairs of the directors)?

(2) I have invited you to attend our regular board meetings but recognise that this may influence your audit opinion.

(3) We have often sought your advice on legal and accounting issues, and I assume that it is in order for us to extend this to the preparation of submissions to the bank for additional finance.

The last point has particular significance as the finance director's letter also indicates that Proper Ltd has been very successful, and intends to improve its status by buying a larger ailing computer company.

Requirements

(a) Write a letter to the finance director which addresses the ethical issues arising from his concerns. The letter should be brief and deal with the major items only, as the intention is not to swamp the client with detail. **(9 marks)**

(b) Describe the ethical repercussions arising from the potential change in size of Proper Ltd in relation to your firm. **(6 marks)**

(15 marks)

10 You are a sole accountancy practitioner. The following situations have arisen.

(1) At the request of Ace Ltd (an audit client) you have agreed to provide advice on the preparation of a tender for a very large contract. Subsequently, client Black & Co (a partnership for whom you prepare accounts and provide a wide range of advice) also asks for your assistance in preparing a tender for the same contract.

(2) Whilst carrying out the final audit of the accounts of Club Ltd (deadline one month after the balance sheet date), you discover a substantial trading debt due from another client, Diamond Ltd. Although it has not been made public, you are aware that Diamond Ltd is in serious financial difficulties and the bank is considering appointing a receiver. The directors of Club Ltd have made no bad or doubtful debt provision against the amount due from Diamond Ltd.

Requirement

Explain the action you would take in each of the above circumstances. **(10 marks)**

Now, go back to the Learning Objectives in the Introduction. If you are satisfied you have achieved these objectives, please tick them off.

Technical reference

1 The need for professional ethics	**n/a**
2 Code of ethics	**ES 1 (similar to IFAC ES)**
3 APB Ethical Standards	**ES 1, ES 2, ES 3, ES 4, ES 5, ESPASE**
4 ICAEW Code of Ethics	**ICAEW Code of Ethics Section 140, 220**

Answers to Interactive questions

Answer to Interactive question 1

Members should:

- Behave with integrity in all professional and business relationships
- Strive for objectivity in all professional and business judgements
- Not accept or perform work beyond own competence (unless obtain adequate advice and assistance)
- Carry out work with due care, skill and diligence and follow expected technical and professional standards
- Respect the confidentiality of information acquired
- Act professionally and comply with relevant laws and regulations

Answer to Interactive question 2

- Total fee income received from Lewis plc > 10% of gross practice income of firm as a whole; therefore there is a risk that perception will be that objectivity impaired
- But ES 4 deals with total fees which 'regularly exceed' the threshold and this is a 'one off' assignment.
- Need to determine whether regular fees will exceed 5% threshold

Conclusion

Assignment may be accepted. Ethics partner should be consulted and those charged with governance informed of the situation.

Answer to Interactive question 3

Threats to objectivity and safeguards:

Alpha Ltd

- Self-interest threat
- Self-review threat
- Firm may be susceptible to pressure for fear of losing work
- Lack objectivity when checking VAT
- Different staff should be used for VAT work and audit

Beta Ltd

- Self-interest threat
- Advocacy threat
- Either company may be uncomfortable with arrangement and exert pressure
- Beta could exert pressure re your knowledge of customer
- Separate audit partners
- Separate audit teams

Answer to Interactive question 4

The auditor must obtain the client's permission before removing any files from the client's offices.

CHAPTER 4

Answers to Self-test

1
- Self-interest
- Self-review
- Management
- Advocacy
- Intimidation
- Familiarity

2
- Reporting of suspected money laundering
- Reporting of terrorist offences
- Defending oneself against negligence charges

3
- Accountability
- Integrity
- Objectivity and independence
- Competence
- Rigour
- Judgment
- Clear, complete and effective communication
- Association
- Providing value

Exam-style questions

4 **Disclosure of information**

- Whether Northend Ltd's permission has been obtained to discuss matters freely with bank
- Extent to which information has already been divulged by the bank to Northend Ltd's management
- Terms of engagement with Northend Ltd and/or bankers for preparation of management accounts
- Duty/responsibility to bankers

5 **Threats**

Threat	How influence objectivity
(1) Self-interest	• Auditor may worry that fees will not be paid if report is qualified or going concern doubts disclosed
(2) Familiarity	• Partner may be reluctant to upset or be too reliant on representations from 'friend'
(3) Self-interest	• Partners and staff may be reluctant to appear ungrateful or hope for further hospitality

General

- Proper audit may not be carried out
- Inappropriate opinion may be given

6 **Principal ethical issue**

- Confidentiality
- East and West may perceive a threat in respect of disclosure/use of information
- Conflict of interest

Procedures to address

- Procedures to ensure staff are aware of confidentiality issues and such issues have been brought to attention of staff (eg Chinese walls)
- Staff to certify awareness of these procedures
- Obtain informed consent of clients
- Use of different partners and teams
- Independent review of arrangements for ensuring confidentiality maintained

7 (1) **Taxation services**

Many audit firms prepare tax computations for their client companies and this should not normally compromise independence.

Where taxation services are provided to the company, a conflict of interest could arise in dealing with the tax affairs of the directors (eg if any of the directors are also shareholders, they may have preferences as to dividends or bonuses, which are not in the best interests of the company's tax or cash flow position).

There may also be independence issues in relation to tax advisory work. For example, the firm may have difficulty in giving an independent view on the acceptability of a scheme to the Revenue or Customs and Excise if the firm designed the scheme itself in the first place.

As a safeguard, a tax manager (or partner) independent of the audit function should be assigned to deal with individual director's tax affairs.

(2) **Accountancy services**

For many audit clients it is common to provide a range of accountancy services including participation in the preparation of accounting records. For listed or other public interest clients, an audit firm should not participate in the preparation of the company's accounts and accounting records except in emergency situations.

Preparing periodic management accounts may draw the auditor, inadvertently, into performing management functions.

Safeguards for non-listed companies include the following.

- The client accepting responsibility for the records as its own.
- The auditor not assuming an operational role.
- Conducting appropriate audit tests on records processed/maintained by the auditor.

(3) **Management consultancy**

An auditor's independence may be compromised if a course of action is recommended to an audit client. For example, if the auditor advises on a new computer system which is then found to be unreliable, the auditor may be reluctant to report the weaknesses to management.

As a safeguard auditors should lay the facts before the directors and let them make the decision. It is important that the auditor is not seen to be acting as part of the management function.

The additional guidance on best practice has also now provided that services involving the design and implementation of financial information technology systems (FITS) should not be provided unless

- Management accept overall responsibility in writing
- Management do not rely on the FITS work as the primary basis for determining the adequacy of internal controls and financial reporting systems, and
- The design specifications are set by management.

In any case separate engagement teams are likely to be necessary to mitigate the potential threat to independence.

(4) **Preparing confidential reports**

Auditors are not prevented from producing confidential reports for banks and other lenders, provided they have obtained the client's authority to do so.

An 'unqualified' confidential report recently issued to a lender may be borne in mind when forming the audit opinion. This may increase pressure not to qualify the audit opinion (to add credibility to the confidential report) when qualification is justified.

A partner other than the audit engagement partner should be responsible for the confidential reports. Unless confidentiality is absolutely necessary, the client should be made aware of the reports to lenders. The quality of these reports may be enhanced by consideration of management's views on matters included.

8 (1) **Share purchase for FD**

Problems

- This constitutes insider dealing which is a criminal offence, as the financial director is benefiting financially from an inside knowledge of the business.
- All chartered accountants and trainees, whether in business or practice, are required to comply with the Code of Ethics. This states that members should act with integrity at all times and not act to bring the profession into disrepute.

Action

- Inform the audit partner but do not approach the finance director directly yourself.

(2) **Exam certificates**

Problems

- The student is guilty of obtaining an employment position under false pretences and by deception. This is not appropriate behaviour for a future chartered accountant.
- It is unlikely that the firm would have taken the student if it had known the class of degree.

Action

- No duty of confidentiality to his friend.
- Encourage the friend to admit to his employer.
- If not, the matter should be discussed with your own partner, who would make contact with the staff partner of the other firm.

(3) **Accepting a gift from an audit client**

Problems

- Firm's independence on the audit may be called into question; need to consider.
- Size and availability to all employees of the client company. (Generally gifts from clients should only be accepted if value modest and available to all employees.)
- Whether own firm's regulations may prohibit this.

Action

- Discuss with partner and only accept if firm's permission is given.

9 (a) **Letter to finance director ABC & Co**

Chartered Accountants
20 Ribble Road
London
SW1B 9GH

Finance Director
Proper Ltd
5-8 Ring Avenue
London
SE9Y 9JA

10 February 20X4

Dear Mr Stewart

Clarification of ethical concerns

I have studied your letter dated 29 January 20X4 and was impressed by your recognition of potential ethical conflicts that may face us as auditors. You will be pleased to know that our professional guidance extends to all the issues raised. Each issue is dealt with in turn below.

(1) **Other services**

It is not unusual for audit firms to provide their clients with other professional services, such as tax advice and, provided they have the technical resources to undertake such work, it is not seen to impact on their objectivity when reaching an audit opinion.

The provision of such advice benefits both parties. It enables the auditors to gain a better insight into client systems, while allowing the management to receive a less costly service than by employing someone who is less familiar with their circumstances.

However, giving tax advice to the directors personally, as well as acting for the company, could lead to a conflict of interest. Similarly, a conflict of interest could arise between giving tax advice to the company and our audit work. If such a conflict were to arise we would have to consider which work to decline. It may be that we would need to decline all tax work in order to continue to act as auditor.

Ethical guidance also requires us to monitor the proportion of gross fee income (audit or otherwise) we receive from a single client. If this exceeds 15% from a limited company, then our objectivity is considered to be at risk, and we must relinquish that client.

(2) **Attending board meetings**

On occasions it may be desirable for the auditor to attend board meetings, for example when management representations on audit issues are to be discussed and minuted.

However, as you have indicated in your letter, it would be wholly inappropriate for a member of our firm to have a permanent seat on the board. It is vital that a reader of our audit report can be confident that we conducted our work with absolute independence and objectivity; this would not be possible if it were known that we also held an executive role. As a director we would be helping to make policy decisions for which at a later date we would have responsibility for auditing.

(3) **Borrowing applications**

The preparation of submissions to the bank creates a potential conflict of interest.

For example, say a client's audit report needs qualifying on the grounds of going concern. If the auditor were also involved in a submission to the bank he would be under pressure to avoid such a qualification in view of the adverse effect it would have on any attempt to raise additional finance.

In these circumstances the most likely precaution would be to invite another partner to oversee the borrowing application.

I hope that the above has addressed and clarified your concerns, but if you would like any additional information please do not hesitate to contact me.

Yours sincerely

ABC & Co

(b) **Impact of client size**

If Proper Ltd goes ahead with its proposed reverse management buy-out, it will undergo a radical increase in size. This could have a number of ethical implications for its auditors.

Fee income

There is likely to be a significant increase in fees; hence a check would be needed to ensure that they do not exceed 15% of the recurring gross fee income of our firm. If this threshold is breached, our ethical guidance proposes resignation from office, as such reliance on one client can affect objectivity.

Company status

One of the most common reasons for undertaking a reverse management buy-out is that it can provide a fast track route to public limited company status (ie target is a plc). In such circumstances the fee income threshold referred to above falls to 10%, with a review needed at only 5%.

Additionally, the reporting requirements on a plc are more stringent, such that the auditors must ensure that they have the technical expertise to address these changes.

Resources

Auditing ethical standards can only be maintained if the firm involved has adequate resources in terms of staff, locations, etc. A significant increase in client size would mean that these would have to be reviewed.

Conflicts of interest

Such a conflict could arise, particularly if the auditors have had any previous involvement with the target company or its management.

10 (1) **Tender preparation**

Additional service

When agreeing to provide any additional services to an audit client it is important to recognise that the independence of the audit may appear to be compromised even though the auditor considers he is able to be objective in executing his work. In general, additional services of an advisory nature are permitted provided no executive function is taken on which might conflict with the office of auditor.

Ace Ltd

The decision to provide advice and assistance in connection with the tender is not unethical provided it is made clear to the directors that any tender ultimately remains their responsibility. The directors should be sent a supplementary engagement letter, distinguishing the nature of an audit from other work and clarifying the extent of the advice to be given.

Black & Co

Independence may also be affected by a conflict of interest between two clients. With Ace Ltd and Black competing by tender for the same contract, it is likely that detailed inside information of both businesses would be obtained which would be of considerable value to the competitor.

Although there is, in theory, nothing improper in having two clients whose interests are in conflict, it must be possible to manage the activities of the firm so that the work on behalf of one client does not adversely affect that on behalf of the other. However, in this case the auditor is a sole accountancy practitioner so safeguards such as 'Chinese walls' which could be put in place in a large firm are unlikely to be feasible.

To advise both clients would not therefore appear to be independent. It would be difficult to be objective and avoid influencing one or other of the tenders unfairly.

It would be preferable to advise only one of the two clients – probably Ace Ltd as already agreed – and thereby avoid conflict. However, the knowledge of Black & Co's business may be seen to impair objectivity, and Black & Co might well object to assistance being provided to Ace Ltd.

It may therefore be best to advise neither client but to explain the predicament to both and suggest that each consults another independent firm of accountants.

(2) **Confidentiality**

To inform the directors of Club Ltd that the accounts will not give a true and fair view unless a provision is made against the debt due from Diamond Ltd would be a breach of confidentiality. It could also have the undesirable effect of precipitating the collapse of Diamond Ltd since the directors of Club Ltd would take steps to obtain payment from Diamond Ltd as soon as possible.

To ignore the information about Diamond Ltd's financial position (since it is not publicly available) and give an unqualified auditors' report, in a situation where the accounts are known (by the auditor) not to give a true and fair view, would be *prima facie* a breach of an auditor's statutory duty under the Companies Act 2006 and in breach of Section 140 Confidentiality of the Code of Ethics.

If the auditor is to continue to act for Club Ltd the conflict must be resolved. To do so normal audit procedures should be followed and enquiries made to enable the information about Diamond Ltd to be obtained from another source. It may be possible to delay forming an opinion until the situation crystallises. Under no circumstances must there be any disclosure of confidential information outside the firm.

Tutorial note

Note how practical this question is. Your answer should not merely be a repetition of the ethical guide but should apply it to the specific circumstances given. Part (2) is really 'unanswerable' and what is required is simply a sensible discussion of the possibilities. In any question on ethics, try to use common sense and come up with practical suggestions, and bear in mind that there may be no 'right' answer.

chapter 5

Quality control

Introduction

Learning objectives

Tick off

- Understand and explain why firms need to have quality control procedures ☐
- Understand and explain what these procedures are and how they operate ☐
- Understand the concept of professional negligence and its potential impact on an assurance firm ☐

Specific syllabus references for this chapter are: 2a, b, d, e, f, g.

Syllabus links

Your understanding of quality control issues will be necessary at the Advanced stage.

Examination context

This is an area of the syllabus that is likely to be examined in conjunction with other issues such as client acceptance or ethics. It has featured as a part of long questions and also as short form questions, for example in January 2009 and March 2009.

In the assessment, candidates may be required to:

- Identify the legal, professional and ethical considerations that an individual or firm must consider before accepting a specified assurance engagement
- Identify the sources of liability (including professional negligence) arising from an assurance engagement and their impact upon the conduct of the engagement
- Formulate the approach suitable for management of the assurance engagement
- Discuss the principles and purpose of quality control of assurance engagements
- Demonstrate how the assurance function within an organisation can be monitored through procedures for review
- Describe how quality can be monitored and controlled through procedures external to the organisation

1 The need for quality standards

Section overview

- Quality control procedures are essential to ensure that an acceptable job is carried out by the assurance firm and assurance engagement risk is reduced to an acceptable level.
- An engagement could go wrong due to client-based problems, or assurance firm based problems, for example that the engagement team has insufficient knowledge of the business or are badly directed and supervised.
- Audit quality is monitored by the Audit Inspection Unit (listed or public interest entities) or by ICAEW under their Practice Assurance scheme.
- There are six key elements of a quality control system (which we shall look at in turn in the next sections of this chapter):
  - Leadership
  - Ethical requirements
  - Acceptance and continuance of client relationships/specific engagements
  - Human resources
  - Engagement performance
  - Monitoring

The main reason the end user wants to have an assurance report prepared is to reduce the risk of making a wrong decision. As a result someone is prepared to pay an assurance firm a fee.

As you know (and we shall look at this in more detail in Chapter 9) the amount of work the firm does is dictated by the need to reduce **assurance engagement risk** to acceptable levels. If the firm does not do this, it has not carried out a job which is acceptable when judged against professional standards.

The firm should ensure that the quality of its work does not fall short by implementing its own quality control procedures.

1.1 What could go wrong?

Worked example: Need for quality

Take a moment to think about what the areas of risk are for the firm. The list you came up with might look something like this.

The terms 'auditor' and 'audit' are used here, because audits are a common form of assurance engagements but the same principles will apply to any assurance engagement.

Let us start, as it were, from the bottom up.

The client

- Could be incompetent
- Could be negligent
- May mislead the audit team

The individual auditor

- May not have adequate understanding of the client's business
- May not perform the right work to an adequate standard
- May not record the work done adequately

The supervisor

- May not have an adequate understanding of the client's business
- May not brief and direct the staff properly
- May not carry out sufficient supervision so that the wrong work is done by the audit team

- May fail to deal with issues raised adequately
- May fail to communicate the issues arising to the engagement partner

The engagement partner

- May have insufficient knowledge of the client and its environment
- May fail to pass knowledge of the business on to the audit team
- May select the wrong team for the audit
- May not adequately brief and supervise the team
- May not consult sufficiently with colleagues and outside experts
- May not review the work carried out by the team with sufficient care
- May fail to deal with issues raised adequately
- May not draw the correct conclusions from the evidence available

1.2 The consequence of quality failure

As we have seen assurance engagements, including audits, do not offer the end user absolute assurance about the subject matter of the assurance report. At best, they offer **reasonable assurance**, a **high** level of assurance.

As a consequence, the firm needs to have quality systems and procedures primarily to ensure that its work is of a sufficiently high standard so that failures simply do not happen.

In the event of a complaint, the firm will have a defence, providing it has followed suitable procedures.

ICAEW firms carrying out audit work have been subject to regulatory inspections for some time, and although inspections of listed company audit files have moved to the Audit Inspection Unit part of the Professional Oversight Board, under the aegis of the Financial Reporting Council, regulatory reviews of non-listed audits remain the responsibility of the ICAEW.

In June 2004 the ICAEW membership approved the introduction of a scheme called 'Practice Assurance' which means that all aspects of a firm's work are subject to periodic review by consultants acting for ICAEW.

During this review, which is designed to be constructive rather than disciplinary in tone, the consultants working on behalf of ICAEW will examine files and procedures in all the firm's departments. They will compare what they find with standards set out by ICAEW, and, where appropriate, make recommendations for improvement.

Clearly, if a firm's working practices were found to be inadequate, there could be disciplinary consequences, but the overall thrust of the scheme is intended to be supportive – in effect to provide the firm with access to consultancy. All members of the ICAEW who hold a practising certificate will be included in the programme of visits.

Audit failures revealed by such visits may result in disciplinary action being taken against the firm. This can lead to fines or, possibly, suspension of the firm's authorisation to carry out audits.

The consequences of failure can be catastrophic as Andersens found out following the Enron affair, but even a complaint which is successfully defended can absorb huge amounts of time and expense. It really is sensible to avoid getting into the situation in the first place.

1.3 Approach to quality control

If you look carefully at the bullet points in the worked example above, you should see that if you were to devise counter-measures against the threats listed, these measures could be listed under a small number of categories:

- Procedures for ensuring only suitable clients are taken on
- Procedures for ensuring only suitable clients are retained

- Procedures for ensuring that the firm's partners and staff have the necessary knowledge and competence
- Guidance on ethics
- Communication skills
- Briefing and supervision skills
- Professional scepticism and judgement
- Monitoring

ISQC 1 *Quality Control for Firms that Perform Audits and Reviews of Financial Statements and other Assurance and Related Services Engagements* lists the following as elements of a firm's quality control system:

- Leadership responsibilities for quality within the firm
- Ethical requirements
- Acceptance and continuance of client relationships and specific engagements
- Human resources
- Engagement performance
- Monitoring

ISQC 1 also requires that the firm documents its policies and procedures and communicates them to the firm's personnel.

In other words, ISQC 1 deals with the sort of procedures you would expect in a straightforward, logical way. We will look in more detail at the elements in the rest of the chapter.

The elements it lists are fairly self explanatory – human resources incorporates issues dealing with staff recruitment, training and appraisal.

In the exam you are not expected to regurgitate lists but the above approach should convince you that you have an understanding of the issues involved.

We will now look at the elements of a quality control system which affect the way the engagement is carried out – 'Engagement performance' under ISQC 1. We will, on the whole, look at the procedures which affect an audit and which are dealt with by ISA 220 because these are broadly applicable to all assurance engagements.

Interactive question 1: Benefits of quality control procedures

[Difficulty level: Exam standard]

Your manager has been asked to brief your department on the new quality control procedures that the firm has introduced. Your manager has asked you to prepare a list of the benefits of quality control procedures in a firm, which he can use as part of his presentation.

See **Answer** at the end of this chapter.

2 Leadership

Section overview

- The ISQC points out the importance of quality being an established part of the culture of the firm.
- This must be instigated by the leaders of the firm, that is, the partners.

It is important that the culture of the firm is that quality is essential in performing assurance engagements. This should be lead by the leaders of the firm, that is, the partners.

In practical terms, the people directing the firm and its resources should ensure that:

- Commercial considerations do not override the quality of work performed.

- The firm's policies in relation to staff promotion, remuneration and performance review incorporate the importance of quality work.
- Sufficient resources are allocated to the development, documentation and support of quality control policies and procedures.

3 Ethics

Section overview

- The firm should have policies and procedures designed to ensure that ethical requirements are met.

We saw in the previous chapter how important ethics are to assurance providers, as they underpin the public trust required to make assurance services viable.

The firm must put together policies and procedures to ensure that it meets ethical requirements.

Worked example: Policy in respect of employees' shareholdings

Freshfields & Co is a large accountancy practice. It has a number of assurance clients. At the beginning of every year it circulates a memorandum to all staff employed in the assurance division requesting that they disclose any shareholdings in a list of named assurance clients. It further emphasises the need for disclosure of such shareholdings should they arise in the year. Every staff member joining the assurance department during the year is also asked to make the disclosure.

4 Acceptance of engagements

Section overview

- The firm should also have policies and procedures designed to ensure that only appropriate clients are accepted in the first place and retained.

The firm should also have policies and procedures designed to ensure that only appropriate clients are accepted in the first place and retained. We shall look in more detail at acceptance issues in Chapter 6. The engagement partner should carry out similar considerations as he did when he accepted the client every year when bearing in mind whether to retain the client.

5 Human resources

Section overview

- As part of the firm's overall culture of quality control, it should have policies and procedures to ensure that it employs and retains staff with the capabilities, competence and commitment to ethical principles necessary to perform the engagements.
- There should be policies on recruitment, career development, performance evaluation and promotion.
- It is also important to allocate staff to assurance engagements appropriately.

As part of the firm's overall culture of quality control, it should have policies and procedures to ensure that it employs and retains staff with the capabilities, competence and commitment to ethical principles necessary to perform the engagements. This means it should have policies on all aspects of employing professional staff. The ISQC lists the following:

- Recruitment
- Performance evaluation
- Capabilities, including time to perform assignments
- Competence
- Career development
- Promotion
- Compensation (that is, how staff are remunerated)
- The estimation of personal needs (for instance, self-appraisal as well as appraisal by others)

These will cover matters such as professional education (for trainees), continuing professional development (for everyone), practical work experience and coaching by more experienced staff.

ICAEW members are required to certify that they have carried out appropriate professional development annually as part of their membership. For members in practice, the ISQC puts professional development on the agenda of firms as well, as part of their overall quality control procedures.

Another important matter in relation to human resources is the allocation of staff to engagement teams. Firms are required to have policies to ensure that:

- Clients are informed of the identity and role of the engagement partner.
- The engagement partner has the capabilities, competence, authority and time to perform the role.
- The responsibilities of the partner in respect of the engagement are clearly defined and communicated to that partner.

The engagement partner should ensure that he allocates appropriate staff to the engagement team. Staff need:

- Understanding of/practical experience with similar engagements
- Understanding of relevant professional and legal requirements in relation to the client
- Appropriate technical knowledge
- Knowledge of the relevant industry
- Ability to apply professional judgement
- Understanding of the firm's quality control procedures and policies

You can see that the types of training and appraisal discussed above will be important as ongoing monitoring of the staff member's abilities and, therefore, capability to be assigned to particular engagements and in what capacity.

6 Engagement performance

Section overview

- Key issues are supervision, direction, review, consultation and resolution of disputes.

6.1 Direction

This is largely the responsibility of the engagement partner who controls how the assurance engagement should be conducted, but this duty will be delegated to the most senior team member on site at the engagement, who will direct the engagement in accordance with the overall strategy.

The engagement partner is responsible for ensuring team members know:

- What work they are supposed to be doing
- The nature of the entity's business
- Any risks relevant to the engagement
- Problems that might arise during the engagement
- The detailed approach to the engagement

6.2 Supervision

ISA 220 *Quality Control for an Audit of Financial Statements* lists four features of supervision:

- Progress tracking
- Considering the competence and capabilities of individual members of the audit team
- Addressing significant matters arising during the audit
- Identifying matters for consultation or consideration by more experienced engagement team members during the audit engagement.

Good supervision can be a difficult skill to master:

- If it is too close it can stifle initiative and waste the time of supervisor and assistant alike
- If it is too loose, mistakes may be made or time wasted in ineffective work

The partner has overall responsibility for supervising the audit, but will normally delegate supervisory duties to a manager or supervisor who will similarly delegate to the 'senior' or 'in charge' who is responsible for the day-to-day management of the engagement.

6.3 Review

Work performed by staff is reviewed by other more senior staff or the engagement partner.

The purpose of the review is to consider whether the work done is in line with the audit strategy and whether:

- The work has been performed in accordance with professional standards and regulatory and legal requirements
- Significant matters have been raised for further consideration
- Appropriate consultations have taken place and the resulting conclusions have been documented and implemented
- There is a need to revise the nature, timing and extent of work performed
- The work performed supports the conclusions reached and is appropriately documented
- The evidence obtained is sufficient and appropriate to support the report and
- The objectives of the engagement procedures have been achieved

6.3.1 Independent review

This review is conducted by a suitably-qualified partner not otherwise involved in the engagement or by an external consultant. The purpose of this independent review is not to re-perform the other reviews in the audit process but to provide an additional safety check about the validity of the firm's opinion on the financial statements.

The following matters need to be considered:

- The evaluation of independence in relation to the engagement that has taken place
- Significant risks identified and responses to those risks
- Judgements made during the engagement, for example, in relation to materiality and significant risks
- Whether appropriate consultation has taken place on contentious issues
- The significance of corrected and uncorrected misstatements
- The matters to be communicated to the client
- Whether the documentation selected for review reflects the work performed in relation to the significant judgements and supports the conclusions reached
- The appropriateness of the proposed report

6.4 Documentation and review

You should remember from your studies for the Assurance paper that ISA 230 *Audit Documentation* requires that audit documentation should contain the following:

What would be necessary to provide an experienced auditor, with no previous connection with the audit, with an understanding of the nature, timing and extent of audit procedures, the results of audit procedures, and the audit evidence obtained, and significant matters arising during the audit and conclusions reached thereon.

One of the key purposes of the documentation of audit procedures is to enable the reviews described in section 6.3 to be carried out. Adequate documentation is also essential to allow the firm to implement overall monitoring of quality (see section 7.1).

6.5 Consultation

When difficult or contentious issues arise, the assurance team must consult properly on the matter and the conclusions drawn as a result of consultation must be properly recorded.

Any differences of opinion must be resolved prior to the assurance report being issued. This may mean that a person independent of the engagement (such as the quality control reviewer) may have to be involved in resolving the difference of opinion.

7 Monitoring

Section overview

- The firm must have policies in place to ensure that their quality control procedures are adequate and relevant, that they are operating effectively and are complied with.
- Management of the assurance firm (that is, the partners) should receive an annual report on the outcome of monitoring activities.
- The most important issues will be systematic or repetitive deficiencies.

The ISQC states that firms must have policies in place to ensure that quality control procedures are adequate and relevant, that they are operating effectively and are complied with. The firm might have a compliance or quality department which carries out such reviews.

Monitoring might take place by ongoing evaluation of the system and also by periodic review of selected engagement files to assess whether policies and procedures were put into place during the engagement.

The partners in the firm (the management board) should receive at least an annual report of the results of monitoring of quality control procedures. Key issues will be systematic or repetitive deficiencies that require corrective action.

Where monitoring reveals a problem with an individual, then remedial action should be taken with that individual, and possibly, additional quality control reviews might be required on that person's work to ensure that corrective action is taken.

The people checking compliance with quality control standards should liaise closely with the training department or partner to ensure that any misunderstandings or problems with controls are corrected during on-the-job training.

7.1 Monitoring (or 'cold' review)

Cold reviews are designed to be a continuing part of the quality control process and take place after the assurance assignment has been completed.

They are usually conducted either:

- As a process, whereby partners in a firm review each other's work

- By a team specifically constituted to conduct such reviews – usually under the direction of a partner, but the work is usually carried out by suitably qualified and experienced managers
- By a suitably qualified external consultant.

The review team should also develop appropriate courses of action where failures are identified, including:

- Communication of the findings within the firm
- Additional training and professional development
- Changes to the firm's policies and procedures
- Disciplinary action against those who repeatedly fail to comply with the firm's standards.

Interactive question 2: Quality control issues on an engagement

[Difficulty level: Intermediate]

You are an audit senior working for the firm Addystone Fish. You are currently carrying out the audit of Wicker Ltd, a manufacturer of waste paper bins. You are unhappy with Wicker's inventory valuation policy and have raised the issue several times with the audit manager. He has dealt with the client for a number of years and does not see what you are making a fuss about. He has refused to meet you on site to discuss these issues.

The former engagement partner to Wicker retired two months ago. As the audit manager had dealt with Wicker for so many years, the other partners have decided to leave the audit of Wicker in his capable hands.

Requirement

Comment on the situation outlined above.

See **Answer** at the end of this chapter.

8 Getting the assurance opinion wrong

Section overview

- Getting the audit opinion wrong could lead to:
  - Being sued for professional negligence
  - Prosecuted and fined
  - Disciplinary proceedings from ICAEW
  - Loss of reputation, clients, key staff
  - Assurance firm collapse
- In the context, quality control procedures are important.
- Risk is another key issue associated with getting the opinion wrong – are some clients too risky to accept?
- Liability limitation agreements for auditors have recently been introduced into UK law.

Think for a moment about the possible cost of getting the audit opinion wrong:

- If someone can demonstrate that you owed them a duty of care and they suffered loss by relying on the financial statements, they could sue you under the tort of negligence, as you saw previously whilst studying for the Law Paper.
- Until the relevant provisions of Companies Act 2006 (see 8.1 below) came into effect, you as auditor, may not be the only person responsible for their loss – the directors, who are responsible for preparing financial statements which give a true and fair view, probably had a hand in it somewhere – but you could find yourself solely liable.
- As a member of the ICAEW you could also face disciplinary proceedings, fines and penalties.

Audit firms must carry professional indemnity insurance, which means that any settlement will be paid out by the insurance company, but there is quite a long list of audit firms which no longer exist – ranging from Spicer and Oppenheim as a result of the British and Commonwealth/Atlantic Computers failure to Andersens, the former auditor of Enron – as a result of the collapse of an audit client.

To some extent the final cost of the settlement is only a part of the overall cost. Lawyers do not come cheap, particularly good corporate lawyers, and the time of partners and staff taken up with defending such an action can also represent a huge cost.

There is a further substantial, but intangible cost, resulting from the damage to a firm's reputation following its involvement with a client collapse. This is the loss of other clients and often key members of staff who no longer want to be associated with the firm.

Remember that many assurance firms operate as partnerships whose partners have unlimited and joint and several liability (which you also will remember from your law studies). If one partner gets it wrong, all the partners could be found liable.

Clearly in this context, quality control policies and procedures, which help to ensure that the wrong opinion is not given, are very important. However, it is not just a question of quality. As you saw in your studies for Assurance, and as we shall look at in more detail in the next chapter, it is a question of risk. Increasingly, assurance firms are concluding that there are some clients which are too risky to take on, leaving companies required to have an audit under the law unable to appoint an auditor.

This situation has needed resolution. One way of trying to restrict liability has been to look at the business vehicles through which many assurance firms operate. As a result, many have incorporated in a limited way, becoming Limited Liability Partnerships (LLPs), which were introduced into UK law in 2001.

However, there has also been a need to review the whole concept of who is to blame when things go wrong. The profession has favoured a scheme of 'proportional liability', whereby the assurance provider only pays for its share of the blame when things go wrong.

8.1 New possibilities for limitation of liability

Companies Act 2006 has brought in a new provision for auditors to agree limits on their liability to companies in respect of statutory audits. For such an agreement to be valid it must:

- Cover only one financial year
- Be approved by a resolution of the company's shareholders

The arrangements are only effective to the extent that they are "fair and reasonable" in the particular circumstances. This means that the Court could override the contractual agreement and amend the liability to a level set by the Court.

The Act does not specify the manner in which liability may be limited. This means that the contractual limits could be set in a variety of ways, for example:

- Based on the auditor's proportionate share of the responsibility for any loss
- Purely by reference to the "fair and reasonable" test
- A cap on liability, which could be either a monetary amount or on the basis of an agreed formula, or
- Some combination of the above methods

As this part of the Companies Act only became effective in April 2008, it remains to be seen how many of these agreements are made, and how the limits are set.

One related development is that the National Association of Pension Funds, which represents a substantial body of institutional investors who carry a great deal of voting power in large companies, has issued the following policy statement:

'investors should consider voting against resolutions which propose any form of liability limitation other than proportionate liability unless there are compelling reasons why that is not appropriate, and why the directors feel that another form of liability limitation would survive a court's judgement of what is fair and reasonable in all the circumstances'.

This provision in the Companies Act has disappointed mid-tier firms, as they believe that this could reduce their chances of competing for audits with larger firms, as they would have to negotiate lower caps as their resources are smaller. The Act theoretically gives the Government power to intervene if this appears to be the case, but we will have to wait and see what the outcome is in practice.

8.2 A new criminal offence

While the liability limitation provisions could be seen to reduce the risks facing audit firms, Companies Act 2006 also introduces a new criminal offence of knowingly or recklessly causing an auditor's report on company accounts to include any matter that is misleading, false or deceptive in a material particular.

The penalty for the offence is a fine although an earlier draft of the law included the possibility of imprisonment.

Members of the profession are worried about the risk here that an honest mistake could attract a criminal penalty but the government's view is that "recklessness" has a very high hurdle and would only catch an auditor who is "aware that an action or failure to act carried risks, that they personally knew that the risks were not reasonable ones to take, and that, despite knowing that, they went ahead".

Summary and Self-test

Summary

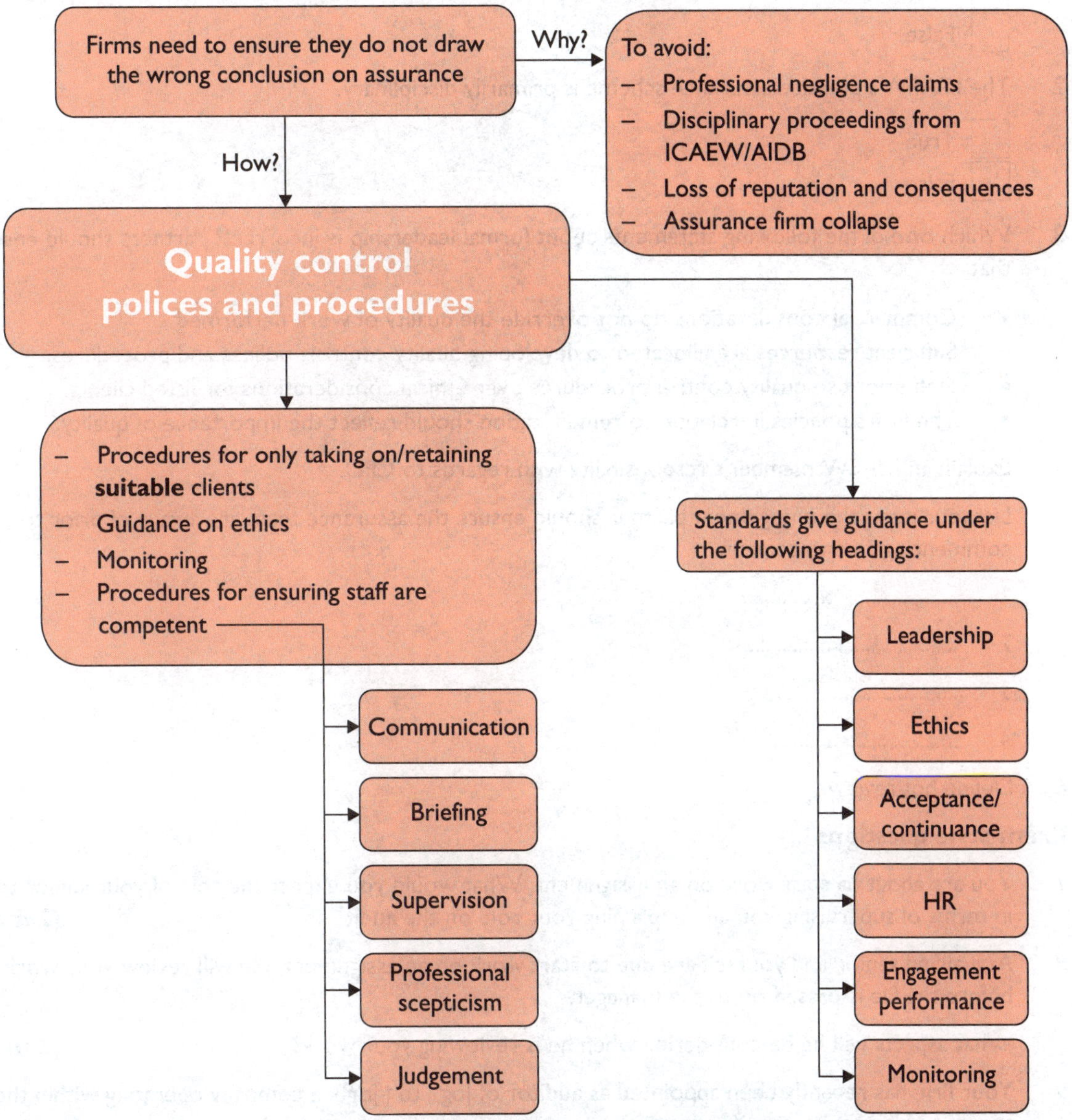
Firms need to ensure they do not draw the wrong conclusion on assurance
Why?
To avoid:
– Professional negligence claims
– Disciplinary proceedings from ICAEW/AIDB
– Loss of reputation and consequences
– Assurance firm collapse
How?
Quality control polices and procedures
– Procedures for only taking on/retaining suitable clients
– Guidance on ethics
– Monitoring
– Procedures for ensuring staff are competent
Communication
Briefing
Supervision
Professional scepticism
Judgement
Standards give guidance under the following headings:
Leadership
Ethics
Acceptance/ continuance
HR
Engagement performance
Monitoring

Self-test

Answer the following questions.

1 Compliance with quality control policies and procedures as required by ISQC 1 will constitute a good defence against allegations that the firm has been negligent.

☐ True

☐ False

2 The ICAEW's practice assurance scheme is primarily disciplinary.

☐ True

☐ False

3 Which **one** of the following statements about formal leadership is incorrect? Partners should ensure that:

- Commercial considerations do not override the quality of work performed.
- Sufficient resources are allocated to developing quality controls polices and procedures.
- Staff prioritise quality control procedures over ethical considerations for listed clients.
- The firm's policies in relation to remuneration should reflect the importance of quality.

4 Explain an ICAEW member's responsibility with regards to CPD.

5 List four items the engagement partner should ensure the assurance team are aware of prior to commencing an engagement.

1 ....

2 ....

3 ....

4 ....

6 Define hot review.

Exam-style questions

7 You are about to start work on an assignment. What would you expect the role of your senior to be in terms of supervising you and explaining your role on the audit? **(2 marks)**

8 A qualified senior and yourself are due to start work on an assignment. He will review your work before the file is passed on to the manager.

What aspects will he be considering when he is reviewing your work? **(2 marks)**

9 Your firm has recently been appointed as auditor of Jog Ltd ('Jog'), a company operating within the sports and leisure sector. Your audit manager has arranged a meeting with the company's finance director for early next week and she has asked you to assist her, in advance of this meeting, with the audit planning for the year ending 30 June 20X6. Your audit manager has also asked you to carry out some preliminary analytical procedures on the year-end financial statements of Jog when these become available.

Jog's business can be split into the following three divisions

- Sports equipment retail outlets: 35 sports equipment retail outlets located in 'out of town' retail parks
- Fitness clubs: 15 fitness clubs, each offering a fully equipped gym together with yoga, aerobics, and circuit training classes
- Machine manufacture: a manufacturing unit in which running machines and rowing machines are assembled using components sourced from overseas.

Further information:

Sports equipment retail outlets

The retail outlets are all located close to major towns and cities throughout the whole of the UK. Each outlet stocks a standard range of products which are supplied from a central warehouse operated by Jog. Salaries for the core staff at the outlets are paid by Jog's head office by direct bank transfer. Each outlet is run on a day-to-day basis by a manager who is responsible for hiring casual staff to cover peak periods. These casual staff members are generally paid using cash from the till.

Jog received some bad publicity during the year following its inclusion in a television documentary which revealed that one of its non-UK sports shoe suppliers was making its employees work long hours for very low wages. In an attempt to manage this adverse press attention, Jog has now had to source these products from alternative suppliers based in the UK.

Fitness clubs

Jog's 15 fitness clubs are all located directly above existing Jog retail outlets. Each club has its own on-site manager and is operated independently of the adjacent retail outlet. Customers of the fitness clubs pay by one of three methods: on a 'pay per session' basis over the fitness club counter; by monthly direct debit paid into Jog's head office bank account; or by annual subscription to head office. Customers are then issued with a membership card which enables them to gain access to the club.

The company operates a bonus incentive scheme for the managers at both its retail outlets and fitness clubs. The size of the bonus is linked to the profitability of their individual operation.

Machine manufacture

During the year Jog started to manufacture its own running machines and rowing machines. It sources the machine components from China and Taiwan. These components are assembled in the UK at Jog's factory for sale both in Jog's own stores under their own 'Jog' brand and also to independent sports shops under the 'Iron Champ' brand. The latter accounts for approximately 80% of Jog's total production of both running and rowing machines. Sales to independent sports shops achieve a gross profit margin of 50%, whereas sales to Jog's own shops are made to that division at cost plus 10%.

Jog is invoiced by its non-UK component suppliers in their respective local currency. The components are sent by sea, which means that Jog's typical lead time for components from the placing of an order to delivery in the UK is three months. Jog is required to pay its suppliers 50% with order and 50% upon receipt of the components in the UK.

Quality control

In line with your firm's system of quality control, procedures were conducted prior to accepting Jog as an audit client, to ensure that it was appropriate to accept such an appointment. Your audit manager has asked you to consider the other objectives of a system of quality control and why they may be particularly relevant to Jog.

Requirements

(a) and (b) omitted until later chapter

(c) (i) State the objectives of a system of quality control within an audit firm.

(ii) Identify, with reasons, which of the above objectives are likely to be particularly relevant to your audit of Jog. **(8 marks)**

Parts (a) and (b) of this question will be included in Chapter 7. Note that much of the information given in the question relates to these parts, but has been left in so that you can use any relevant information for the purposes of answering Part (c)(ii).

Now, go back to the Learning Objectives in the Introduction. If you are satisfied you have achieved these objectives, please tick them off.

Technical reference

1 The need for quality standards	
• Requirement for quality control procedures	**ISQC 1.16 and ISA 220.6**
2 Leadership	**ISQC 1.18 – 19**
3 Ethics	**ISQC 1.20 – 25**
4 Acceptance of engagements	**ISQC 1.26 – 28**
5 Human resources	**ISQC 1.29 – 31**
6 Engagement performance	**ISQC 1.32 – 47, ISA 220**
7 Monitoring	**ISQC 1.48 – 56**
8 Getting the assurance opinion wrong	**Companies Act 2006 ss. 532 – 538 and ss. 507 – 509**

Answers to Interactive questions

Answer to Interactive question 1

The benefits of quality control procedures include:

- Standard of all audit work completed is high and consistent
- Registered auditors are regarded as professionals who follow standards
- Quality of the work completed can be measured against a standard
- Individuals within firms know if the work they have completed is acceptable

Answer to Interactive question 2

Several quality control issues are raised in the scenario:

Engagement partner

An engagement **partner** is usually appointed to each audit engagement undertaken by the firm, to take responsibility for the engagement on behalf of the firm. Assigning the audit to an experienced audit manager is not sufficient.

The lack of an audit engagement partner also means that several of the requirements of ISA 220, about ensuring that arrangements in relation to independence and directing, supervising and reviewing the audit, are not in place.

Conflicting views

In this scenario the audit manager and senior have conflicting views about the valuation of inventory. This does not appear to have been handled well, with the manager refusing to discuss the issue with the senior.

ISA 220 requires that the audit engagement partner takes responsibility for settling disputes in accordance with the firm's policy in respect of resolution of disputes required by ISQC 1. In this case, the lack of engagement partner may have contributed to this failure to resolve the disputes. In any event, at best, the failure to resolve the dispute is a breach of the firm's policy under ISQC 1. At worst, it indicates that the firm does not have a suitable policy concerning such disputes as required by ISQC 1.

Answers to Self-test

1 True

2 False, although disciplinary action may be taken as a result of a review if required.

3 Staff prioritise quality control procedures over ethical considerations for listed clients.

4 Every member is required to certify that he/she has carried out appropriate professional development annually.

5 From:

- What work they are supposed to be doing
- The nature of the entity's business
- Any risks relevant to the engagement
- Problems that might arise during the engagement
- The detailed approach to the engagement

6 A hot review is a review carried out by a partner not otherwise involved in the engagement or an external consultant before the audit report is signed.

Exam-style questions

7 **Supervision**

- Inform you of your responsibilities
- Explain the objectives of the work you are carrying out
- Explain the nature of the entity's business
- Highlight possible accounting and auditing problems which may affect the procedures you carry out

8 **Review of work**

- Work properly conducted in accordance with plan/programmes
- Working papers to a standard/evidence recorded
- Conclusions valid
- Matters identified for further consideration
- Working papers headed, initialled, dated

9 (c) **Objectives of quality control**

The objectives of an audit firm's system of quality control are to ensure that the auditor performs the right work to a high standard and adequately records the work done. It involves selecting the appropriate team, supervising staff, consulting sufficiently with colleagues and outside experts and reviewing the work carried out by the team with sufficient care.

A system of quality control will also ensure that the auditor draws the correct conclusions from the evidence available, forms the appropriate audit opinion and deals adequately with issues raised including reporting to management.

Quality control is also designed to protect the auditor from risks arising as a result of incompetence or negligence of the client's staff and will protect the firm from the risk of litigation.

Objectives relevant to the audit of Jog

Jog operates out of many locations and because it has a number of diverse activities, the audit firm may not have staff with relevant expertise. It is therefore particularly important that a team with appropriate skills and experience is selected for the audit and that the work is supervised closely.

As Jog is a new audit client and because its business is diversified it is particularly important that the audit team has an adequate understanding of the business. The risks arising from the client's staff being incompetent or negligent are particularly relevant to Jog as the auditor does not yet know the client very well.

As Jog is a new audit client and because its business is diversified it is particularly important that the audit team has an adequate understanding of the business. The risks arising from the client's staff being inexperienced and negligent are particularly relevant to Jog as the auditor does not yet know the client very well.

chapter 6

Accepting engagements

Introduction

Learning objectives

Tick off

- Understand and explain the legal requirements for appointment and removal of auditors ☐
- Identify the professional and ethical matters a firm should consider when accepting appointment as assurance providers ☐
- Understand the need to clarify the terms of engagement in writing and understand and explain the issues involved ☐
- Discuss the process by which an auditor obtains an engagement ☐

Specific syllabus references for this chapter are: 1h, 2a, c, h, i, j.

Syllabus links

Many of the considerations set out in this chapter have already been introduced in the Assurance paper. In this paper, you are required to consider the matters at a higher level, and be able to explain and discuss the matters in more detail.

Examination context

You may be asked to apply the principles discussed in this chapter to a scenario question in the exam. For instance, in the December 2008 and March 2009 exams, matters to consider when accepting engagements were examined as part of 40 mark questions.

In the assessment, candidates may be required to:

- Explain the main ways in which national legislation affects the appointment and removal of auditors
- Identify the legal, professional and ethical considerations that an individual or firm must consider before accepting a specified assurance engagement
- Discuss the issues which underlie the agreement of the scope and terms of an assurance engagement (new or continuing)
- Discuss the process by which an auditor obtains an audit engagement
- Discuss the issues and risks that an individual auditor or audit firm must consider with regard to the acceptance of an audit engagement (new or continuing) with a client, including terms of engagement and their documentation
- Identify the legal, professional and ethical considerations that an individual auditor or audit firm must consider before accepting a specified audit engagement

1 Tendering

Section overview

- An assurance firm might be invited to accept an engagement or to tender for an engagement.
- A tender is in effect a 'bid' for an engagement.
- The firm will set out the reasons why it is best placed to provide the engagement and the fee at which it can do it.
- Lowballing may occur during a tender process, and while this is not ethically wrong, it may require ethical safeguards to be put in place.

An assurance firm might obtain an engagement by the following methods:

- Being approached by a potential client and being asked to accept the engagement
- Being approached by an existing client and being asked to accept the engagement
- Being approached by a potential or existing client and being asked to tender for the engagement

In practice, the most common method of obtaining an audit is by tender. In a tender process, several assurance firms are in effect asked to 'bid' for the engagement, by setting out the attributes their firm possesses that makes them the best placed to carry out the engagement, and, sometimes very importantly, by indicating the level of fee that they are likely to charge. The company seeking auditors then considers the bids (which may be written or presented orally or both) and invites the successful party to accept the audit.

Although the price of the proposed engagement can be very important, it is not the only consideration for the company in a tender process. Other important considerations are:

- The quality of the service the prospective auditors are likely to provide
- The knowledge of the business they possess
- The experience of the industry they have
- The proposed personnel on the audit team
- References obtained about the audit firm

An issue to consider briefly in the context of tendering is lowballing. Lowballing is the name given to the practice of charging less than the 'market rate' for the audit. In other words, say five comparable-sized firms were tendering for an audit, it is likely that their proposed fees would be similar. If one were significantly lower than the others, then it might be that the firm was quoting at a low rate in order to obtain the engagement on those grounds, in other words, lowballing.

The ICAEW Code of Ethics states that a firm may quote any fee it considers acceptable. In other words, the practice of lowballing is not unethical in itself. However, ethical safeguards should be considered as lowballing does increase the self-interest threat of not being able to complete the audit to the appropriate standards in a commercial way.

The Code of Ethics suggests that the basis for fee computation should be disclosed to and discussed with the client/potential client as soon as possible, so this would probably be incorporated into a tendering document. It states that fees should be determined with reference to:

- The seniority and professional experience of the persons necessarily engaged on the work
- The time expended by each
- The degree of risk and responsibility which the work entails
- The nature of the client's business, the complexity of its operation and the work to be performed
- The priority and importance of the work to the client
- Together with any expenses properly incurred

Giving the client such details about the basis of the fee will help the client determine if he is getting value for money, particularly in comparison with other tenders.

2 Risk analysis

Section overview

- Firms carry out risk analysis prior to accepting engagements.
- This is in order to ensure that the risk of giving an inappropriate opinion on the engagement is not too high.
- Matters to consider are whether the directors appear to have integrity, the company has a good financial record and prospects, the attitude to internal control and the nature of the client's transactions.

As you learnt in Assurance, assurance firms will carry out a risk analysis before accepting clients. This is partly to determine what fee they think is appropriate for the engagement (the higher risk the client, the greater the benefit that the firm will want from undertaking the engagement) but also to lay foundations for understanding the risks associated with the engagement if it is taken on and the amount of work that will have to be undertaken to reduce assurance risk to an acceptable level for that assignment. As noted in Chapter 5, it may be that an engagement is too risky for a firm to risk taking on.

Worked example: Two clients

Imagine two clients of a similar size, in the same industry:

Client A

You have never had to make any adjustments to client A's financial statements, which are produced by their qualified chief accountant and his experienced and competent staff from proprietary software which both you and they know and understand well. The company's chief executive is a stickler for deadlines, but takes a genuine interest in the financial statements so that accurate numbers are produced on time on a regular basis.

Client B

The chief executive of client B is a 'seat of the pants' man, who has little time for accountants and the financial statements they produce. The accounts department is understaffed, those working there are unqualified and using an accounting package on which they have received no formal training. Every year you go through a lengthy process of correcting the trial balance before you can even start to think about analytical procedures and audit work proper. You are always under pressure to finish the engagement on time and there is always an argument about the fee.

Which of these clients presents the higher risk?

Clearly client A is better organised than client B on the accounting front. Client A therefore starts out as a lower risk proposition than client B, based on the firm's experience of client A, its organisational culture and its reliable systems.

After the financial statements for both clients are finalised, however, you may feel more confident about the figures for client B because you had analysed them in more depth.

Another question

If:

- You were a fraudster, hoping to inflate the value of your company so that a venture capital fund would invest, or a bank would continue with finance, or a large multinational would purchase it, or
- You were a money launderer wanting to introduce the profits from your drug smuggling and dealing activities into an otherwise legitimate business;

would you prefer to be operating client A or client B?

You could argue that things are so chaotic at client B that no one would notice a few stray transactions.

Or you might think that the auditors have to spend so much time on the detail that they would have quite a good chance of picking something up.

Perhaps the well organised, reliable client A, where the auditors don't seem to do very much detailed checking, might be a better bet.

The most that can be said therefore is that the assessment of risk is something of a balancing act between your judgement of how reliable the information coming from the client is likely to be and the things you can actually do.

The example illustrates that such judgements are not simple, but generally speaking when carrying out risk analysis prior to accepting a client, assurance providers will be seeking to determine:

- Whether the directors/management of the company appear to have integrity: this can be assessed by looking at the accounting policies of the company (are they prudent and conservative or imprudent?) and the qualifications of the finance director it employs, or by obtaining references for key personnel from parties known to the assurance firm, such as bankers or solicitors, or the previous auditors.
- Whether the company has a good financial record, resources and outlook: this can be assessed by looking at recent financial performance and reports and by making enquiries (with permission) from its bankers.
- Whether the company appears to have good internal control, or, at minimum, a good control environment: this might be indicated by the existence of an internal audit department, or assessed through inquiries of management.
- Whether the company has unusual transactions: this can be assessed by reviewing published financial statements.

In general terms, if the directors appear to have integrity, the financial record is strong and prospects look good, there is a good attitude to internal control in the company and it has few unusual transactions, then it is lower risk than a company for which those things are not true.

Remember, that if a firm determines that a company is a high risk client, this does not necessarily mean that the firm will not accept the engagement, but this preliminary assessment of risk will be incorporated into the audit procedures when risk assessment identification and procedures are carried out on the engagement.

Another area constituting risk to the auditor, as indicated in the example above, is the risk that the client may be money laundering. As you know, accountants are required to report suspicions of money laundering and failure to report a suspicion is a criminal offence. The auditors are also required to carry out client due diligence with respect to money laundering at the start of an engagement. This was all set out in your manual for Assurance, and you should refer back to it for the details.

3 Acceptance and legal issues

Section overview

- Auditors must consider:
  - The results of risk analysis
  - Any ethical barriers to acceptance
  - Whether the firm has the resources to undertake the assignment
  - Legal issues

When deciding whether to accept an assurance engagement, the auditors need to consider the following:

- The results of risk analysis (discussed above)
- Whether there are any ethical issues which prevent acceptance (discussed in Chapters 4 and 5)

- Whether the firm has sufficient experience and resources (mainly staff who are appropriately qualified, experienced and available) to undertake the engagement
- For an audit engagement, whether all the legal requirements associated with the appointment of the incoming auditors and the removal or resignation of the outgoing auditors have been met.

3.1 Ethical issues

The ICAEW Code of Ethics sets out the following points in relation to changes in professional appointment.

3.1.1 Prospective auditors

When a prospective auditor is first approached by a prospective client or nominated, he should explain to the prospective client that he has a professional duty, if asked to act or be nominated, to communicate with the existing auditor. (This may be mentioned in replying to requests to submit tenders.)

The client should give the existing auditor written authority to discuss the client's affairs with the prospective auditor.

The prospective auditor should then write to the existing auditor, seeking information which could influence his decision as to whether or not he may properly accept appointment.

If the existing auditor fails to respond within a reasonable time, the prospective auditor should write to the existing auditor by recorded delivery stating an intention to accept the appointment in the absence of a reply within a specified period. The existing auditor's silence would imply that there were no adverse comments.

Once the prospective auditor has received confirmation that there are no reasons not to act, or has become satisfied that he can properly act, and is prepared to accept nomination/appointment, he should inform the client.

3.1.2 Existing auditor

The existing auditor should get written authority from the client to communicate with the prospective auditor. In the absence of specific instructions by the client an existing auditor should not ordinarily volunteer information, as he is bound by confidentiality.

The existing auditor or adviser should quickly answer the communication from the prospective auditor. However care must be taken in situations where the existing auditor knows or suspects that his or her client is involved in money laundering as it is a criminal offence to 'tip off' a money launderer.

If there are no matters of which the latter should be aware, the existing auditor should write to say that this is the case.

If there are such matters, he should inform the prospective auditor of those factors within his knowledge of which, in his opinion, the latter should be aware. It is not sufficient to state that unspecified factors exist.

Matters may include:

- Unlawful acts by the client
- Unpaid fees
- Differences of opinion between the auditor and the client

The fact that there are issues that should be brought to the attention of the prospective auditor does not preclude him or her from accepting appointment; it merely identifies issues that need to be considered.

This communication between the prospective and existing auditors should also provide evidence to the prospective auditor of both the identity and integrity of the client. This is additionally valuable in the light of new requirements on accountants to verify the identity of clients to guard against money laundering.

3.1.3 Client refuses permission to contact previous auditors

If the client fails or refuses to grant the existing auditor or adviser permission to discuss the client's affairs with the proposed auditor, the existing auditor or adviser should report that fact to the prospective auditor or adviser, who should carefully consider the impact of this on his decision whether to accept the appointment/nomination or not.

3.1.4 Additional work

A professional accountant invited to undertake work which is additional to and related to continuing work carried out by another professional adviser should notify that other professional adviser of the work he has been asked to undertake.

It is generally in the interest of the client that the existing auditor or adviser be aware of the nature of the additional work being undertaken.

The existing adviser will be provided with the opportunity to communicate with the professional accountant to provide information, lack of which might otherwise prevent the additional work from being carried out effectively.

Additionally, such notification could affect the way an existing auditor or adviser discharges his continuing responsibilities to his client.

Notification should always be given unless the client advances reasons which persuade the firm that, in all the circumstances, the existing adviser should not be informed.

An example of such a situation might be where a client disagrees with the proposed audit opinion of its auditors and engages a second accountant to give him a second opinion on the matter. A key danger in this situation is that the second accountant does not have all the information necessary to give an appropriate second opinion, thus communication is vital. Auditors should always be wary of giving second opinions as they may compromise the position of the first auditor, trying to give an appropriate, independent opinion.

3.2 Legal issues

3.2.1 Appointment of auditors by the members

In order to carry out the audit of a company, the auditor first needs to be appointed by ordinary resolution.

The members (ie shareholders) of a company appoint the auditor at an annual general meeting (AGM), or other general meeting of the company at which the financial statements are put forward for approval by members. The appointment must be made by the end of the 28 days after the last date on which the account must be filed. If an auditor is not appointed within this time, the existing auditor is deemed to be reappointed, subject to certain conditions.

3.2.2 Appointment of auditors by the directors

The exception to the above rule is where the directors appoint the auditor either to:

- Fill a casual vacancy, for example when the existing auditor resigns during the year, or
- Appoint the first auditor between the date of incorporation and the first AGM or if the company qualifies to require an audit, before the next AGM.

As noted above, however, in both cases the members must then reappoint the auditors at the next AGM, by ordinary resolution.

3.2.3 Appointment of auditors by the Secretary of State

In rare circumstances where no auditor has been appointed at the appropriate time, the company must inform the Secretary of State within one week of the relevant timing expiring and the Secretary of State will then appoint an auditor.

3.2.4 Removal of auditors

If the members of the company wish to remove the existing auditor and appoint a new one, they can do so by ordinary resolution with special notice at a general meeting.

Where this happens the auditors must make a statement of circumstances (see below) and they have certain rights, which include the right:

- To receive notice, attend and speak at the meeting where they would have been appointed, or the proposed new auditor is appointed
- To have a written representation of a reasonable length circulated to all members. Such a representation might explain why they should not be removed as auditors.

In practice, it tends to be the directors who decide that they would like the existing auditor removed, but to achieve this they must put up a resolution for the members to vote on.

One of the possible reasons why directors might wish to make this change is because they have had a disagreement in principle with the existing auditor over the accounting treatment of an item in the financial statements, but have no such disagreement with the new auditor. (Finding auditors who are more acquiescent is a process known as 'opinion shopping'). It is to protect the existing auditor (by giving him a right to argue his case) that company law provides for an auditor being removed to make written representation to members and to speak at the meeting at which the resolution is voted on.

3.2.5 Resignation of auditors

If the auditor resigns during his year of office, he must submit written notice to the company. The auditor must also send a statement of circumstances (see below).

The auditor has certain rights here, which include the right:

- To request an extraordinary general meeting (EGM) to set out the reasons for their resignation
- To require the company to circulate the statement of circumstances in advance of the meeting which:
  - The auditor requested (ie the EGM)
  - Appoints new auditor, or
  - Coincides with when his term of office would have expired

On receipt of the auditor's resignation the company must then notify:

- The Registrar of Companies
- Anyone entitled to receive a copy of the company's accounts

As an alternative to resignation the auditor may simply not seek reappointment, or the company may decide against reappointment. In either of these two circumstances, the auditor is still required to prepare a statement of circumstances or confirm in writing that there are no circumstances of which members should be aware.

3.2.6 Statement by auditor ceasing to hold office as auditor

An auditor who ceases to hold office as auditor of an unquoted company is required to deposit at the company's registered office:

- A statement of the circumstances connected with his ceasing to hold office which he considers should be brought to the attention of the members or creditors of the company; or
- A statement that there are no such circumstances if he considers this to be the case.

The requirements of Companies Act 2006 are stricter for an auditor who ceases to hold office as auditor of a quoted company. That auditor must deposit a statement of the circumstances connected with his ceasing to hold office at the company's registered office. There is no option to deposit a statement that there are no circumstances.

This makes it very difficult for an auditor who thinks something is wrong at a company, but is not sure, to walk away quietly without telling the members.

Interactive question 1: Disagreement with directors

[Difficulty level: Exam standard]

You have recently had a serious disagreement with the directors of one of your major audit clients who, as a result, have threatened to recommend another firm of auditors for appointment at the next AGM.

What statutory rights do you have if they carry out their threat?

See **Answer** at the end of this chapter.

4 Terms of an audit engagement

Section overview

- As part of engagement acceptance, the assurance providers will negotiate the terms of the engagement. For assurance engagements, this will include:
  - The scope of the engagement
  - The subject matter of the engagement
  - The criteria by which the subject matter is being judged
  - The level of assurance required and therefore the type of opinion to be given
  - The timings associated with the engagement
  - Any restriction in liability
  - The fee for the engagement

With regard to audits, the scope of the engagement is determined by law and professional standards, but the auditors must ensure that these terms are understood by the client. In addition, the following matters will need to be agreed:

- The fee or the basis by which the fee will be determined
- The limited liability agreement, that is, the cap on the auditors' liability for the engagement (discussed in the previous chapter)

4.1 Audit engagement letters

You were introduced to the concept of an engagement letter in your studies for Assurance. Engagement letters are required under ISA 210 *Agreeing the Terms of Audit Engagements*. As you may remember, it is a requirement of this standard that the terms of the engagement are put in writing.

The form and content of an engagement letter will vary, but should cover the following matters:

- The objective and scope of the audit of financial statements (including reference to applicable legislation, regulations, financial reporting framework and auditing standards)
- Management's responsibilities (including responsibility for the financial statements and the company's system of internal control)

The auditor's responsibilities

- The form and content of reports and communications that will arise from the audit
- The fact that due to the test nature and other limitations of an audit, there is an unavoidable risk that some material misstatement may remain undiscovered
- The fact that auditors are entitled to unrestricted access to records, documents and other information requested in connection with the audit

The expectation that management will provide written representations

The letter may also cover practical matters, such as arrangements relating to planning, using the work of experts, liaising with the internal audit department, the fee and restriction of auditor liability.

4.2 Recurring audits

When the audit is a recurring audit, it is not necessary to issue a new letter each year. However, the auditors should consider every year whether a new letter is required. The following factors may indicate a new letter is required:

- Indications that the client misunderstands the terms of the engagement
- Revised or special terms of the engagement
- A recent change in senior management or directors
- A significant change in ownership of the company

- A significant change in the nature or size of the company
- Legal or regulatory requirements

4.3 Changes in engagement

If the auditor is asked to change the engagement to one which provides a lower level of assurance then he should consider the appropriateness of doing so. Obviously, if the audit is a statutory audit, the auditor must provide an appropriate audit as required by law, that is one giving reasonable assurance on the truth and fairness of the engagement.

If the terms are changed, the auditor and the client must agree the terms. If the auditor and the client cannot agree, the auditor should withdraw from the existing arrangement.

4.4 Disclosure of the terms of agreement

The Companies Act 2006 makes provision for potential future regulations requiring disclosure of the terms of the audit engagement. Currently there are no such regulations in place.

Interactive question 2: Engagement letter [Difficulty level: Intermediate]

Mr Angry of Gonzo Animations Ltd has approached your audit firm to undertake the audit of his company. When the partner held the initial meeting with Mr Angry, the client refused to sign the engagement letter as he said that it was merely a means of the firm abdicating its responsibility for the audit.

Requirement

Your partner has asked you to draft a letter to the client explaining the need for a letter of engagement.

See **Answer** at the end of this chapter.

5 Terms of other assurance engagements

Section overview

- It is important to agree terms in the context of a statutory audit
- Think how much more important this is if a firm is appointed to carry out some other type of assignment
- Where there is no detailed regulatory framework there will be a much greater risk of misunderstanding so the negotiation and formal documentation of terms becomes much more important

5.1 Engagement letter for review of financial statements

Interactive question 3: Engagement letter for review of financial statements [Difficulty level: Intermediate]

Explain the purpose of each of the numbered paragraphs.

To the Board of Directors (or the appropriate representative of senior management):

(1) This letter is to confirm our understanding of the terms and objectives of our engagement and the nature and limitations of the services we will provide.

We will perform the following services:

(2) We will review the balance sheet of ABC Company as of December 31 19XX, and the related statements of income and cash flows for the year then ended, in accordance with the International Standards in Review Engagements (ISRE) 2400 (or refer to relevant national standards or practices

applicable to reviews). We will not perform an audit of such financial statements and, accordingly, we will not express an audit opinion on them. Accordingly, we expect to report on the financial statements as follows:

(3) Based on our review, nothing has come to our attention that causes us to believe that the accompanying financial statements do not give a true and fair view (or are not presented fairly, in all material respects) in accordance with International Accounting Standards.

(4) Responsibility for the financial statements, including adequate disclosure, is that of the management of the company. This includes the maintenance of adequate accounting records and internal controls and the selection and application of accounting policies. As part of our review process, we will request written representations from management concerning assertions made in connection with the review.

(5) Our engagement cannot be relied upon to disclose whether fraud or errors, or illegal acts exist. However, we will inform you of any material matters that come to our attention.

(6) Please sign and return the attached copy of this letter to indicate that it is in accordance with your understanding of the arrangements for our review of the financial statements.

XYZ and Co

Acknowledged on behalf of ABC Company by

(Signed)

Name and Title

Date

5.2 Agreement of terms on engagements to examine prospective financial information

If a firm is appointed, for example, to review a cash flow forecast that a client has prepared to support an attempt to raise finance from a bank, there are further issues to consider and to include in the engagement letter:

- The intended use of the information
- Whether the information will be for general or limited distribution
- The nature of the assumptions, that is whether they are best-estimate or hypothetical assumptions
- The elements to be included in the information
- The period covered by the information
- A caveat warning that there could be differences between the forecast and actual performance due to unforeseen circumstances.

Summary and Self-test

Summary

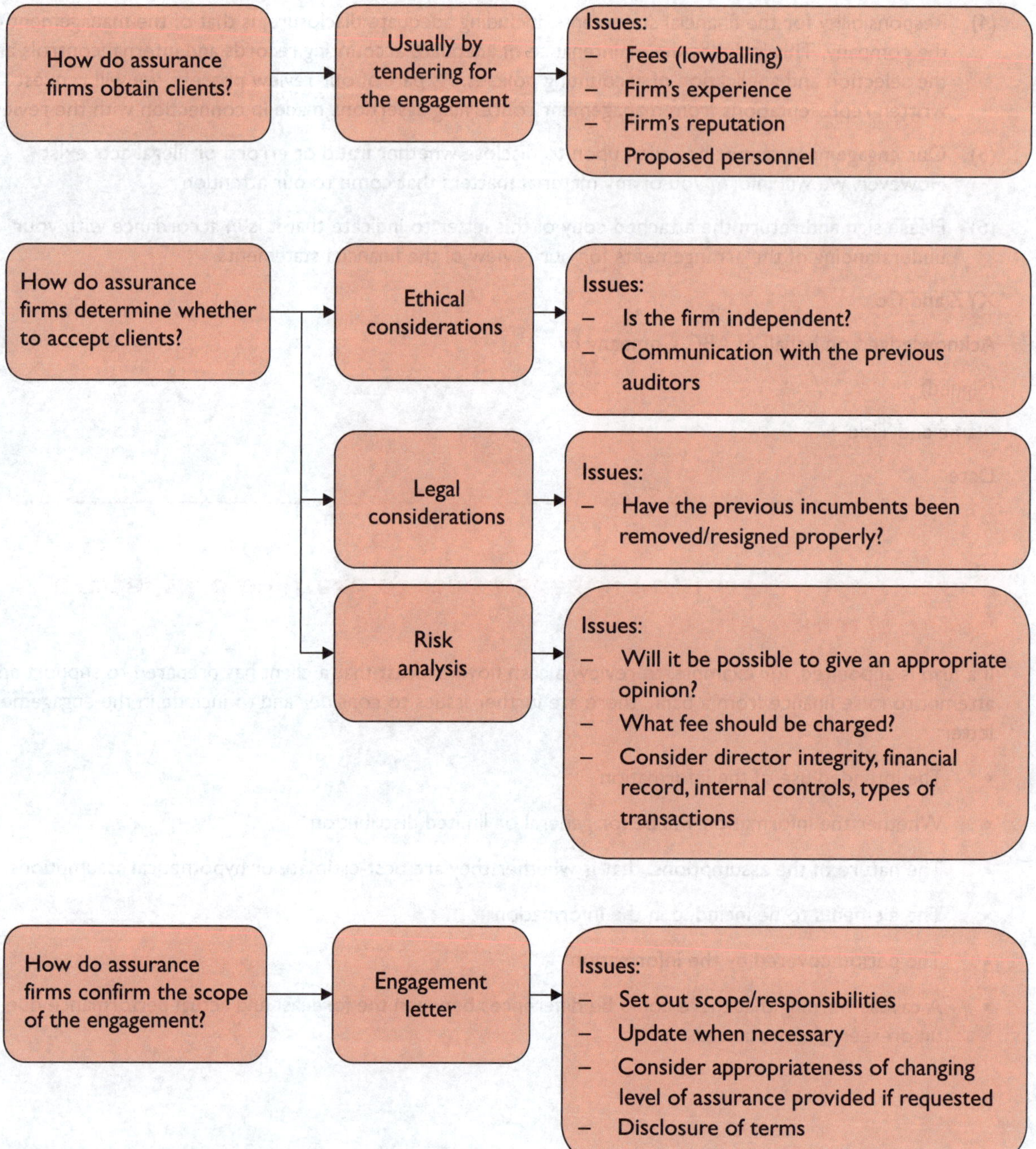
How do assurance firms obtain clients?
Usually by tendering for the engagement
Issues:
– Fees (lowballing)
– Firm's experience
– Firm's reputation
– Proposed personnel
How do assurance firms determine whether to accept clients?
Ethical considerations
Issues:
– Is the firm independent?
– Communication with the previous auditors
Legal considerations
Issues:
– Have the previous incumbents been removed/resigned properly?
Risk analysis
Issues:
– Will it be possible to give an appropriate opinion?
– What fee should be charged?
– Consider director integrity, financial record, internal controls, types of transactions
How do assurance firms confirm the scope of the engagement?
Engagement letter
Issues:
– Set out scope/responsibilities
– Update when necessary
– Consider appropriateness of changing level of assurance provided if requested
– Disclosure of terms

Self-test

Answer the following questions.

1 Define lowballing.

2 List four issues that ICAEW states should be referred to when determining fees

1 ....

2 ....

3 ....

4 ....

3 Why do firms undertake risk analysis?

4 If the client refuses the existing auditor permission to communicate with the prospective auditor, the prospective auditor should decline the appointment.

☐ True

☐ False

5 An auditor can be appointed by which of the following methods?

☐ Ordinary resolution by shareholders

☐ By directors to fill a casual vacancy

☐ By directors to appoint first auditor

☐ By Secretary of State

6 If a client requests that an auditor reduce the level of assurance offered on a statutory audit, an auditor may agree and reduce procedures accordingly.

☐ True

☐ False

Exam-style questions

7 Acer Ltd is a client of your firm and is seeking funding in order to expand the business. The directors have prepared profit and cash flow forecasts for the next three years ending 30 June 20X9 in support of the request for funding. The company's bankers require this information to be reviewed by independent accountants and the board of directors has requested that your firm undertakes this review.

Set out the matters that you would include in the engagement letter in relation to the respective responsibilities of the directors and the reporting accountant. **(2 marks)**

8 **Wrapper Ltd**

Your firm, which has six partners, has been invited by Mr Packer, the managing director and majority shareholder of Wrapper Ltd, to accept appointment as auditor of the company and also provide assistance with the preparation of the financial statements and the corporation tax computation.

The principal activity of Wrapper Ltd is the production of paper carrier bags, serviettes, coffee cups and lids which are sold to customers operating in the fast food sector. Wrapper Ltd was incorporated on 1 October 20X4 and the financial statements will cover the 15 month period to 31 December 20X5. Although the company's revenue and assets are below the thresholds for statutory audit purposes, the company's bankers require the annual accounts to be subjected to a full audit.

Mr Packer started the business using a combination of money inherited from his grandfather and a bank loan. The loan agreement includes a covenant specifying that the company's debt equity ratio should not exceed parity (ie 1:1).

The accounting records are computerised and the company uses software which was developed by IT Systems Ltd, a company owned by Mr Packer's brother. The software has been customised to integrate inventory control with receivables and payables. IT Systems Ltd also provides support for the company's computer systems. The accounting records are maintained by Mrs Carlton, assisted by Mrs Biggs who works one day a week and is responsible for payroll processing.

Requirements

(a) State, with reasons, the matters to be considered and procedures to be performed prior to your firm accepting and commencing the audit of Wrapper Ltd for the period ending 31 December 20X5. **(8 marks)**

(b) Identify, from the information provided above, the factors which should be taken into account when assessing the risk of misstatement in the financial statements of Wrapper Ltd and explain why such factors should be taken into account when conducting the audit. **(10 marks)**

(18 marks)

9 The directors of Harmony Ltd ('Harmony') have approached you with a view to your firm accepting appointment as its auditor for the year ending 31 July 20X6. Harmony manufactures satellite navigation systems which it supplies to many of the major motor car manufacturers with UK-based factories.

Harmony has a wholly-owned subsidiary undertaking located overseas which manufactures 'high-end' audio systems for locally based motor car manufacturers. The subsidiary, which is of a similar size to Harmony, is located in a country where there is no audit requirement for companies whose shares are not publicly held. Harmony prepares consolidated financial statements.

The shareholders of Harmony are actively involved in the day to day running of the business and that of the wholly-owned subsidiary.

The directors of Harmony have told their existing auditors that they will not be re-appointed at the company's forthcoming annual general meeting. They have not given them a reason for this, but the existing auditors suspect that it is due to a dispute that arose during the audit of last year's financial statements. At 31 July 20X5 Harmony was carrying inventory totalling £375,000 in respect of a cancelled order for a satellite navigation system from a motor car manufacturer that had gone into liquidation. During September 20X5, modifications were made to the inventory, at a cost of £75,000, to enable them to be sold to another customer for £195,000 that same month. The directors of Harmony were concerned at the effect that any provision against the inventory in the financial statements would have on their distributable profits for the year. The directors accordingly insisted on including the inventory in the financial statements at £375,000, which gave rise to a modified audit report.

In addition to your appointment as auditor, the directors of Harmony have also requested:

(i) That you, as the proposed engagement partner, attend the company's monthly board meetings; and

(ii) That your firm be appointed to provide internal audit services to Harmony.

Your firm has seven partners in total and has an office in each of three cities in the South of England.

Requirements

(a) Outline the reasons for and against the subsidiary of Harmony having an audit on its own basis despite being owner-managed. **(6 marks)**

(b) Set out the key issues specific to Harmony that may prevent you from accepting the appointment solely as its external auditor, and state what action you could take to resolve these issues. **(6 marks)**

(c) Discuss the potential threats to objectivity caused by the provision of the additional services requested by Harmony and describe what safeguards could be put in place to mitigate those threats. **(8 marks)**

(20 marks)

Now, go back to the Learning Objectives in the Introduction. If you are satisfied you have achieved these objectives, please tick them off.

Technical reference

Terms of an audit engagement

• Audit engagement letters	ISA 210.9 – 10
• Recurring audits	ISA 210.13
• Changes in engagement	ISA 210.14 – 17

Answers to Interactive questions

Answer to Interactive question 1

Rights

- To receive notice of the resolution to appoint another auditor
- To have written representations circulated to all members, or read out at the meeting
- To attend the meeting
- To be heard at the meeting

Answer to Interactive question 2

ABC & Co Chartered Accountants
123 High Street
Bristol
BS6 7HJ
5 April 20X2

V Angry Esq
Gonzo Animations Ltd
Muppet Road
Bath
BA18 9LL

Dear Mr Angry

Engagement letters

We are required by International Standards on Auditing (UK and Ireland) to send you a formal engagement letter before conducting the audit. All firms of auditors should abide by this procedure.

The letter is there as much to protect the client, as it is the auditor, and we would suggest that legal advice is taken prior to you accepting the terms.

Purpose of engagement letter

The purpose of the letter is to:

- Define clearly the extent of the our responsibilities, and your responsibilities.
- Minimise the possibility of any misunderstanding between ourselves and Gonzo Animations Ltd.
- Provide written confirmation of our acceptance of appointment, the scope of the audit and the form of the report.

We believe that it is important for both parties to clearly understand their roles within the external audit function.

Contents of engagement letter

The contents of the letter are set out below, together, where necessary, with the justification of the inclusion of the section.

- Our respective relevant statutory and professional responsibilities (to avoid misunderstanding).
- An explanation of the scope of the audit (so that we inform you of what we will do). This covers a number of issues.
  - The audit will be carried out in accordance with the International Standards on Auditing (UK and Ireland) issued by the Auditing Practices Board.
  - We need to obtain an understanding of the accounting system in order to assess its adequacy as a basis for the preparation of the financial statements.

- We need to obtain relevant and reliable evidence sufficient to enable us to draw reasonable conclusions therefrom.
- The nature and extent of our procedures will vary according to the assessment of the accounting system and, where we wish to place reliance upon it, the system of internal control.
- We will endeavour to plan the audit so that we have a reasonable expectation of detecting material misstatements in the financial statements or accounting records resulting from fraud, error or non-compliance with law or regulations but that the examination ought not to be relied upon to disclose all frauds, errors or instances of non-compliance which may exist (as some may be immaterial).
- Due to the test nature and other inherent limitations of an audit, together with the inherent limitations of any system of internal control, there is an unavoidable risk that even some material misstatement may remain undiscovered.
- An explanation that management representations may be required in writing during the audit (this will only be in the case of audit areas where we have to rely on your representations).
- The fact that we may send a letter of comment, adding value to the audit, by outlining ways in which we discussed the business may be improved.

- Other matters such as
  - Our billing arrangements
  - Any arrangements in the future concerning the involvement of
    - Other auditors and experts
    - Internal auditors
    - Previous auditors
  - Management's responsibility to detect and prevent fraud
  - Your complaints procedures
  - A proposed timetable for the engagement (which will vary each year).

I hope this clarifies the need for the letter. Except for the timetable, we will only send out such letters in future where absolutely necessary.

Yours sincerely
Mr A Accountant

Answer to Interactive question 3

(1) Establishes the purpose of the letter.

(2) Describes the nature of the services to be performed and professional standards that will be followed. The paragraph also emphasises that this is not an audit assignment, and that the nature of the opinion will differ from an audit opinion. This is included to minimise the risk of misunderstandings.

(3) A review gives moderate assurance and the opinion will be expressed as negative assurance. It is important that the directors understand this before the assignment starts, again to eliminate misunderstandings as to the level of assurance that will be provided.

(4) This paragraph sets out the responsibilities of management in respect of the subject matter of the review.

(5) One of the roles of the engagement letter is to limit the liability being taken on by the practitioner. Here the practitioner is trying to protect himself from being held liable if fraud and errors exist.

(6) It is important that the terms are formally agreed by the two parties so the practitioner requires signed confirmation from the directors that they are in agreement.

Answers to Self-test

1 Lowballing is the practice of charging less than the market rate for assurance services.

2 From:

- The seniority and professional experience of the persons necessarily engaged on the work
- The time expended by each
- The degree of risk and responsibility which the work entails
- The nature of the client's business, the complexity of its operation and the work to be performed
- The priority and importance of the work to the client
- Together with any expenses properly incurred

3 • To ensure that the assurance provider believes an appropriate conclusion can be drawn.
- To assist in determining an appropriate fee (that reflects the risk of the assignment).

4 False. Not necessarily, although this might be an indicator that the auditor should have concerns about director integrity.

5 All of them.

6 False. A statutory audit provides a reasonable level of assurance.

Exam-style questions

7 **Directors**

Responsible for

- Forecasts including the assumptions on which they are based
- Cooperating with the reporting accountant by making available records, documents and personnel

Reporting accountant

- Forecast is properly prepared on the basis of the assumptions made
- Provide negative assurance that nothing has come to reporting accountant's attention to cause them to believe that the assumptions do not provide a reasonable basis for the forecast

8 **Wrapper Ltd**

(a) **Matters/procedures prior to acceptance of audit**

(i) Check adequacy of resources to enable

- Work to be completed to a high standard on a timely basis/use of competent staff
- Provision of tax/accountancy services without compromising independence (ie. safeguards can be put in place) eg:
  - Use of separate personnel to perform accountancy and tax
  - Review by an independent partner/senior staff member with appropriate expertise if tax computation prepared by audit team
  - Review of the audit by an audit partner who is not involved in the audit engagement

(ii) Establish/document existence of informed management – to ensure auditor does not take management role

(iii) Consider relationships/familiarity threat – to ensure independence/objectivity not impaired

(iv) Consider potential conflicts of interest (eg competing clients) – to ensure act in the best interest of clients

(v) Consider integrity of client – to reduce risk of misstatements due to fraud/misrepresentation

(vi) Client identification procedures – to reduce exposure to money laundering/comply with money laundering requirements

(vii) Send letter of engagement – to ensure client understands nature and scope of the work to be undertaken/narrow expectations gap

(b)

Factors	Why taken into account
• New client	• Lack of familiarity – may not identify events and transactions which have an impact on the financial statements/higher detection risk
• Start-up	• Going concern risk • Doubts/material uncertainty will require disclosure in the financial statements • Lack of going concern status will require financial statements to be prepared on a break-up basis
• Lack of prior year figures	• Lack of comfort/corroboration from use of analytical review procedures • Require more extensive use of tests of detail (substantive tests)
• Bank covenant	• Risk that profits may be overstated in order to preserve the debt equity ratio
• Trading with IT Systems Ltd	• Need to ensure complete disclosure of related party transactions
• Customised accounting software	• May not be reliable, resulting in errors
• Lack of segregation of duties	• Misstatements may not be prevented or detected and corrected on a timely basis/higher control risk • Determine the audit approach which is likely to be substantive based

9 (a) **Arguments for Harmony's subsidiary having an audit**

An audit requires all similar-sized companies to be treated the same, regardless of ownership. It provides assurance that the company has complied with the Companies Act and accounting standards. Many would consider that an external audit is a fair price to pay for limited liability.

There are more stakeholders in a company than simply its shareholders who can use the assurance generated by the audit work. The tax authorities can place more reliance on the financial statements and an audit affords some measure of protection to creditors that the company is not trading whilst insolvent. It also means potential investors can place similar reliance on the financial statements whether or not the company is listed.

Arguments against Harmony's subsidiary having an audit

Harmony's shareholders are actively involved in the management of the subsidiary and therefore an audit will be of little value to them. The auditor's report will be addressed to shareholders and therefore contribute little to their knowledge and understanding of the business. Furthermore, an audit can cause unnecessary red tape and expense.

(b) The audit of Harmony will include the results of the subsidiary, which are material as the subsidiary is the same size as Harmony. The audit firm must consider whether it has adequate resources to audit the overseas subsidiary itself and whether it has the required level of competence. Harmony should appoint a local audit firm and undergo an audit of its subsidiary voluntarily. This local firm would use the firm's UK audit packs and the UK firm would review the work of the local auditor in detail.

The dispute with the previous auditors may also cast doubt over the integrity of management and whether accepting the appointment will put the firm at risk of management intimidation. In an attempt to resolve this issue, permission should be sought to speak with the outgoing auditors and enquire of them whether there are any other issues of which the incoming auditor should be aware.

The engagement partner assigned must ensure that members of the audit team have appropriately consulted on difficult or contentious issues. It is also recommended that an independent second partner review of the audit file is undertaken in the first year, before the audit report is signed.

(c) **Threats to objectivity**

In some cases, for example when management representations are discussed, it may be desirable for the auditor to attend board meetings. However, an auditor must not under any circumstances make management decisions. Attending board meetings is allowed if the auditor is acting in an advisory capacity only or is reporting the results of audit work.

Safeguards

To safeguard against this threat, the auditor should ensure that there is 'informed management' at the company. The auditor should inform the directors that they alone are responsible for decision-making and he should get their written confirmation of agreement to this. In the interests however of being 'seen to be independent' it may be best to decline the offer of attendance at monthly board meetings.

Threat to objectivity

The provision of internal audit service causes a self-review threat to the external auditor as the external audit staff members may overlook errors made by their internal audit colleagues or may place too much reliance on their work.

Safeguards

The external audit firm can only act as internal auditor if the external auditor does not place significant reliance on the work or relies on it only after rigorous and objective assessment of the work completed by the internal auditors. Additional safeguards include separate engagement partners, separate engagement letters and different teams for the two respective roles.

Finally, the directors must confirm in writing that they are responsible for the overall system of internal control including the work of internal audit, and that they are responsible for acting on the recommendations of internal audit.

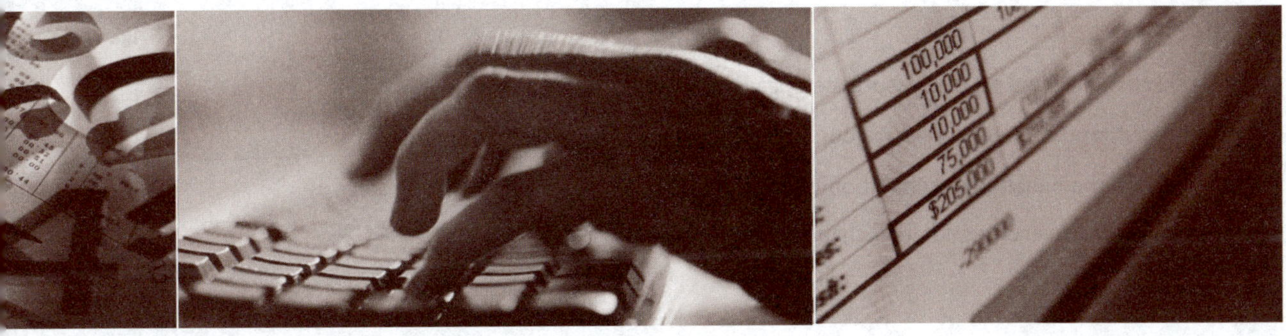

chapter 7

Planning

Introduction

Learning objectives

Tick off

- Discuss the need to plan assurance engagements ☐
- Understand and explain what goes into the key audit planning documents ☐
- Explain the benefits and limitation of analytical procedures at the planning stage ☐

Specific syllabus references for this chapter are: 3h, i, o.

Syllabus links

You have studied these matters for your Assurance paper, so much of the technical detail covered here is revision. It is important at this Application stage to be able to explain and apply the techniques outlined in the chapter.

Examination context

A question which deals with planning in the exam is also very likely to deal with risks, which we shall look at in more detail in the next chapter, hence the question practice given in this chapter is limited and more practice will be given in the next chapter.

In the assessment, candidates may be required to:

- Assess the impact of risk and materiality on the engagement plan, including the nature, timing and extent of audit procedures, for a given organisation
- Discuss the benefits and limitations of analytical procedures at the planning stage
- Specify and explain the steps necessary to plan the audit of the financial statements of a non-specialised profit oriented entity in accordance with the terms of the engagement including appropriate auditing standards

1 The need to plan

Section overview

- Audits are planned so that auditors know what to do so that the appropriate conclusion can be drawn.
- It is a requirement of ISA 300 *Planning an Audit of Financial Statements* that audits are planned.

Audits (and other assurance engagements) are planned because if they are not:

- Time might be wasted doing the wrong work
- The really important work might not be done at all
- Ultimately, the wrong conclusion might therefore be drawn

Planning an engagement is a key aspect of the quality control associated with that audit. If an audit is planned, then the right work is done, it is easier to supervise and review that work, and therefore it adds to the quality of the whole engagement.

In addition, as you know from your studies for Assurance, audits are planned because it is a requirement of auditing standards. ISA 300 *Planning an Audit of Financial Statements* requires audits to be planned so that they can be carried out 'effectively'.

Much of the material we look at in this chapter, you have covered in your lower level studies. In this area, you need to be able to apply your knowledge to the scenarios presented in the exam.

In summary, planning helps the auditor know:

- What to do
- How much to do
- Where to focus resources
- What the important matters that need dealing with

Interactive question 1: The need to plan [Difficulty level: Easy]

State the reasons why auditors need to plan audits.

See **Answer** at the end of this chapter.

2 Overall audit strategy and audit plan

Section overview

- The key planning document is called the overall audit strategy.
- It covers matters such as materiality, risk, audit approach, use of experts/internal audit, timings, team, budget and deadlines.
- Many audit firms have 'audit packs' containing example audit strategies and plans, but care should be taken when using them.
- The other key document in audit planning is the audit plan.

As you know from your studies for Assurance, the key planning document is called an overall audit strategy. This covers the main general areas of planning: materiality, risk, audit approach, use of experts and internal audit, timing, team, budgets and deadlines.

The technical details of many of these issues will be covered in later chapters.

Most audit firms have 'audit packs' which have a specific planning section and set out the key areas that auditors must consider when planning an audit. However, care should be taken when using any standard forms, as there is a risk that matters particular to the client might be forgotten. It is important to tailor the plan to the client, not the other way around. Identifying key issues relating to the client and then adjusting the audit approach will be necessary. This is why understanding the business (Chapter 8) and risk assessment (Chapter 9) are very important.

The overall audit strategy should be updated as necessary during the course of the engagement.

As you also know from your earlier studies, the other key document in audit planning is the audit plan, which is more detailed that the audit strategy, and sets out the nature, timing and extent of planned audit procedures (including risk assessment procedures) to fulfil the requirements of the overall audit strategy and auditing standards.

The audit plan should be updated as necessary during the course of the engagement.

3 Materiality

Section overview

- An item is material if its omission or misstatement could influence the economic decisions of users taken on the basis of the financial statements.
- Items might be material by value or nature.
- Materiality is a matter of auditor judgement.

You learnt about materiality and the principles of ISA 320 *Materiality in Planning and Performing an Audit* in your studies for Assurance. The following is therefore revision.

Definition

Material: Information is **material** if its omission or misstatement could influence the economic decisions of users taken on the basis of the financial statements. Materiality depends on the size of the item or error judged in the particular circumstances of its omission or misstatement. Thus, materiality provides a threshold or cut-off point rather than being a primary qualitative characteristic which information must have if it is to be useful.

Auditors should consider materiality when determining the nature, timing and extend of audit procedures.

Items might be material due to their:

- Amount/value/quantity
- Nature/quality

Hence, during planning, the auditors will often set a computed level of materiality, often based on the following ranges:

Revenue:	0.5% – 1%
Profit before tax:	5% – 10%
Gross assets:	1% – 2%

In addition, some matters might be material by nature, for example:

- The £1 that turns a profit into a loss might be considered very important by some companies/shareholders
- The £1 that changes the thresholds the company operates in (for example, becoming a medium-sized rather than small company) might also be very important
- Some matters are automatically material, such as matters relating to directors, or related parties because these matters have to be disclosed in financial statements regardless of the value of them.

Auditors should always bear in mind that materiality is a matter of professional judgement. Materiality is also important at the completion stage of an audit, when the auditors are evaluating the effect of discovered misstatements. We shall look at this in Chapter 12.

4 Analytical procedures

Section overview

- Analytical procedures must be used in risk assessment.
- The benefits of analytical procedures in planning are the 'overall' perspective, the use of information outside of the accounting records and the comparison of different elements of the financial statements.
- The limitations of analytical procedures in planning are:
  - Substantial knowledge of the business is required for results to be meaningful (therefore experienced staff may be required to carry them out)
  - They can be performed mechanically
  - The relevant information may not be available

You looked at analytical procedures in some detail in your studies for Assurance. You should be able to explain what analytical procedures are and carry out basic analytical procedures. If not, you should refer back to Chapter 3 of your Assurance manual, which contains a worked example you may like to work through again.

ISA 315 *Identifying and Assessing the Risks of Material Misstatement through Understanding the Entity and Its Environment* states that the auditor should use analytical procedures in risk assessment in order to obtain an understanding of the entity and its environment. We shall look at this in detail in the next chapter.

In this syllabus you are required to be able to discuss the benefits and limitation of analytical procedures at the planning stage.

Interactive question 2: Benefits and limitations of analytical procedures

[Difficulty level: Easy]

Analytical procedures must be carried out at the planning stage of an audit to help identify risk areas requiring extra work.

Set out the benefits and limitations of using analytical procedures to identify risk areas during audit planning.

See **Answer** at the end of this chapter.

These are the ratios students need for applying analytical procedures.

Heading/Ratio	Formula	Purpose
Performance		
Return on capital employed	$\frac{\text{Profit before interest and tax}}{\text{Equity + net debt}}$	Effective use of resources
Return on shareholders' funds	$\frac{\text{Net profit for the period}}{\text{Share capital + reserves}}$	Effective use of resources
Gross profit percentage	$\frac{\text{Gross profit} \times 100}{\text{Revenue}}$	Assess profitability before taking overheads into account

Heading/Ratio	Formula	Purpose
Cost of sales percentage	$\frac{\text{Cost of sales} \times 100}{\text{Revenue}}$	Assess relationship of costs to revenue
Operating cost percentage	$\frac{\text{Operating costs/overheads} \times 100}{\text{Revenue}}$	Assess relationship of costs to revenue
Net margin/operating margin	$\frac{\text{Profit before interest and tax} \times 100}{\text{Revenue}}$	Assess profitability after taking overheads into account
Short-term liquidity		
Current ratio	Current assets : Current liabilities	Assess ability to pay current liabilities from current assets
Quick ratio	Receivables + Current Investments + cash : liabilities	Assess ability to pay current liabilities from reasonably liquid assets
Long term solvency		
Gearing ratio	$\frac{\text{Net debt}}{\text{Equity}}$	Assess reliance on external finance
Interest cover	$\frac{\text{Profit before interest payable}}{\text{Interest payable}}$	Assess ability to pay interest charges
Efficiency		
Net asset turnover	$\frac{\text{Revenue}}{\text{Capital employed}}$	Assess revenue generated from asset base
Inventory turnover	$\frac{\text{Cost of sales}}{\text{Inventories}}$	Assess level of inventory held
Trade receivables collection period	$\frac{\text{Trade receivables} \times 365}{\text{Revenue}}$	Assess ability to turn receivables into cash
Trade payables payment period	$\frac{\text{Trade payables} \times 365}{\text{Credit purchases}}$	Assess ability to pay suppliers

Worked example: analytical procedures

A distribution and warehousing company is seeking to increase its overdraft and the bank has requested to review its audited financial statements. The company's contracts cover periods of between 3 and 5 years. Invoicing takes place after the service has been provided and terms of trade require payment in 30 days. Revaluation of land and buildings has occurred during the financial year. The company owns its own vehicles and trailers.

The following information has been extracted from the financial statements for years ended 31 May:

Extracts from the income statement

	Draft	*Actual*
	20X8	*20X7*
	£'000	£'000
Revenue	25,417	23,867
Cost of sales	(21,895)	(20,924)
Gross profit	3,522	2,943
Administrative expenses	(2,205)	(2,011)
	1,317	932
Loss on sale of vehicles and trailers	(232)	–
Profit from operations	1,085	932
Finance cost	(345)	(302)
Profit before tax	740	630

Extracts from the balance sheet

	£'000	£'000
Non-current assets		
Property, plant and equipment	7,987	6,528
Current assets		
Trade receivables	3,156	2,681
Non-current liabilities		
Borrowings – bank loan	3,000	2,500
Current liabilities		
Trade payables	1,553	1,922
Borrowings:		
– Overdraft	499	454
– Bank loan	500	250

From this information the auditor may wish to highlight the following factors, and to consider the audit risk that they pose:

- Revenue has increased by 6.5% which may be indicative of overstatement due to early recognition of income or cut off errors.
- There has been a significant increase in the gross margin from 12.3% to 13.8%. This may be indicative of inflated sales or unrecorded purchases.
- There is a significant loss in sales of vehicles which may be indicative of inappropriate asset lives and consequently overstatement of carrying amounts.
- The revaluation of land and buildings may have been undertaken in order to inflate the assets figure.
- There has been an increase in trade receivables days from 41 to 45 days. This is greater than the normal terms of trading of 30 days and may be indicative of overstatement. This may be due to inclusion of sales invoices relating to the next accounting period or unrecoverable debts.
- There has been a reduction in payables days from 33.5 to 25.9 days, which may be indicative of understatement. This may be due to a failure to record all supplier invoices relating to the period.

Summary and Self-test

Summary

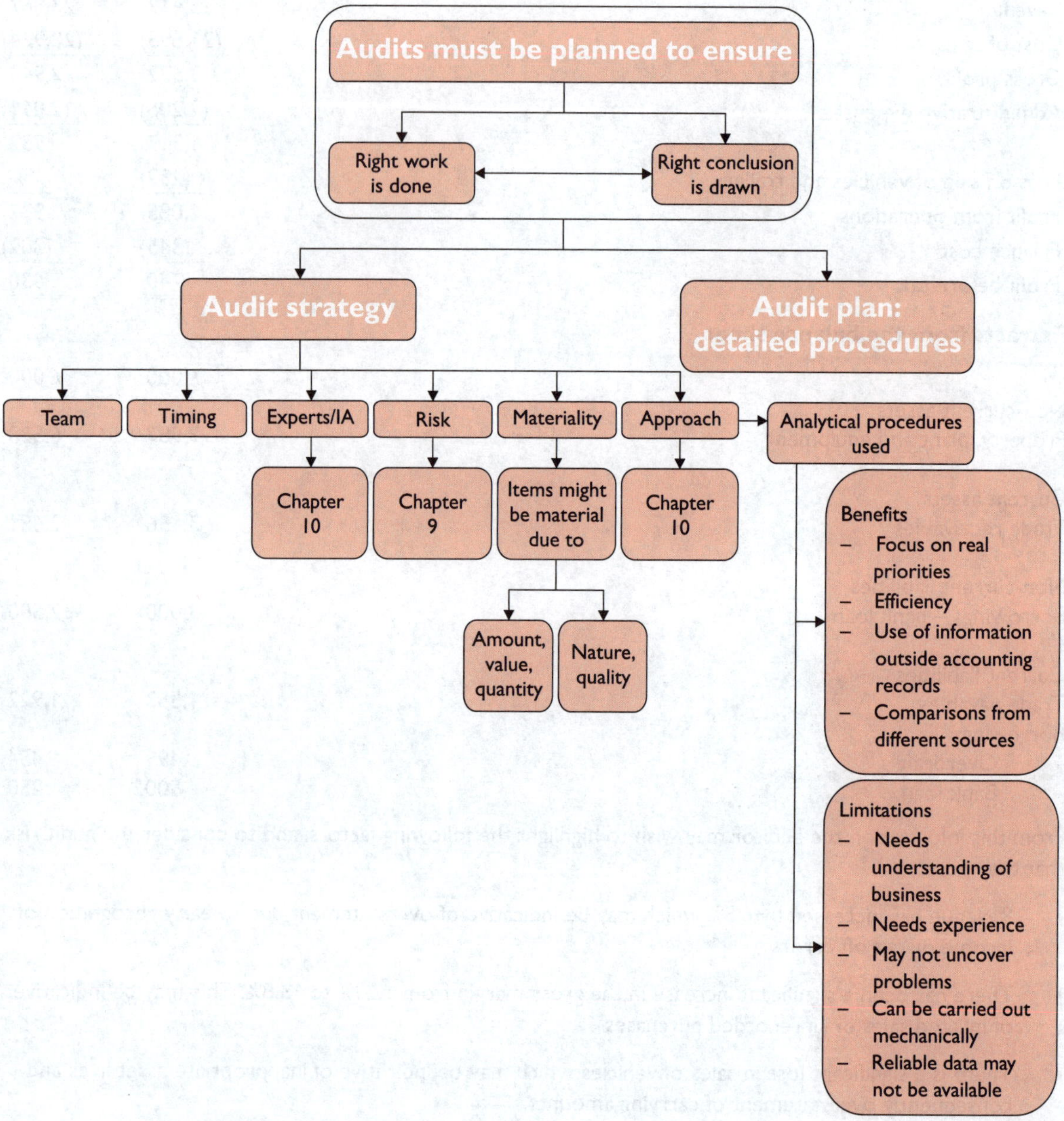

Self-test

Answer the following questions.

1 State why audits are planned.

2 Why should care be taken if using a standardised audit pack?

3 Give an example of an item being material by its nature.

4 Analytical procedures should be carried out by an audit junior.

☐ True

☐ False

Exam-style questions

5 The gross profit percentage in your client's draft financial statements is the same as in the previous year.

What further information would you require in order to use this fact at the planning stage of the audit? **(1 mark)**

6 Described below are situations which have arisen in three audit clients of your firm. The year end in each case is 31 March 20X6.

Jay plc ('Jay')

The directors have included the following note to the financial statements for the year ended 31 March 20X6:

'Although the company has incurred significant trading losses and cash outflows during the last two years, the directors believe that the effects of internal restructuring and corporate disposals undertaken will bring about improved results as indicated in the detailed profit and cash flow forecasts for the period to the end of March 20X7. These forecasts indicate that the company will be able to trade within its agreed working capital facility for at least the next 12 months from the date of this report. Considerable progress has been made on the financial restructuring of the company.

On the basis of the above factors the directors consider it is appropriate that the financial statements are prepared on the going concern basis. Should the company fail to meet its forecasts, the going concern basis may prove to be inappropriate. In such circumstances adjustments are likely to have to be made to the net assets shown in these financial statements to reduce assets to their recoverable amounts, to reclassify non-current assets and payables due after more than one year to current assets and current liabilities and to provide for further liabilities that may arise.'

Finch plc ('Finch')

Finch has included the results of Wren Ltd ('Wren'), a subsidiary, in the consolidated financial statements. Wren is audited by a different firm of auditors who have modified their opinion on Wren's financial statements for the year ended 31 March 20X6 because a fire at the company's premises destroyed the physical inventory count sheets which were the only record of the year end inventory. Wren has included inventory at its estimated cost of £500,000 in the financial statements for the year ended 31 March 20X6.

The consolidated pre-tax profit of Finch is £33.4 million and the pre-tax profit of Wren is £1.2 million for the year ended 31 March 20X6.

Sparrow Ltd ('Sparrow')

On 30 April 20X6, the board of directors decided to undertake a restructuring programme which would commence in June 20X6. A provision of £1.8 million in respect of the restructuring costs has been included in the financial statements for the year ended 31 March 20X6.

The pre-tax profit of Sparrow for the year ended 31 March 20X6 is £7.2 million.

Requirements

(a) Discuss what is meant by the concepts of materiality and a true and fair view. **(6 marks)**

(b) Explain why there can be difficulties for auditors regarding materiality and true and fair in relation to the three cases above: Jay, Finch and Sparrow. **(6 marks)**

(12 marks)

7 Your firm has recently been appointed as auditor of Jog Ltd ('Jog'), a company operating within the sports and leisure sector. Your audit manager has arranged a meeting with the company's finance director for early next week and she has asked you to assist her, in advance of this meeting, with the audit planning for the year ending 30 June 20X6. Your audit manager has also asked you to carry out some preliminary analytical procedures on the year-end financial statements of Jog when these become available.

Jog's business can be split into the following three divisions

- Sports equipment retail outlets: 35 sports equipment retail outlets located in 'out of town' retail parks
- Fitness clubs: 15 fitness clubs, each offering a fully equipped gym together with yoga, aerobics, and circuit training classes
- Machine manufacture: a manufacturing unit in which running machines and rowing machines are assembled using components sourced from overseas.

Further information:

Sports equipment retail outlets

The retail outlets are all located close to major towns and cities throughout the whole of the UK. Each outlet stocks a standard range of products which are supplied from a central warehouse operated by Jog. Salaries for the core staff at the outlets are paid by Jog's head office by direct bank transfer. Each outlet is run on a day-to-day basis by a manager who is responsible for hiring casual staff to cover peak periods. These casual staff members are generally paid using cash from the till.

Jog received some bad publicity during the year following its inclusion in a television documentary which revealed that one of its non-UK sports shoe suppliers was making its employees work long hours for very low wages. In an attempt to manage this adverse press attention, Jog has now had to source these products from alternative suppliers based in the UK.

Fitness clubs

Jog's 15 fitness clubs are all located directly above existing Jog retail outlets. Each club has its own on-site manager and is operated independently of the adjacent retail outlet. Customers of the fitness clubs pay by one of three methods: on a 'pay per session' basis over the fitness club counter; by monthly direct debit paid into Jog's head office bank account; or by annual subscription to head office. Customers are then issued with a membership card which enables them to gain access to the club.

The company operates a bonus incentive scheme for the managers at both its retail outlets and fitness clubs. The size of the bonus is linked to the profitability of their individual operation.

Machine manufacture

During the year Jog started to manufacture its own running machines and rowing machines. It sources the machine components from China and Taiwan. These components are assembled in the UK at Jog's factory for sale both in Jog's own stores under their own 'Jog' brand and also to independent sports shops under the 'Iron Champ' brand. The latter accounts for approximately 80% of Jog's total production of both running and rowing machines. Sales to independent sports shops achieve a gross profit margin of 50%, whereas sales to Jog's own shops are made to that division at cost plus 10%.

Jog is invoiced by its non-UK component suppliers in their respective local currency. The components are sent by sea, which means that Jog's typical lead time for components from the placing of an order to delivery in the UK is three months. Jog is required to pay its suppliers 50% with order and 50% upon receipt of the components in the UK.

Quality control

In line with your firm's system of quality control, procedures were conducted prior to accepting Jog as an audit client, to ensure that it was appropriate to accept such an appointment. Your audit manager has asked you to consider the other objectives of a system of quality control and why they may be particularly relevant to Jog.

Requirements

(a) (i) List, with reasons, the information you would require in order to carry out analytical procedures on the draft financial statements of Jog for the year ending 30 June 20X6.

(ii) Set out the limitations of using analytical procedures at the planning stage of an audit.

(8 marks)

(b) Identify which of the circumstances outlined above, should be taken into account when planning the audit of Jog. Explain clearly why these matters are important and set out their effect on your proposed audit work. **(24 marks)**

You attempted Part (c) of this question (for 8 marks) in Chapter 5.

(32 marks)

Now, go back to the Learning Objectives in the Introduction. If you are satisfied you have achieved these objectives, please tick them off.

Technical reference

1 The need to plan	**ISA 300.2**
2 Preliminary engagement activities	**ISA 300.6**
3 Overall audit strategy	**ISA 300.7–8**
4 Audit plan	**ISA 300.9–11**
5 Materiality	
• Concept of materiality	**ISA 320.2**
• When materiality is relevant	**ISA 320.5**

Answers to Interactive questions

Answer to Interactive question 1

Purpose of planning:

- To enable the audit to be performed in an effective and timely manner
- To ensure that:
  - Appropriate attention is directed to important areas of the audit
  - Potential problems are identified
  - Work is completed expeditiously
- Assists in:
  - Proper assignment of work to the team
  - Co-ordination of work done by others
- Facilitates review

Answer to Interactive question 2

Benefits:

- Identifies items for attention that detailed tests may miss
- Uses information outside accounting records, for example, budgets
- Allows comparison of data from different sources

Limitations:

- A good knowledge of the business is required to understand results
- Consistency of results may conceal a material error
- There may be a tendency to carry out procedures mechanically, without appropriate professional scepticism
- Requires an experienced member of staff to be done properly
- Reliable data may not be available

Answers to Self-test

1 To ensure that the right work is carried out resulting in the right conclusion being drawn.

2 It is important for the audit plan to be tailored to the client.

3 Examples include:

- Related party transactions
- Directors' transactions
- £1 that makes a company small/medium/large
- £1 that turns a profit into a loss

4 False, as experience and understanding are required to carry out analytical procedures properly.

Exam-style questions

5
- Client's expectation of GP%
- Changes in year that affect GP%

6 (a) **Materiality**

Information is material if its omission or misstatement could influence the economic decisions of users taken on the basis of the financial statements.

Materiality

(i) Is not capable of mathematical definition

(ii) Can be quantitative (size) or qualitative (nature)

(iii) May be considered in the context of any individual primary statement within the financial statements or of the individual items included within them

(iv) Depends on the size of the item or error judged in the particular circumstances of its omission or misstatement.

True and fair

True is generally accepted as meaning in accordance with the facts and fair as meaning objective or unbiased and concerned with the presentational aspects of information including substance over form. True and fair is not defined by statute, however, Counsel's opinion is that financial statements prepared in accordance with GAAP will give a true and fair view. Furthermore, there may be more than one true and fair view for a given set of circumstances.

The concepts of materiality and true and fair require the exercise of professional judgement.

(b) **Jay**

Materiality/true and fair

The difference between the figures prepared on each basis may not be significantly different. However, the effect on the business is so significant that the user needs to be made aware of the situation. The auditor needs to judge whether the disclosures are sufficient for the user to understand the circumstances.

Finch

Materiality/true and fair

Although material to Wren as 42% of pre-tax profits, it is unlikely to be considered material in the context of the consolidated pre-tax profit as it is only 1.5% of consolidated pre-tax profit. Materiality should be considered in the context of the entity on which the auditor is reporting. However, it may be material by nature if a key ratio (eg current ratio) is affected.

Sparrow

Materiality/true and fair

There is no obligation at the balance sheet date in respect of restructuring costs. The financial statements therefore do not comply with GAAP as they include a provision in respect of restructuring costs. The amount of the provision for restructuring costs is considered material by size as it is 25% of pre-tax profit, thereby exceeding the commonly used yardstick of 5-10% of pre tax profit.

7 (a) **Information required**

Individual statements of comprehensive income and split of the statement of financial position for each division are required. Each division has different profit margins and the split of the statement of financial position figures will enable the calculation of inventory and trade receivable days for each division.

Budget information for each division is required, together with the date from which the machine division commenced trading, so that its figures can be adjusted to take account of a trading period of less than one year. Comparative information by division from Jog's previous financial statements will also be needed. This information will allow actual and budget performance to be compared. This could identify material or significant items, potential misstatements or variations from expected results.

If available, financial information from companies in the same industries could be used to identify where the company has performed well or badly and prompt areas for further enquiry by the auditor.

Limitations of using analytical procedures

One limitation of analytical procedures at the planning stage of an audit is that the auditor needs a good understanding of the business to interpret the results of analytical procedures. If analytical procedures are performed mechanically, a consistency of results from one year to the next may in fact conceal a material error which may not be identified. Effective analytical procedures need to be carried out by experienced members of staff and they rely upon good quality and reliable information being available from the client which may not always be available.

(b) This is a new audit client which means that there is a lack of cumulative prior knowledge which in turn increases the risk of an undetected misstatement in the financial statements. The audit work will include an evaluation of the company's accounting systems and internal controls in addition to consideration of opening balances. Adequate planning will be essential to avoid over-auditing in the first year.

The company operates from 35 locations at which it holds material balances of inventory and non-current assets. The risk of a breakdown in head office controls is higher in multi-site locations. The year-end attendance at inventory counts should cover all material locations and it would be efficient to take the inventory count attendance as an opportunity to inspect material non-current assets and carry out selected cash counts. If the audit approach relies upon controls, it must be ensured that the tests of controls sample covers all material locations.

The company makes cash sales in its retail outlets and fitness clubs and it pays its casual staff in cash. Cash transactions increase the risk of misappropriation of cash and the understatement of revenue in the financial statements. The employment of casual staff may also mean that the company is failing to declare the appropriate amounts of PAYE, which could lead to penalties from the tax authorities. The effect of this on the audit work is that controls over cash must be evaluated and audit effort should be directed to confirming the completeness of recorded sales. In addition, the company's compliance with PAYE regulations should be considered and the wages included in the financial statements should be checked to ensure that this agrees with the company's payroll records.

The company has received adverse publicity over the use of "sweatshops". This may damage the reputation of the company which could in turn affect the status of Jog as a going concern. The audit work should attempt to assess the effect of the publicity on Jog's business. The cost implications of the switch by Jog to alternative suppliers in the UK also need to be considered as part of the audit work.

Jog fitness clubs receive annual subscriptions which may cause revenue to be recognised in the wrong accounting year. The company's accounting policy for revenue recognition will need to be considered and audit work should include testing of new subscriptions close to the year end to ensure that an appropriate proportion of income is deferred at the year end.

The company has a profit-related bonus scheme increasing the risk of manipulation of profit by the company's management. Audit work should include checks on income recognition to ensure it has not been accelerated to boost profits. For similar reasons purchase cut-off should be checked to identify any potential suppressed invoices.

The company purchases its machine components in a foreign currency, under payment terms which specify 50% be paid with order. Foreign currency transactions may lead to the incorrect translation of these transactions in the financial statements. The existence of a three-month delivery lead time on these transactions may also give rise to adverse foreign currency exposure. Component payment terms may also lead to cut-off errors arising from incorrect treatment of the first 50% paid with order. The audit work should include sample checks of the company's foreign exchange translation to an independent source such as the FT. The steps taken to minimise the company's exposure to foreign exchange risk needs to be discussed with management. Careful consideration should be given to cut-off for any goods in transit at the year end.

Some of the machines manufactured using imported components are transferred to the company's retail outlets at cost plus 10%. This inter-divisional trading means the value of the retail outlet inventory may contain some unrealised profit. In addition, the practice of adding only 10% onto the cost price, may cause outlets to under price these products, damaging the gross profit margin of the company as a whole. The audit approach should ensure all inter-divisional trading is separately analysed so that any unrealised profit can be identified.

chapter 8

Understanding the entity and its environment

THE INSTITUTE OF CHARTERED ACCOUNTANTS IN ENGLAND AND WALES

Introduction

Learning objectives

Tick off

- Understand the crucial role of understanding the entity in the assessment of engagement risk ☐
- Understand what knowledge is required ☐
- Understand how such knowledge should be obtained ☐

Specific syllabus references for this chapter are: 3a, b.

Syllabus links

We introduced this topic in Assurance, where you learnt the basic content of ISA 315 *Identifying and Assessing the Risks of Material Misstatement through Understanding the Entity and Its Environment*. In this syllabus you need to consolidate and build on this knowledge.

Examination context

Understanding the entity is a key component of risk assessment. Risk assessment is the subject of chapter 9, which is big exam topic.

In the assessment, candidates may be required to:

- Explain, in the context of a given scenario, why it is important to have a knowledge and understanding of the business when planning an engagement
- Identify ways of gaining knowledge and understanding of a client's business

1 Why?

Section overview

- It is important to understand the client's business:
  - In order to assess risk
  - In order to comply with auditing standards

You know from your previous studies and from what has already been said in this Study Manual that assessing risk is very important in assurance engagements.

In general terms, it is clearly impossible to be sure how risky a client may be if you do not understand:

- Who they are
- What they do
- How they do it
- Whether there are any special circumstances (like specific laws and regulations) which govern their business
- The integrity and competence of their staff

If you understand a client's business properly you will:

- Be able to assess the skills and competence which the audit team needs
- Be able to plan your audit work so that it is appropriate and efficient
- Be able to assess what controls have been put in place by the client which may reduce the level of control risk
- Be able to assess any significant risks which need special attention
- Be able to perform analytical procedures
- Comply with professional requirements (the reports by the ICAEW, ICAS and ICAI to the DTI about the results of monitoring visits to firms in the last five years have commented, every year, about the need for recording and disseminating knowledge of the business)

Also, assessing risk is compulsory – ISAs 315 and 330 require it.

Finally, consider **fraud** – understanding the entity may not guarantee that you will uncover a clever, well laid fraud, but not understanding the entity certainly will guarantee that you have very little chance of finding it.

Auditors need to be particularly vigilant during a period of economic downturn and uncertainty, when company directors and accountants may be under pressure to present favourable results by artificially increasing revenues or profits. Whilst a variety of treatments may be permitted by legislation and accepted standards, aggressive earnings management, as this practice is known, is a form of fraud.

2 How?

Section overview

- Understanding of the client's business can be obtained from:
  - External sources of information (such as industry surveys/publications)
  - The firm (permanent files (including previous years' audited financial statements), correspondence files, personnel associated with the engagement in previous years)
  - The client (personnel, correspondence/procedures manuals, watching procedures, current year management accounts)
- Auditors are required to carry out a combination of procedures to understand the business:
  - Inquiries of client personnel
  - Analytical procedures
  - Observation and inspection

It is important to understand where the information comes from.

2.1 External sources

There are reports auditors can look at:

- Credit reference agencies
- Industry surveys
- Industry publications such as trade journals
- HM Revenue and Customs produces Business Economic Notes (the 'BEN' series). Beware, some of these are not terribly up-to-date
- The Irish Revenue produces similar information which is available on its website
- Companies House searches.

Remember, for an existing client, assurance staff have a better source of information much closer to home.

2.2 The firm

Remember, the firm should not have taken the client on in the first place if it does not have the competence to service it in line with ethical and professional standards. So, it follows that someone in the firm must know something about the client and its environment. Usually the person who has most knowledge will either be the engagement partner or, for firms dealing with industries where specialist knowledge is required, the industry expert.

It is the firm's responsibility to ensure that audit staff are properly briefed, but it is also the responsibility of each member of the team to ensure he is properly briefed. Team members should read:

- Last year's file
- The permanent file
- The correspondence file
- The tax file

and should talk to:

- The partner
- The manager
- The tax person
- Last year's senior
- The firm's industry specialist

This may appear both obvious and a bit woolly, but it is specifically dealt with in ISA 315. As you know, there is a requirement for a discussion of the client's business as part of the planning process, and for that discussion to be documented.

You also need to consider your own knowledge and background.

- Have you worked on similar clients before?
- What do you know of the industry?
- How would you expect it to work?

2.3 The client

Then move out to the client:

- Talk to the people responsible for the area you are auditing – the people actually doing the work and their bosses.
- Read internal correspondence and minutes of board/committee meetings – you have rights of access, subject to your professional duty of confidentiality.
- Read internal audit reports (if there is an internal audit function).
- Observe what goes on around you, how transactions are recorded and how processes are operated.
- Look at the website, brochures etc.

To be professional, auditors must be wary of ignorance combined with pride. If something is difficult to understand – ask. If it is still difficult, it is possible that you should not be doing the audit, but it is also possible that there is a fraud going on.

You learnt about the specific requirements of ISA 315 in relation to obtaining the information in your Assurance studies. Remember, you are required to use a combination of the following procedures:

- Inquiry of management and others within the entity
- Analytical procedures
- Observation and inspection

2.4 Summary

Figure 8.1 provides a general summary of how understanding the client's entity can be achieved.

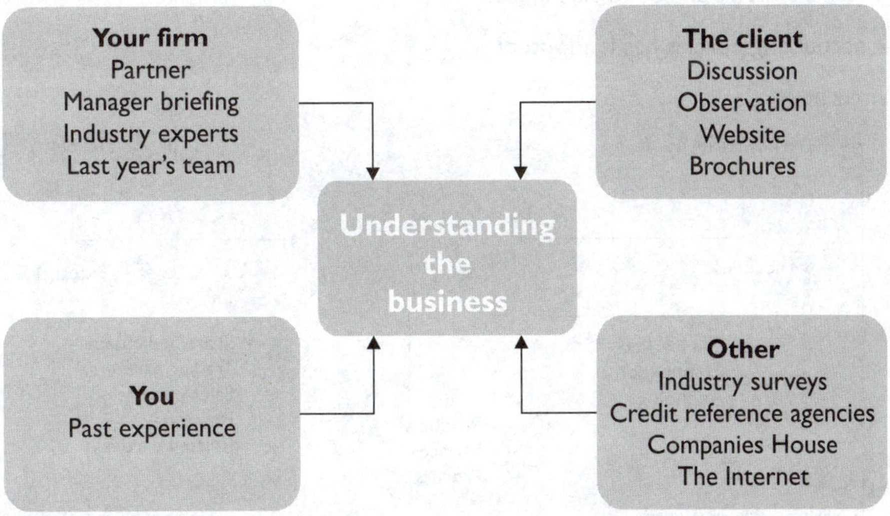

Figure 8.1: Sources of information

Interactive question 1: Sources of information [Difficulty level: Easy]

From what sources of information can auditors obtain a knowledge of the entity they are about to audit and the industry in which that entity operates?

See **Answers** at the end of this chapter.

3 What?

Section overview

- The auditors need to understand any aspect of the business which might affect the audit.
- ISA 315 contains a list of potential areas to be understood in paragraphs 11 and A11.

3.1 The basics

If the following nine questions have been answered in sufficient depth, the audit file should contain sufficient evidence that the auditors have satisfied the requirements of ISA 315 *Identifying and Assessing the Risks of Material Misstatement through Understanding the Entity and Its Environment.*

- What does the client do?
- What are the characteristics of the industry/environment in which it operates?
- Is it governed by specific laws and regulations, or is it at greater risk than other businesses from the incidence of more general laws and regulations?
- What are the characteristics of its relationships with external parties, shareholders, other stakeholders, trading partners and providers of finance?
- Is it under threat from takeover or lack of finance?
- Are there any dealings with related parties?
- How competent is its management?
- Are suitable systems and controls in place?
- What accounting policies has it adopted?

Figure 8.2 may help.

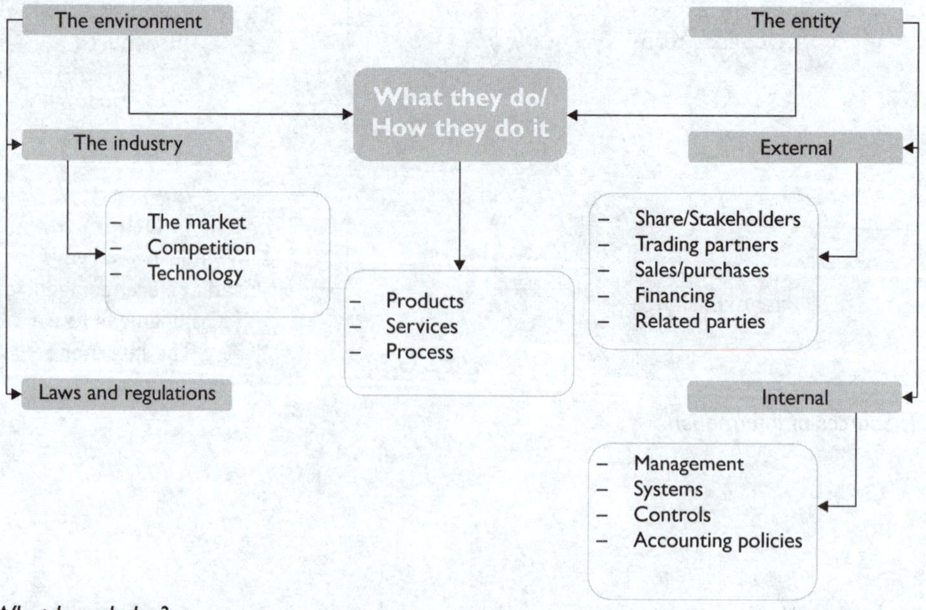

Figure 8.2: What knowledge?

3.2 Laws and regulations

To understand the client, auditors need to have a good understanding of any laws and regulations which have an impact on its operations.

Laws and regulations are considered to be of two types:

- Those which affect the preparation of financial statements
- Those which affect the way the client conducts its business

Clearly the auditor should know about relevant laws and regulations, such as the Companies Act 2006 and Accounting Standards, which affect the way the financial statements are prepared. The auditor is not expected to be an expert in all the laws and regulations which affect the client, but, it is not quite as simple as this, if a client fails to comply with the laws and regulations which govern its business:

- It will very soon go out of business; and
- This will have a material impact on its financial statements

It follows, therefore, that if an audit firm has a client in the haulage industry, it cannot simply ignore what the law says about tachographs and vehicle maintenance. If a client runs a restaurant the auditors need to know something of the food hygiene enforcement regime operated by local authorities.

How much knowledge an assurance provider should have and in what depth is another question of risk.

- If the likely impact of non-compliance is assessed as low, auditors will ask management for background information and that will be sufficient.
- If the likely impact is assessed as high, but management has good systems for controlling the risk, auditors will confirm that the systems appear to operate effectively.
- If the risk is high and management appears to do nothing about it……let us simply say it will have a direct impact on audit work.

Paragraph A13 in ISA 250 gives the following list of indicators of non-compliance:

- **Investigation** by a **government department**
- **Payment of fines or penalties**
- **Payments** for **unspecified services** or loans to consultants, related parties, employees or government employees
- **Sales commissions** or agents' fees that appear excessive in relation to those normally paid by the entity or in its industry or to the services actually received
- **Purchasing** at **prices significantly above** or **below market price**
- **Unusual payments** in **cash**, purchases in the form of cashiers' cheques payable to bearer or transfers to numbered bank accounts
- **Unusual transactions** with companies registered in **tax havens**
- **Payments for goods or services made other than to the country from which** the goods or services **originated**
- **Payments without proper exchange control documentation**
- **Existence** of an **information system** that **fails**, whether by design or by accident, to **provide adequate audit trail** or sufficient evidence
- **Unauthorised transactions** or improperly recorded transactions
- Adverse **media comment**

3.3 Fraud

ISA 240 *The Auditor's Responsibilities Relating to Fraud in an Audit of Financial Statements* stresses that auditors have no responsibility for the prevention and detection of fraud as such – that is management's job, but fraud can have a material impact on financial statements, so it becomes a part of audit after all!

Remember, the ISA makes a crucial distinction between two types of misstatements arising from fraud:

- Misstatements arising from fraudulent financial reporting
- Misstatements arising from misappropriation of assets

In understanding the client's business there are some key questions that need to be asked:

- Can the figures be manipulated and if so how?
- Which areas are most susceptible to manipulation?
- Can assets be misappropriated and if so how?
- Which areas are most at risk?

3.4 Service Organisations

Increasingly, companies are outsourcing processes and operations to third party organisations. Some examples of activities that may be outsourced are:

- Information processing
- Maintenance of accounting records
- Facilities management

ISA 402 *Audit Considerations Relating to an Entity Using a Service Organisation* highlights the issues that must be considered if the auditor discovers during the planning phase of the audit that the client has outsourced, for example, its payroll accounting function. In broad terms the main requirements are to:

- Obtain an understanding of the services provided by a service organisation, including internal control, specifically:
  - The nature of the services provided by the service organization
  - The nature and materiality of the transactions processed
  - The degree of interaction between the activities of the service organization and those of the company
  - The nature of the relationship between the user entity and the service organization, including the relevant contractual terms
- Consider access to sources of evidence
- Assess the risks arising

Interactive question 2: What matters? [Difficulty level: Easy]

Auditors should use their knowledge of the business to assess the risks arising from fraud, error and non-compliance with laws and regulations.

What matters should they consider in making this assessment?

See **Answer** at the end of this chapter.

Summary and Self-test

Summary

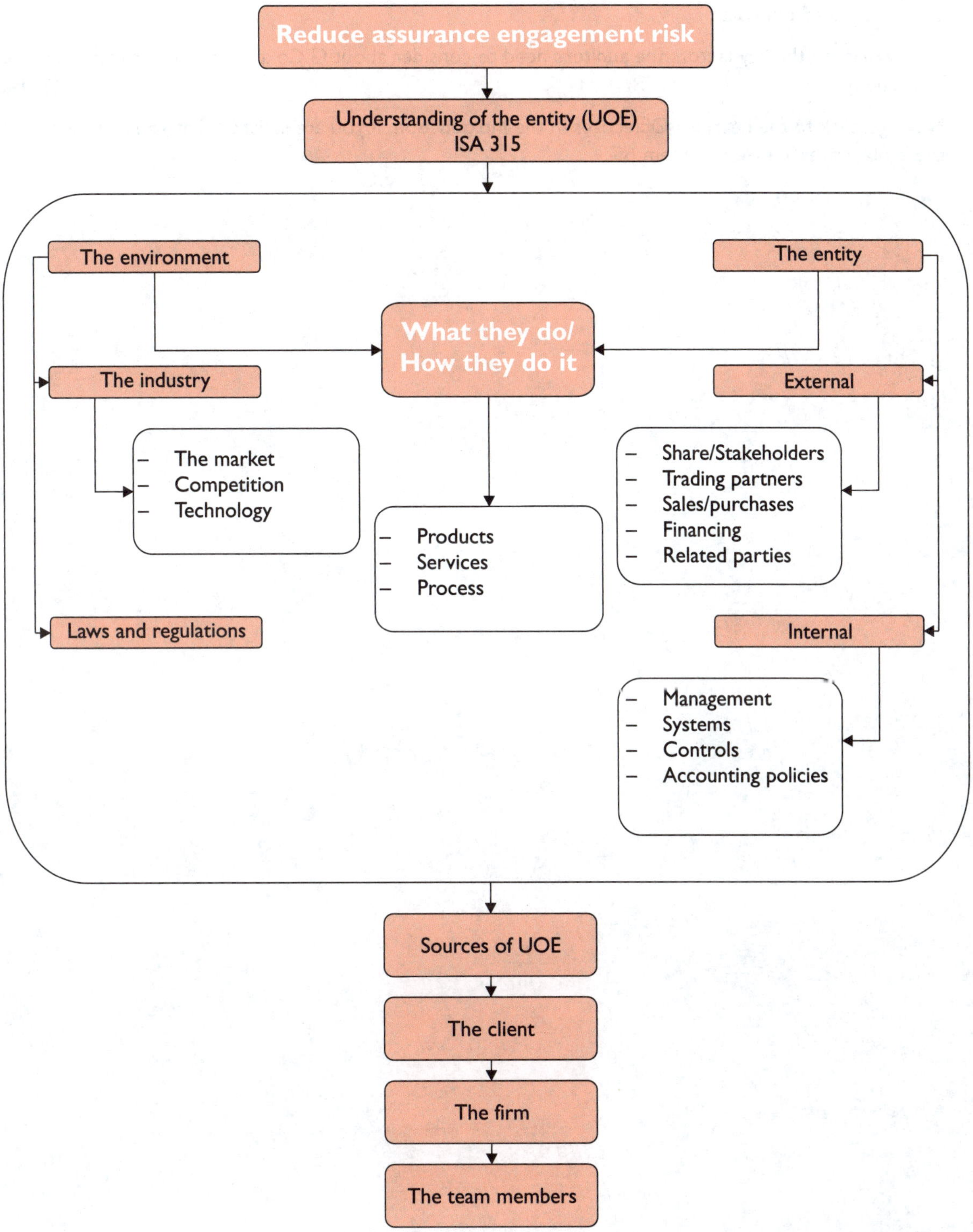

Reduce assurance engagement risk
Understanding of the entity (UOE)
ISA 315
The environment
The entity
What they do/
How they do it
The industry
External
– The market
– Competition
– Technology
– Share/Stakeholders
– Trading partners
– Sales/purchases
– Financing
– Related parties
– Products
– Services
– Process
Laws and regulations
Internal
– Management
– Systems
– Controls
– Accounting policies
Sources of UOE
The client
The firm
The team members

CHAPTER 8

Self-test

Answer the following questions.

1 What key knowledge should an audit firm obtain about its client and why is this understanding of the entity important? **(3 marks)**

2 G Co is a manufacturing company which has one factory and two warehouse sites. It imports raw materials from Asia.

What are the key factors the auditors need to consider about G Co and how this may impact their audit? **(3 marks)**

Now, go back to the Learning Objectives in the Introduction. If you are satisfied that you have achieved these objectives, please tick them off.

Technical reference

1	**Why it is important to understand the client's business**	**ISA 315.3**
2	**How to gain an understanding of the client's business**	**ISA 315.6**
3	**What aspects of the client's business should be understood**	**IAS 315.11** **ISA 250.A13** **ISA 402**

CHAPTER 8

Answers to Interactive questions

Answer to Interactive question 1

- Previous experience with entity and its industry
  - Last year's file/audit team
  - Permanent file
  - Tax file
  - Correspondence file
- Visits to entity's premises and plant facilities
- Discussion with people within entity
- Discussion with other auditors and with legal/other advisers who have provided services to the entity or within the industry (eg industry specialists)
- Publications related to the industry legislation and regulations that significantly affect the entity, eg industry surveys
- Industry publications such as trade journals and HM Revenue and Customs publications for the relevant industry
- Documents produced by the entity/entity website
- Companies House searches

Answer to Interactive question 2

Non-compliance (ISA 250 A13)

- Previous experience
- Incidents which call into question integrity or competence of management or other staff, eg
  - Investigations
  - Payment of fines/penalties
- Unusual transactions/payments
- Payments for/of
  - Unspecified services/loans
  - Excessive commission
- Unauthorised/improperly recorded transactions
- Accounting system which fails to provide adequate audit trail/sufficient evidence
- Adverse media comment

Fraud/error (ISA 240 Appendix 3)

- Discrepancies in the accounting records, eg
  - incomplete recording of transactions
  - significant last-minute adjustments
- Conflicting or missing evidence, eg
  - missing documents
  - unexplained items on reconciliations

- Problematic or unusual relationships between the auditor and management, eg
  - denial of access to records or delays in producing information
  - complaints about the conduct of the audit
- Other, eg
  - accounting policies at variance with industry norms
  - frequent, unnecessary changes in accounting estimates

CHAPTER 8

Answers to Self-test

1 **Key knowledge to obtain**

- Nature of the business
- Key personnel and their integrity/competence
- Whether there are any laws or regulations which apply to the entity
- Whether there are any pressures on the directors which may lead them to show the company in a more favourable light than might otherwise be the case – for example
  - Directors' profit related bonuses
  - Cash flow/financing concerns
  - Stock market pressures
- Strength of internal control systems
- Existence of related parties and related party transactions
- Complex account transactions

Why important?

The above knowledge is important in order for the auditor to assess the level of risk associated with the client and the potential likelihood that an incorrect opinion may be given.

2

- As a manufacturing company G Co will hold inventory of raw materials, work in progress and finished goods at the end of the year

  The auditor will need to consider whether the valuation of work in progress is appropriate given its stage of completion and that only production overheads are included.

- G Co has two warehouse sites.

  The auditor should obtain an understanding as to how G Co ensures all inventory items held are counted only once and how goods moving between sites are dealt with to ensure they are properly recorded.

- G Co imports raw materials.

  Inventory items may well be in transit at the end of the year. The auditor will need to consider when title to the goods passes to G Co in order to assess when the goods should be included in inventory at the year end.

  It is also possible that the raw materials attract import duties and so the auditors should consider whether the cost of raw materials is fairly stated.

chapter 9

Risk assessment

Introduction

Tick off

Learning objective

- Identify and assess risks in a given scenario

Specific syllabus references for this chapter are: 3d, f, g, k.

Syllabus links

Risk assessment has already been covered in some detail in the Assurance syllabus. At this Application level, the key issue is being able to carry out risk assessment, that is, identify and assess, not merely understand the components of risk and be able to identify them.

Examination context

Risk assessment is a very important area for your exam. There were 24 marks available in the 40 mark question in the sample paper for risk assessment, and has featured in all the exam papers set under this syllabus.

In the assessment, candidates may be required to:

- Identify the risks arising from, or affecting, a given set of business processes and circumstances and assess their implications for the engagement
- Identify the risks arising from error, fraud and non-compliance with law and regulations and assess their implications for the engagement
- Assess the significant business risks identified for their potential impact upon an organisation, in particular, their potential impact on performance measurement
- Identify the components of risk for a specified assurance engagement
- Identify the components of risk for a specified audit engagement, including the breakdown of audit risk into inherent risk, control risk and detection risk

1 Business risk

Section overview

- There are three general categories of business risk:
  - Financial risk
  - Operational risk
  - Compliance risk

Business risk was introduced in your Assurance studies.

Definitions

Business risk is the risk inherent to the company in its operations. It includes risks at all levels of the business. ISA 315 defines business risk as a 'risk resulting from significant conditions, events, circumstances, actions or inactions that could adversely affect an entity's ability to achieve its objectives and execute its strategies, or from the setting of inappropriate objectives and strategies.' There are three general categories of business risk:

- **Financial risks** are the risks arising from the financial activities or financial consequences of an operation, for example, cash flow issues or overtrading
- **Operational risks** are the risks arising with regard to operations, for example, the risk that a major supplier will be lost and the company will be unable to operate
- **Compliance risk** is the risk that arises from non-compliance with laws and regulations that surround the business, for example a restaurant failing to comply with food hygiene regulations might face fines, enforced closure, legal action from customers and so on.

Directors are required to manage business risks. The Turnbull Report sets out recommendations for business in how to manage those risks.

Business risk management is an area in which assurance can be required. Why? Because the risk that the company accepts has a direct impact on the risk of the investment that anyone purchasing shares in a company (a minority share or a company takeover) or loaning money to a company is making.

However, it is not simply shareholders and lenders that will want assurance in this area. Management might want assurance services to provide an indication of how well they are performing in controlling the risks to the company, to ensure it continues in business, but also as evidence that it is operating efficiently and cost-effectively. Criteria for assurance services could be the Turnbull guidelines, or management's own written policy on risk. Management may employ an internal audit department to (among other things) monitor internal controls or may seek external assistance.

Auditors are interested in business risk because issues which pose threats to the business may in some cases also be a risk of the financial statements being misstated (which is a component of audit risk). For example, if a particular division of a business was threatened with closure, the valuation of all the assets associated with that division would be affected. In more general terms, if an economic downturn puts pressure on a company to meet the expectations of providers of finance, management might be tempted to manipulate the financial statements.

2 Audit risk

Section overview

- There are three components of audit risk:
  - Inherent risk
  - Control risk
  - Detection risk

You have already covered audit risk (the risk of giving an inappropriate opinion in relation to the financial statements) in detail.

Remember that it has three components:

- Inherent risk
- Control risk
- Detection risk

2.1 Inherent risk

Definition

Inherent risk is the susceptibility of an assertion to misstatement that could be material, individually or when aggregated with other misstatements, assuming that there were no related internal controls.

In other words, how likely is it that the account balance or transaction will be wrong? And how likely is it that, as a result, the financial statements will be misstated by a material amount? Inherent risk can be analysed on a number of levels which are covered in turn below.

2.1.1 At industry or sector level

Different industries have different levels of inherent risk.

Worked example: Industry level risk

The obvious example of a sector which in relatively recent years, was characterised by high risk was the 'dot com' boom of the 1990s.

- You could argue that this was not a sector at all – as the various players in the market were dealing in a wide variety of goods and services, and the only thing they had in common was that they were all attempting to deal over the Internet.
- You could argue that the problems in the sector were really systems and controls problems, and that the people setting up dot com businesses did not have the experience or acumen to run any business successfully.

Nevertheless all the dot com businesses needed a high level of start-up capital because not only did they have to fund the normal things which a business has to do – marketing, research and development, the purchase of initial inventory, the financing of working capital needs – they also had to develop the IT platform which was so fundamental to the business.

Remember that the inherent risk attached to different sectors changes over time – for example yesterday's dot com industry, the day before's biotechnology.

2.1.2 At entity level

At entity level there will also be different levels of inherent risk.

Worked example: Entity level risk

For two similar clients A and B, if one of the companies was:

- A takeover target
- Up to its overdraft limit
- Had a major supplier or customer in difficulties

it would clearly be more inherently risky than the other.

Again you should remember that the picture does not remain static.

2.1.3 At balance level

Different balances can also carry different inherent risks.

Worked example: Balance level risk

The inventory at a jewellers, for example might be considered higher risk than the same company's non-current assets, consisting of shopfittings, office equipment and, hopefully, some rather impressive safes and security equipment.

Remember that the inventory itself will still be inherently risky, even though the company may have well thought out security arrangements. The impact of these fall into the category of 'control risk' which we will revisit in a moment.

2.2 Control risk

Definition

Control risk is the risk that a misstatement that could occur in an assertion and that could be material, individually or when aggregated with other misstatements, will not be prevented or detected and corrected on a timely basis by the entity's internal control.

So the key questions are:

- What is management doing to stop things going wrong?
- If measures have been taken, are they effective?

Control risk will be lower where effective control measures are taken. However there will always be control risk due to the limitations of internal controls:

- Cost > benefit
- Routine/non-routine transactions
- Human error
- Management override
- Circumvention by collusion
- Changes in procedures

2.3 Detection risk

Judgements about inherent risk and control risk, depend on the assurance provider's understanding of the client's business and the systems and controls set up by the client's management.

The third component of audit risk – detection risk – depends on matters which are under the assurance provider's control.

Definition

Detection risk is the risk that an auditor's procedures will not detect a misstatement that exists in an assertion that could be material, individually or when aggregated with other misstatements.

It is up to the auditor to organise the way the engagement is handled, so that the risk of material misstatement is reduced to acceptable levels.

This will include:

- Ensuring the audit team (including the engagement partner) has the necessary mix and depth of experience and skills
- Devising an audit plan which tackles the audit risks

The audit approach (which we shall look at in Chapter 10) is the way in which the auditor assembles sufficient audit evidence to build up a satisfactory level of audit confidence, and which can come from tests of controls, analytical procedures and tests of details.

Because the auditor cannot check every transaction, audit work is carried out on a test basis. The auditor will select a sample.

The possibility that the opinions you form, perfectly validly, from the results of your sample, are different from those you would have formed if you had been able to examine the whole population is called **sampling risk.**

Non-sampling risk is the possibility of coming to the wrong conclusion about the financial statements for any other reason, for example

- Lack of understanding of the nature of your client's business
- Use of invalid sampling techniques
- Failure to investigate a particular class of assets, liabilities or transactions

3 Assessing the risks of material misstatement

Section overview

- The best way to learn the skill of identifying and assessing risk of misstatement is to practice doing it in exam questions.

Try the interactive questions that follow.

Interactive question 1: Assessing the risks of material misstatement

[Difficulty level: Exam standard]

Your firm has recently been appointed auditor of Trendy Products Ltd, a wholesaler of clothing and fashion accessories geared to the younger market. You are responsible for planning the audit, and have obtained the following background information.

The company imports most of its goods from manufacturers in the Far East. The suppliers issue invoices in dollars, payable within 30 days. The finance director uses a mixture of forward exchange contracts and spot purchases of dollars to pay these suppliers.

Most of the company's customers are small retailers. However, the company has increased its sales by 50% in the last quarter due to a new contract to supply a large retailer. In order to secure this new business, credit terms had to be relaxed from the standard 30 days to 60 days for this customer.

As a result of this expansion the company is finding it difficult to stay within its overdraft limit and is currently negotiating with the bank to increase the facility.

The company recently upgraded its PC-based modular purchases, sales and nominal ledger systems to an integrated system. The accounting package was supplied by a software company which had recently commenced trading.

The software supplier assisted the company with the changeover from the old system to the new. As a result management decided that there was no need to involve the previous auditor or to have a parallel run.

Mrs Evans is solely responsible for the input of data, but due to the changeover she is several weeks behind with her work. She hopes to be up-to-date by the time of the audit as she intends to work overtime to clear the backlog.

The company has introduced an incentive scheme under which the directors are entitled to a bonus on achieving a certain level of profit. The bonus will be paid 30 days after the audited accounts are available.

Requirements

Identify the factors that impact on audit risk in respect of the above matters, and state what effect these would have on audit procedures.

See **Answer** at the end of this chapter.

Interactive question 2: Vax plc **[Difficulty level: Exam standard]**

You are the manager responsible for the audit of Vax plc which has a year end of 31 May. This is the first year that your firm has undertaken the audit of Vax plc, having succeeded the previous auditors at the last annual general meeting following a successful tender for the audit. Your firm has an office in Manchester and in 25 other locations throughout the United Kingdom.

You have had preliminary discussions with the management of Vax plc and obtained some background information about the company. The company produces fertiliser in a factory on the outskirts of Liverpool. The head office is situated in Manchester. There are ten depots throughout the country which hold large stocks of fertiliser so that local demand for its products can be met quickly. Inventory records are not maintained and a full count is carried out at the year end.

You have also read a recent government press release that indicates that 'Liso', a product which forms a major part of the company's sales, contains a chemical that has been identified as being potentially dangerous to those who handle it. An official government working party has been set up to review the situation.

Requirements

(a) Identify the risk factors that should be taken into account when planning the audit of Vax plc, and set out for each factor the effect on audit procedures.

(b) Explain the objectives of audit planning.

See **Answer** at the end of this chapter.

---

4 Significant risks

Section overview

- Significant risks are referred to in IAS 315.
- Significant risks are items that are unusual or one-offs.

ISA 315 refers to what it calls significant risks.

Definition

A **significant risk** is a risk of material misstatement that, in the auditor's judgement, requires special audit consideration.

These are usually items that are unusual or one-offs.

Worked example: Significant risks

- Property purchases and sales
- Acquisition and disposal of businesses
- Decision to factor receivables
- Potential sale of the business
- Diversification into new sectors

Of course, remember that what is unusual for one company is not necessarily unusual for another. Hence, we are reminded of the importance of knowledge of the particular business being audited.

5 Documentation

Section overview

- ISAs 315 and 330 contain a number of requirements regarding documentation.

You know about the need for auditors to document their audit work from your Assurance studies. ISAs 315 and 330 contain a number of requirements about documentation, and we shall briefly run through those here.

The following matters should be documented.

- The discussion among the audit team concerning the susceptibility of the financial statements to material misstatements, including any significant decisions reached
- Key elements of the understanding gained of the entity including the elements of the entity and its control specified in the ISA as mandatory, the sources of the information gained and the risk assessment procedures carried out
- The identified and assessed risks of material misstatement
- Significant risks identified and related controls evaluated
- The overall responses to address the risks of material misstatement
- Nature, extent and timing of further audit procedures linked to the assessed risks at the assertion level
- If the auditors have relied on evidence about the effectiveness of controls from previous audits, conclusions about how this is appropriate

Summary and Self-test

Summary

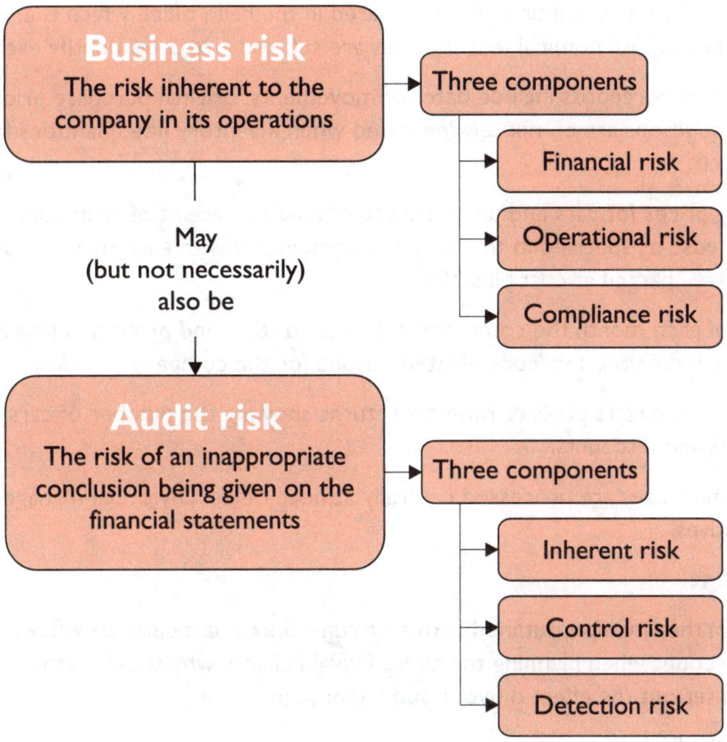

Self-test

Answer the following questions.

1 As part of the audit planning for a client the auditor has evaluated the components of audit risk, namely, control risk, detection risk and inherent risk.

His tests of controls reveal deficiencies in the operation of the system of internal control, and he is now reassessing the risks to the audit.

Since control risk has increased, describe the effect of this on the other components of risk.

2 What is the meaning and implication of high inherent risk?

3 What is the meaning and implication of high detection risk?

4 If an auditor decides that an acceptable level of audit risk is 5%, what does this mean?

5 Auditors should plan and perform their audit procedures recognising that fraud and error may materially affect the financial statements.

Give four examples of indicators in a business that the risk of fraud and error may be high.

6 Earthmovers Ltd is a civil engineering company that provides a pipe-laying service to the energy, water and telecommunications industries. It uses much heavy plant and machinery, and is subject to the strict provisions of health and safety at work regulations.

Identify the risks to which breaches of these regulations could expose the company, and the implications for the audit in the event of such breaches.

CHAPTER 9

Exam-style questions

7 Your new client, Wheeler Ltd, sells new cars, parts and accessories and undertakes workshop repairs. The company operates through five divisions/locations in the Midlands.

Each division deals with a different overseas vehicle supplier and has three managers, one for each trading activity. Each division makes sales to companies and individuals, but only corporate customers are granted credit terms.

The computer-based accounting system is based in the head office which is annexed to the premises of the largest division. All nominal ledger codes are suffixed 1 to 5 to identify each division's transactions.

Detailed inventory records include dates of movements, original purchase price and latest selling price. Purchase requisitions are computer-generated when inventory line quantities fall to pre-determined re-order levels.

Gross selling prices for cars and parts are established on receipt of each consignment at standard markups on cost, as specified in the franchise agreements with each manufacturer. Parts transferred to workshops are charged at cost plus 10%.

At the end of each month the computer generates trading and profit and loss accounts and balance sheets for each division, and 'consolidated' results for the company.

New car sales managers prepare monthly returns showing the number of cars sold, gross selling prices, extras and discounts.

All salaries and wages are processed centrally at head office. Divisional managers all have profit-related bonus incentives.

Requirement

Identify, from the situation outlined above, circumstances particular to Wheeler Ltd that should be taken into account when planning the audit. Explain clearly why these matters should be taken into account and set out the effect on your audit approach. **(20 marks)**

8 **Golden Pond Fisheries**

Richard Pine is a senior audit manager for Ratcliffe, Barnes and Soammes, a firm with offices around Birmingham and Exeter. These split locations have arisen from the merger two years previously of Barnes, Soammes & Co (Birmingham), a firm specialising in the audit of property and service companies, with Ratcliffe & Co whose fee income was based on the audit of farms and holiday resorts in the South West. The merger was seen as an opportunity for both firms to break away from their restricted markets.

Richard moved from Birmingham to take up a new portfolio of clients in Cornwall and Devon, including Golden Pond Fisheries Ltd. This is a family business with John Carnes running the 80-acre farm, and his wife, Claire, taking responsibility for the holiday cottages, fishing lakes and completion of the books and records.

The farming operation has been significantly curtailed in recent years and now comprises a small beef herd and, as a recent addition, two geese sheds. These birds are fed on a chemical-free diet to offer a high quality alternative to turkeys over the Christmas period. John supplements the farm revenue by letting pastures on a rotational basis to neighbouring farms for sheep grazing.

John is also considering the introduction of rare breeds (pigs and goats) to provide an additional attraction to holidaymakers with young families.

Claire Carnes trained as a bookkeeper before her marriage 30 years ago, and has informed Richard that the accounts are now maintained to a 'high standard' on her son's PC. This has apparently saved a lot of time, and much of the previous paperwork is now superfluous.

Five years previously the family had borrowed a substantial sum to convert three derelict barns into luxury holiday cottages, and these have proved to be a huge success, being fully booked from late May to November. During this period two extra helpers are employed on a part-time basis to assist with cleaning and maintenance. Both are paid in cash at the end of each week.

Most of the visitors are fishermen and their families, as the farm boasts excellent fishing. John Carnes is keen to maintain this quality and is always on the lookout for big fish to stock. He has recently become interested in the possibility of introducing from China some 60lb blue carp, which could be 'sneaked in' with a batch of koi carp being imported for a local garden centre.

A good relationship has always existed with the auditors and the Carnes are confident that this will be another quick audit.

Requirement

Identify, from the information above, the potential audit risks, and for each risk explain why it is a risk.

(14 marks)

9 **Shades Ltd**

You are planning the audit of Shades Ltd for the year ending 30 June 20X9. The principal activities of the company are the manufacture and distribution of a range of window blind systems and of the component parts for window blinds. Approximately 50% of revenue is generated from overseas customers.

During your preparation for the planning meeting with the finance director, the following matters have been highlighted as significant.

(1) Operating results

The company has had a successful year to date with revenue, gross and operating margins up on the previous year.

	10 months to 30 April 20X9	*10 months to 30 April 20X8*	*Year to 30 June 20X8*
	£'000	£'000	£'000
Revenue	22,656	19,597	22,557
Cost of sales	13,367	12,472	14,313
Gross profit	9,289	7,125	8,244
Operating expenses	4,531	4,115	4,732
Operating profit	4,758	3,010	3,512
Gross profit margin	41%	36%	37%
Operating profit margin	21%	15%	16%

Inventories at 30 April 20X9 were £4.3 million compared with £3.6 million at 30 April 20X8 and £3.4 million at 30 June 20X8.

(2) New computer system

During the year the company replaced its accounting software with a fully integrated standard package modified by the supplier to the company's requirements.

(3) Incentive scheme

During the year the company introduced an incentive scheme under which the executive directors are entitled to a bonus based on pre-tax profits. The bonus will be paid thirty days after the audited accounts are available.

Requirement

In respect of the above, identify and explain the potential audit risks and indicate the matters you would discuss with the finance director at your planning meeting. **(20 marks)**

Now, go back to the Learning Objectives in the Introduction. If you are satisfied you have achieved these objectives, please tick them off.

CHAPTER 9

Technical reference

1 Business risk	**ISA 315.4 (b)**
2 Audit risk	**ISA 200.13 (c)**
3 Assessing the risks of material misstatement	**IAS 315.25–29**
4 Significant risks	**ISA 315.4 (e)**
5 Documentation	**ISA 315.32** **ISA 330.28–30**

Answers to Interactive questions

Answer to Interactive question 1

Factor and risk	Effect on audit procedures
• This is a new audit appointment. New appointment increases detection risk due to lack of cumulative/prior knowledge from previous audits	• Accounting systems and internal controls need to be ascertained. • Current period audit work should have regard to the opening balances and comparatives. ISA 510 and ISA 710 will assist the auditor.
• Trendy Products Ltd operates in the fashion industry. The nature of the industry contributes to high inherent risk, as clothes and accessories do not stay in fashion and year end inventory provisions may be inadequate.	• Evaluate inventory count instructions for procedure to identify obsolete items. • Review post year-end order book to establish adequacy of inventory provisions.
• Most purchases are imported and paid for in dollars. Inherent risk is increased by exposure to dollar fluctuations.	• Any gains and losses on dollar transactions/year-end balances should be taken to the income statement and monetary items should be translated at the year-end rate.
• Economic dependence on a principal customer. Pressure from the new customer may increase inherent risk.	• Having expanded to accommodate this customer, ensure the going concern assumption remains appropriate if the new contract is terminated.
• The company is currently renegotiating its overdraft. Deterioration of cash flows increases going concern risk, which will be made worse if the overdraft is withdrawn.	• The auditor should review management assessment of going concern. • The effect on liquidity ratios, debtor days etc should be calculated and actions to remedy the cash flow problems discussed with directors.
• The bank may seek to place reliance on the audited accounts before negotiations are finalised. This increases risk as management have a motive to manipulate the accounts.	• Particular attention should be given to – Bank overdraft/creditor cut-off – Most likely areas of misstatement and significant areas where judgement is involved, eg provisions – Impact of potential audit adjustments on key ratios • If a satisfactory outcome to the negotiations is not reached before the audit is completed, a qualification is likely.
• The software company being used has only recently commenced trading. Inherent risk may be increased by the inexperience of the software company.	• The level of audit testing of the new system is likely to be higher than for an accounting package with a good track record.

CHAPTER 9

Factor and risk	Effect on audit procedures
• There is a potential risk that data transfer was inaccurate or incomplete. If any significant problems with the changeover are encountered then, in the absence of a parallel run, proper accounting records may not have been kept.	• The lack of proper accounting records may need referring to in the audit report.
• There is a backlog of data input. Human error is more likely if overtime working is excessive, therefore inherent risk is increased.	• Cut-off should be carefully reviewed as errors are more likely if data processing is not up-to-date at the year end.
• The introduction of the incentive scheme may cause management to overstate the profit.	• Extended checks and/or increased sample sizes to look for potential understatement of liabilities and expenses, and overstatement of assets and income.

Answer to Interactive question 2

(a)

Risk factor	Effect on audit procedures
• This is the first year that the firm has undertaken the audit of Vax plc.	• In order to be satisfied about the previous financial statements – Hold consultations with management – Review client's records, working papers and accounting and control procedures for the previous period – (Possibly) hold consultations with the previous auditor. • Familiarisation with the nature of the business, market, accounting systems etc by – Discussions with management – Review of interim/management accounts.
• Vax plc has – A head office in Manchester – A factory in Liverpool – Ten depots throughout the country.	• Staff must be planned to carry out the audit from the firm's offices throughout the country. • They must all be adequately briefed and provided with a copy of the audit plan detailing their specific tasks and deadlines.
• No inventory records have been maintained but a full inventory count is to be carried out at the year end.	• It is vital that the auditors are satisfied with the inventory count. • The written count instructions must be reviewed well in advance of the year end, so that improvement can be suggested by the auditors and incorporated into the client's instructions. • The auditors should ensure that sufficient staff with the necessary experience are available to attend the count at all material locations.

Risk factor	Effect on audit procedures
• 'Liso', a major product of the company, has been identified as being potentially dangerous.	• Ascertain – For how long Vax plc has been selling 'Liso' and in what quantity – How much 'Liso' the company now holds in inventory. • Ensure that the firm keeps up-to-date with the findings of the government working party. • Consider whether any Vax plc employees may have been harmed and, if so, the consequential liability of the company to them.

(b) **Objectives of audit planning**

To ensure that appropriate attention is devoted to important areas of the audit

This is done via a formal written audit plan, laying down the objectives and the procedures to be followed in order to meet those objectives.

To facilitate review

Work should be delegated to staff with the appropriate level of experience. All work should be properly supervised and reviewed by a more senior member of staff.

To ensure that potential problems are identified

The auditor must ensure that resources are directed towards material/high risk areas.

To assist in the proper assignment of work

This may be to members of the audit team or to experts or other auditors. It helps the audit to proceed in a timely and efficient manner.

Answers to Self-test

1 **Effect of increased control risk (CR)**

On inherent risk (IR)

- No direct impact → IR and CR largely independent of each other

On detection risk (DR)

- Impact dependent upon IR assessment
  - If IR also high, increased testing required to render DR low
  - If IR low, control weakness impact may not be as significant on audit risk (AR). May increase work required to reduce DR to ensure AR is acceptable
- Provided DR is managed, control weaknesses should not affect AR

Other components must cancel impact of control weaknesses on AR

2 **Meaning and implication of high inherent risk**

- Meaning = risk of material errors arising is high
- Implication = detection risk must be rendered low

3 **Meaning and implication of high detection risk**

- Assessed levels of inherent and control risk are low
- High risk that substantive procedures do not detect material misstatement
- Implies small sample sizes

4 **Meaning – audit risk 5%**

- 5% chance of an invalid conclusion (audit opinion) being drawn after all procedures completed; or
- 95% confident that audit opinion will be valid

5 From:

- Previous experience of integrity or competence of management
- Financial reporting pressures (profit-based rewards)
- Weaknesses in design or operation of systems
- High staff turnover
- Industry characteristics, for example, cash handling
- Unusual transactions
- Problems in obtaining audit evidence
- Inadequate control over information systems data

6

Risks	Audit implications
• Civil liabilities to victims	• Possibility of:
• Statutory fines and penalties	– Unrecorded liabilities
• Increased insurance premiums	– Impairment of property, plant and equipment
• Loss of reputation	
• Forced closure	• Going concern doubts

Exam-style questions

7

Circumstance	Why taken into account	Effect on audit approach
• This is a new audit client.	• Lack of cumulative/prior knowledge, from which assurance can be derived, increases inherent risk. • Adequate planning is essential for audit efficiency to prevent over-auditing in first year.	• Accounting systems and internal controls need to be ascertained. Flowcharting will probably be appropriate. • Current period audit work should have regard to the opening balances to provide assurance as to the accuracy of the opening position.
• The accounts of each division are not being reported on individually.	• Materiality, risk, the audit approach and extent of audit procedures must be assessed in the context of the company ('consolidated') accounts.	• Sample sizes should be apportioned between divisions (eg by stratifying populations to divisions) to curb tendency to overaudit.
• The company operates from five locations.	• Assets which are material to the balance sheet (inventory and possibly premises, equipment, fixtures, etc) are kept at five different locations.	• The year end attendance at inventory counts should cover all locations and take the opportunity to verify other assets, including tangible non-current assets and cash.
• Cash sales are made to individuals.	• Increases the risk of misappropriation of cash and understatement of sales.	• Controls over cash must be evaluated and any weaknesses reported to management. • Audit effort should be directed to confirming the completeness of recorded sales for parts and accessories, and workshop in particular.

Circumstance	Why taken into account	Effect on audit approach
• Computerised inventory information includes dates of movements, cost and selling price relevant to determining the adequacy of inventory provisions.	• Computerised inventory records should be materially accurate and up-to-date (otherwise they would not be appropriate for raising purchase requisitions).	• If there are no significant differences between physical and book inventories – Reliance may be placed on the accuracy of accounting entries to inventory records – Annual count need not be confined to year end as 'roll-forward' is possible – Continuous inventory checking may be facilitated. • Audit software may be used to produce an inventory ageing and report by exception – Slow-moving items (eg no movements in x months) – Actual selling price less than original purchase price.
• Standard mark-ups are used.	• Standard mark-ups facilitate budgetary control of divisional activities.	• Analytical procedures including 'proof in total' may confirm the completeness (or otherwise) of recorded revenue.
• Parts transferred to workshops are charged at cost plus 10%.	• Divisional trading at lower mark-ups gives incentive to inter-divisional trading and could – Distort GP% subjected to analytical procedures – Conceal parts sales at more than the allowed margin.	• Inter-divisional trading should be separately identified.
	• Value of parts inventories held by workshop is inflated by 10% unrealised profit.	• Although this is unlikely to be sufficiently material to warrant a year end adjustment, consideration should be given to the level of parts inventories held in the workshops. Quantities should be sufficient (to meet most immediate requirements) but not excessive (giving rise to risk of damage/theft).

Circumstance	Why taken into account	Effect on audit approach
• Sales are made under franchise agreements with each manufacturer.	• A breach of franchise terms and conditions (eg concerning prescribed mark-ups) could bring penalty clauses into effect.	• This aspect of inherent risk must be assessed, eg – If low, there may be no implications for the financial statements (eg any contingent liability may be disregarded as being remote) – If high (see also management bias) a provision for penalties could be required. • The appropriateness of the going concern assumption should be considered in the light of – Any known breaches – Foreseeable renewals.
• Monthly accounts and returns are prepared	• These indicate a control-conscious head office to mitigate the inherent risk attributable to divisional operations.	• The disaggregated financial information (by divisions and certain activities) should highlight key audit areas and fluctuations requiring investigation. • For analytical procedures on the company's 'consolidated' accounts, the inter-divisional trading and balances must be eliminated.
• Divisional managers have profit-related bonus incentives.	• Inherent risk is increased by possible management bias to overstate profit by – Overstating sales – Understating expenses.	• This bias may reduce other aspects of inherent risk (eg of loss of cash/inventory through unrecorded sales). • Risk of sales overstatement may not be great, since – Maximum prices set by franchise agreement, and – Market is fiercely competitive at present time. • Risk of expense understatement is restricted (eg because head office controls payroll expenditure). • Audit tests should be directed to most likely area of misstatement (eg cut-off 'errors' arising through suppression of invoices).

CHAPTER 9

8 Golden Pond Fisheries

Factor	Why a risk
• Richard Pine, the new audit manager is from the property and service client base.	• Errors in the financial statements may be missed due to Richard's non-familiarity with the Carnes' business.
• The Carnes are expecting 'another quick audit'.	• Richard is likely to need to carry out more work than usual to become familiar with the client. This may be interpreted by the Carnes as mistrust, with the consequence that they are reluctant to volunteer assistance.
• The business is run and managed by a husband and wife team.	• There is limited scope for supervisory or authorisation controls and segregation of duties. • Those controls in place are likely to be unreliable due to the risk of management override.
• There has been a loss of revenue from the original farming operations, which the Carnes are addressing by diversification.	• The loss of revenue from the original business may threaten the viability of the farm as a going concern. Although the Carnes are addressing this by diversification, the process of change also carries a risk as it involves adapting to new markets and learning new skills.
• The Carnes are raising organically fed geese as an alternative to turkey.	• This source of revenue assumes that customers of the meat distributors used can be persuaded to change from the traditional turkey. There is a significant possibility that this market will not materialise. • Organic food supplies for the geese will carry a higher price tag. There is no evidence to suggest that John Carnes has evaluated if this cost can be recouped. It is possible that in spite of generating revenue the sale of geese may realise no overall profit. • This is a markedly seasonal business. Income will have ceased before the first holidaymakers arrive in May, thereby putting a strain on the servicing of debt.
• Pastures are being let for sheep grazing.	• If John Carnes has entered into contracts for the supply of grazing, this could prohibit future expansion of holiday/fishing facilities by restricting the availability of land. • As these are the most successful elements of Gold Pond Fisheries Ltd, their curtailment could threaten the going concern status of the company. If no such contracts exist, then grazing revenues could cease at any time – there is no evidence that such a prospect has been considered.

Factor	Why a risk
• John Carnes appears to imply that blue carp are to be imported illegally.	• Any such breach of import regulations when discovered will result in severe penalties, extending to fines, quarantine of inventories, etc. • The consequence would be a loss of revenue and reputation in the core business. • The importing of alien species will threaten existing inventories with diseases and parasites to which they are not resistant.
• In the UK holiday cottages are a seasonal business.	• Cash flows will fluctuate widely over a 12 month period. This places strain on debt repayment terms and going concern.
• The development of the holiday cottages was financed by borrowing.	• Financing a business by way of borrowing always carries the risk that repayment of capital and interest does not cease in less successful periods. • The provider of finance will want to review the financial statements, increasing the risk of management bias in preparing the financial statements to show a favourable position.
• Accounting records are maintained on a PC.	• The use of a PC, with its associated risks of data corruption and lack of sufficient controls, increases risks re the completeness and accuracy of accounting records.
• The amount of paperwork has decreased.	• Audit trails may be lost without hard copies, increasing the risk that insufficient evidence will be available.
• Data has recently been transferred to the computer system.	• Increased risk of errors due to inaccurate transfer of data onto the PC.
• Claire trained as a bookkeeper 30 years ago.	• Claire's bookkeeping training may prove to be of limited advantage as there has been a significant amount of change over recent years. Again, this reduces confidence in the accuracy of the financial statements.
• Part-time staff are employed for six months of the year and are paid in cash.	• It is important to ensure that these individuals appear on the payroll, and that PAYE/NI regulations have been complied with. • Insufficient records may be available due to the cash nature of transactions.
• The current audit firm has resulted from a merger of two firms with very different client bases from different parts of the country.	• It will take time to create and adopt a truly uniform audit approach, and this will increase the detection risk associated with all work undertaken. • This arises from non-familiarity, and increases the risk of procedures being omitted or conducted inefficiently. • Mergers of any type always create the risk of 'culture clashes', and this can reduce the efficiency of audit work undertaken.

9 Shades Ltd

Audit risks	Matters to discuss
Manufacturing company	
• Inventories may be materially misstated due to difficulties in estimating the degree of completion of work in progress (WIP). • Estimating the net realisable value (NRV) of certain window blind systems.	• The methods used by the company to determine the stage of completion and valuation of WIP. • The NRV of window blind systems awaiting sale or installation.
Overseas customers	
• Sales in foreign currencies may not be translated at an appropriate rate, resulting in revenue and receivables being misstated in the financial statements.	• The rate used to translate transactions on foreign currencies. • The procedures adopted to ensure compliance with accounting standards.
Bad debts	
• There may be insufficient provision made for bad debts as a result of increased difficulties in assessing credit worthiness and recoverability for overseas customers.	• The techniques used to assess credit worthiness of customers, particularly those based overseas. • Method used to monitor and chase slow payers. • Whether there are any known bad or doubtful debts. • The reasons for any seasonal variations within the company's sales. • The methods of managing cash flow and working capital to address the impact of seasonal variations.
Seasonal business	
• Misstatements in monthly revenue and expenditure figures may be more difficult to detect as a result of seasonal variations in the business.	
Revenue growth	
• Revenue may be overstated. The increased volume of sales may increase the extent of errors arising within the accounting records.	• The reasons for the increase in revenue this period. • Whether any noticeable increase in error rates within the accounting records has occurred.
Gross profit increase	
• Gross profit may be overstated as a result of items in transit to overseas customers being included in both year end inventories and revenue purchases being understated.	• The reasons for the increase this period. • Procedures used to ensure that transactions just before or after the year end are recorded in the correct accounting period. • How adequate provision is made for purchases, particularly those invoiced post year end.

Audit risks	Matters to discuss
Operating profit increase	
• Operating expenses may be understated due to recording being incomplete and the client failing to fully accrue for such expenses.	• The procedures for ensuring the completeness of recording expenditure. • The methods used for identifying and making adequate provision for accruals.
Increasing inventory values	
• The company may have difficulty in selling certain lines of inventory if items are made to customer specification and then orders cancelled. Such lines may be overvalued in the financial statements.	• The proportion of lines of inventory made specifically to order. • The adaptability of such lines in the event of order cancellations. • The anticipated future revenue from sales of the type of blinds. • The level of advanced orders received.
Change in accounting system	
• Misstatements may increase as a result of information being lost or incorrectly transferred from the old to new systems.	• The procedures used to ensure that all accounting information was correctly transferred from old to new systems. • The type of changeover which was used eg parallel running, stepped changeover direct changeover.
New computer system	
• Modifications to the new computer software may reduce its reliability. This, together with the relative unfamiliarity of client staff with the new system, will increase the risk of errors arising.	• The extent and nature of any problems being experienced with the new system. • The extent of training and system support given to staff operating the new system. • The criteria used to choose the new system and the reason for the change.
Bonus scheme	
• The scheme provides an incentive for directors to overstate income and understate expenditure.	• The nature of any conditions attached to the bonus. • The effect on profits since the introduction of the scheme. • The anticipated level of bonus payable this period.
Disclosure	
• The audited accounts may fail to properly disclose such bonuses within directors' emoluments. • Similarly, failure to properly include such bonuses may result in current liabilities being understated.	• The proposed treatment and disclosure of the directors' bonuses within the financial statements. • Whether the directors are aware of the auditors' legal duty to make good any disclosure lapses in this area in the audit report.

chapter 10

Audit approach

Introduction

Learning objectives

Tick off

- Understand the sources of audit confidence and be able to determine audit approach ☐
- Understand when an auditor may rely on the work of others as part of the audit ☐
- Identify practical issues that need to be included in the overall audit strategy ☐

Specific syllabus references for this chapter are: 3h, j.

Syllabus links

This area was introduced, in connection with evidence, in Assurance.

Examination context

In the exam, you could be asked to identify risks and then justify an approach towards those risks.

In the assessment, candidates may be required to:

- Assess the impact of risk and materiality on the engagement plan, including the nature, timing and extent of assurance procedures, for a given organisation
- Determine an approach appropriate for an engagement for a specified organisation which addresses:
  - Possible reliance on controls (including those within the IT system)
  - Possible reliance on the work of internal audit or other experts
  - Possible reliance on the work of another auditor
  - Probable extent of tests of controls and of substantive procedures, including analytical procedures
  - Nature and extent of client-generated information
  - Probable number, timing, staffing and location of assurance visits

1 Responding to the risk assessment

Section overview

- The auditor must formulate an approach to assessed risks of material misstatement.
- Overall responses include issues such as emphasising to the team the importance of professional scepticism, allocating more staff, using experts or providing more supervision.
- The auditor must also determine further audit procedures to address the risks of material misstatement.
- There are three sources of audit confidence: tests of controls, tests of details and analytical procedures.
- Remember, some substantive procedures (that is, tests of details and/or analytical procedures) must be carried out.

The main requirement of ISA 330 *The Auditor's Responses to Assessed Risks* is that in order to reduce audit risk to an acceptably low level, the auditor should determine overall responses to assessed risks at the financial statement level, and should design and perform further audit procedures to respond to assessed risks at the assertion level.

In other words, having assessed the risks of material misstatements in the financial statements, the auditor has to **plan the work** that will be carried out **to ensure** that **he can draw a conclusion** about whether the financial statements give a true and fair view, that is, that any material misstatements have been identified and amended if necessary.

1.1 Overall responses

Overall responses to risks of material misstatement will be changes to the general audit strategy or re-affirmations to staff of the general audit strategy. For example:

- Emphasising to audit staff the need to maintain professional scepticism
- Assigning additional or more experienced staff to the audit team
- Using experts, the work of internal auditors or other auditors
- Providing more supervision on the audit
- Incorporating more unpredictability into the audit procedures

The evaluation of the control environment that will have taken place as part of the assessment of the client's internal control systems will help the auditor determine whether they are going to take a substantive approach (focusing mainly on substantive procedures) or a combined approach (tests of controls and substantive procedures).

1.2 Responses to the risks of material misstatement at the assertion level

The ISA says that 'the auditor shall design and perform further audit procedures whose **nature**, **timing** and **extent** are based on and are responsive to the assessed risks of material misstatement at the assertion level'. Nature refers to the purpose and the type of test that is carried out. The extent of audit tests is determined by sampling, which we covered in our Assurance studies. The auditors must also have to consider the timing of tests – before the year end or after, or possibly, continuously throughout the year using CAATs.

1.3 Sources of audit confidence

To reduce the level of risk that the financial statements might be wrong, the auditors have to build up audit confidence based on sufficient appropriate audit evidence.

We have looked at the nature and sources of audit evidence in your Assurance studies. In summary, there are three sources of audit confidence.

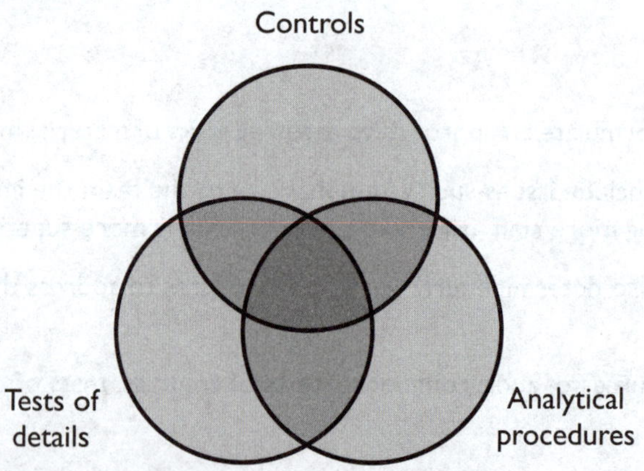

Figure 10.1: Sources of audit confidence

You know what internal controls are from your Assurance studies.

To derive audit confidence from the client's controls, auditors have to ascertain them (by enquiry), document them and then test them to make sure that:

- They operate in the way they think they do (by walkthrough testing); and
- They are effective (by tests of controls).

You covered the nature of controls and their strengths and weaknesses in your Assurance studies. We will revisit some key issues in section 2 of this chapter.

During the planning process the audit team decides on the use of these sources to give sufficient audit confidence and what the mix should be.

The audit plan will record the approach to be used as decided on by the audit team.

1.4 Additional guidance

ISA 501 *Audit Evidence – Specific Considerations for Selected Items* illustrates how the principles of ISA 500 *Audit Evidence* should be applied to certain items in the financial statements. Two areas that it covers are particularly relevant in this syllabus:

- Attendance at physical inventory counting
- Litigation and claims

You will have looked at the procedures normally performed at an inventory count in your studies for the Assurance paper.

Worked example: Audit of inventories

You could audit inventory by counting it all and working out what it is worth by exhaustive checking to invoices etc – **reliance on tests of details** (substantive approach)

Alternatively you could look at the client's systems for recording purchases and sales, for checking goods into the warehouse, and for ensuring security of the warehouse site. Should you conclude that the systems are sound you may wish to place **reliance on controls.**

You could also look at the breakdown of inventory over the last few years, consider the normal inventory levels the client carries and their relationship to purchases and cost of sales, the basis for overhead and labour recovery, and you might think that, all in all the inventory figure looks about right – **reliance on analytical procedures**

In practice you are likely to do a combination of all three. Auditing standards require you to carry out some substantive procedures (tests of details or analytical procedures) so **placing reliance solely on controls is not an option**. Carrying out some controls testing reduces the amount of substantive testing to be carried out but it does not eliminate the need for substantive tests. The precise mix changes depending on the nature of the client:

- For a small scale client at a single location it may be just as efficient to observe the inventory count and to carry out a number of test counts as it is to spend a great deal of time evaluating the system, or calculating ratios. You will be relying on controls such as the reliability of the inventory checkers to a limited extent, but you will also have a good deal of confidence about the final figure deriving from the substantive work you have done; ie your own test counts.
- For a large national building supplies company with a large number of depots, you are likely to rely to a greater extent on your assessment of controls and analytical review.

Interactive question 1: Reliance on controls [Difficulty level: Easy]

List the factors that you would consider in deciding at the planning stage of the audit whether to seek to rely on internal controls as part of the audit.

See **Answer** at the end of this chapter.

2 Reliance on controls

Section overview

- The auditors carry out tests of controls when:
  - They are intending to rely on controls; or
  - They are unable to derive sufficient evidence from substantive procedures
- In summary, ISA 330 says that if auditors want to rely on a control:
  - They have to test it
  - The have to obtain evidence that it is effective
  - They have to obtain evidence that it operated throughout the period under review
  - They have to flex their approach in accordance with the nature of the control and the risk it is seeking to mitigate

ISA 330 says auditors need to carry out tests of controls under two sets of circumstances:

- When they are intending to rely on controls to reduce audit risk; or
- When they are unable to derive sufficient evidence from substantive procedures.

The type of testing will depend on the nature of the control.

The client's procedures for authorising expenditure, for example could take many forms:

- There could be an approval box in a grid rubber stamped on invoices – auditors would check that the stamp had been applied and the box signed or initialled on a sample of invoices
- Expenditure over a certain level may need to be approved by the board, or by a committee – auditors would check the minutes of the relevant meetings
- The client may operate a budgetary control system, where managers have responsibility for particular projects, and where the board, or a committee will periodically review actual performance against budget.

Procedures here may be more difficult to devise.

- The auditors could review the minutes of the relevant meetings.
- The auditors could select a sample of projects and make actual/budget comparisons and then follow up to see what the client did in response to any overruns.

- The auditors could attend the relevant meetings and observe how they are conducted – but would need to be careful about whether the auditors' presence at the meeting will affect the way the meeting is conducted.

In respect of IT controls the following questions are relevant.

- How do these operate?
- Is the auditor justified in assuming that they function properly?
- If a client uses a recognised accounting package such as Quickbooks or Sage Line 50, is the auditor justified in assuming that, for example VAT will be calculated correctly and that control accounts will be updated properly?

It may be necessary to use CAATs to prove these assumptions. We considered testing controls in Assurance.

Interactive question 2: Reliance on internal controls **[Difficulty level: Easy]**

In the course of planning an audit several internal controls in the company's systems have been identified. List the conditions that each control must satisfy if it is to be relied upon in reducing the extent of substantive procedures to be performed.

See **Answer** at the end of this chapter.

Interactive question 3: Bix plc **[Difficulty level: Exam standard]**

You are the senior auditor in charge of the audit of Bix plc, a manufacturing company. You have been talking with the payroll supervisor who has commented on the strength of the company's payroll internal control system. She has assumed that this internal control system guarantees the completeness, accuracy and validity of the payroll accounting records.

Requirements

(a) State whether you agree with the supervisor's assumption that an internal control system can guarantee the completeness, accuracy and validity of the records, supporting your answer by using examples from a payroll system.

(b) The supervisor has also asked you to explain some internal control terminology which she does not understand.

Explain the meaning of the following terms, using payroll examples different from those you have given above.

(i) Segregation of duties
(ii) Approval and control of documents

See **Answer** at the end of this chapter.

3 Substantive approach

Section overview

- Substantive procedures constitute tests of details and/or analytical procedures.
- Auditors always carry out a number of substantive procedures.
- The number of substantive procedures carried out will depend on the level of risk, the amount of reliance on controls and the results of controls testing.

As you know, substantive procedures fall into two categories: analytical procedures and tests of details.

The auditor must always carry out substantive procedures on material items.

ISA 330 says 'irrespective of the assessed risk of material misstatement, the auditor shall design and perform substantive procedures for each material class of transactions, account balance and disclosure'.

In addition, the auditor **must** carry out the following substantive procedures:

- Agreeing the financial statements to the underlying accounting records
- Examining material journal entries
- Examining other adjustments made in preparing the financial statements

The auditor must determine when it is appropriate to use which type of substantive procedure.

Analytical procedures tend to be appropriate for large volumes of predictable transactions (for example, wages and salaries). **Other procedures** (**tests of detail**) may be appropriate to gain information about account balances (for example, inventories or trade receivables), particularly verifying the assertions of existence and valuation. Substantive procedures were covered in detail in your studies for Assurance where you studied the principles of audit evidence outlined in ISA 500 *Audit Evidence* as well as specific procedures such as those described in ISA 505 *External Confirmations*.

Tests of detail rather than analytical procedures are likely to be more appropriate with regard to matters which have been identified as **significant risks**, but the auditor must determine procedures that are specifically responsive to that risk, which may include analytical procedures. Significant risks are likely to be the most difficult to obtain sufficient appropriate evidence about.

How much substantive testing is carried out will depend on:

- Whether the auditor wants to rely on controls in the first place (in which case substantive testing might be reduced)
- Whether controls testing reveals that controls can be relied on (if they cannot, the auditors will have to increase substantive testing)

In the Assurance paper you studied ISA 530 *Audit Sampling* and saw how sample sizes are determined based on the assessment of audit risk.

Interactive question 4: Substantive testing [Difficulty level: Easy]

King Ltd is a new audit client of your firm. The finance director has attended a seminar on 'Understanding how your auditors work', and has come away convinced that you will be able to rely on the internal controls within the company to reduce the overall amount of work done.

Identify the circumstances in which this approach may not be possible, leading you to undertake full substantive testing.

See **Answer** at the end of this chapter.

Interactive question 5: Hydra Ltd **[Difficulty level: Exam standard]**

Your firm acts as auditor to Hydra Ltd, which manufactures and bottles non-alcoholic drinks in the UK under licence from a Swiss company.

Hydra Ltd has two products only: 'Eau Vital', a sparkling cold drink made from fruit juices, herbal extracts and mineral water, and 'Glowvine', which is to be served hot, made from grape juices, herbs and spices.

Royalties are payable to the Swiss company, which is not related to Hydra Ltd, at the rate of 20p per bottle of Eau Vital or Glowvine sold. Royalties are included in cost of sales, and Hydra Ltd expects to make an average mark-up on total cost of 150% for Eau Vital and 120% for Glowvine.

To reflect environmental concerns the customer is charged a deposit of 10p, which is reimbursed on return of the bottle. This scheme was introduced during the year. The theme of concern for the environment is echoed in Hydra Ltd's advertising, which emphasises the natural ingredients.

The final audit is scheduled to commence in two weeks' time. You have recently received a copy of Hydra Ltd's management accounts, which reflect the position for the current year.

	20X6	*20X5*
	£'000	£'000
Revenue	3,280	1,876
Gross profit	1,940	1,042
Profit from operations	1,345	807

Requirements

(a) Prepare a schedule that indicates the analytical procedures which would form part of your year end substantive procedures. Where relevant, suggest possible reasons for the changes between 20X6 and 20X5.

(b) Explain what impact the new scheme involving deposits on bottles will have on the audit of liabilities at the year end.

See **Answer** at the end of this chapter.

4 Reliance on the work of others

Section overview

- External auditors may make use of work internal audit have done when carrying out their own external audit procedures.
- External auditors may make use of the work of an expert when carrying out audit procedures.
- Principal auditors have a duty to report on the truth and fairness of group accounts.
- Principal auditors have the right to require from auditors of subsidiaries the information and explanations they need, and to require the principal company to obtain the necessary information and explanations from subsidiaries.
- Principal auditors should consider whether their involvement in the group audit is sufficient for them to act as principal auditors.

4.1 Reliance on the work of internal audit

ISA 610 *Using the Work of Internal Auditors* states that as part of their planning procedures, auditors must determine whether or not they wish to use the work of the audit client's internal audit function. While the external auditor has sole responsibility for the opinion expressed, some internal audit work may be helpful to him in forming a decision.

As you learnt in your Assurance Study Manual, the scope and objectives of internal auditing can vary widely. Normally however, internal audit operates in one or more of the following broad areas.

- Review and monitoring internal control systems
- Examination of financial and operating information
- Review of operating activities, e.g. economy, efficiency and effectiveness of operations
- Review of compliance with laws and regulations
- Risk management
- Governance

An effective internal audit function may reduce, modify or alter the timing of external audit procedures, but it can **never** eliminate them entirely. Even where the internal audit function is deemed ineffective, it may still be useful to be aware of the internal audit conclusions. The effectiveness of internal audit will have a great impact on how the external auditors assess the whole control system and the assessment of audit risk.

The ISA says that the external auditor shall determine 'whether the work of internal auditors is likely to be adequate for purposes of the audit' and if so shall perform an assessment of the internal audit function.

4.1.1 Making an assessment of internal audit

The following table is a summary of paragraph A4 of ISA 610, which considers the factors that the external auditors will take into account when making their assessment of internal audit.

Assessment of internal audit	
Objectivity	Consider the **status** of the function within the entity, who they **report** to, whether they have any **conflicting responsibilities** or **restrictions** placed on their function. Consider also to what extent management acts on internal audit **recommendations**
Technical competence	Consider whether internal auditors have adequate **technical training** and proficiency
Due professional care	Consider whether internal audit is **properly planned**, **supervised**, **reviewed** and **documented**
Communication	Consider the frequency and form of contact between internal audit and **external audit**

When reporting, internal auditors should report to the whole board or the audit committee and should be free to discuss their concerns with external auditors. They should not report to management upon whose work or responsibilities they are likely to comment; this may mean for example that they should not report to the finance director.

Interactive question 6: Using the work of internal audit [Difficulty level: Exam standard]

You are currently involved in planning the audit of Midget Ltd. At the beginning of the year that you are auditing, the company set up an internal audit department, and this is the first visit since you were aware of its existence. From your initial discussions with the managing director, you have established that Mr Gnome, the internal auditor, has undertaken a number of assignments across the company, and fed back to the board on his findings.

Requirements

What factors should you take into account when considering whether you can rely on the work undertaken by Mr Gnome and his staff?

See **Answer** at the end of this chapter.

4.1.2 Using the work of internal audit

The **objectives** of internal audit will differ from those of the external auditors. However, some of the **means** of achieving their respective objectives are often **similar**, and so some of the internal auditors' work may be used by the external auditors. External auditors may use internal auditors' work on the following areas.

Recording an accounting system	The external auditor should carry out walkthrough tests on the records to ensure that the recording undertaken by the internal auditor is accurate (rather than record the accounting system themselves).
Evaluating and testing internal control	If the external auditors are to rely on the work done, say the completion of an internal control evaluation questionnaire, they should check that the method of evaluation is appropriate. They should confirm that internal audit has satisfactorily tested controls in detail by re-performing a sample of internal audit's tests; if internal audit's work is satisfactory, external auditors can make a reduced assessment of control risk as a consequence. In particular external audit may be able to rely on internal audit's assessment of computer systems, since internal audit may have carried out extensive testing on aspects of the system including controls over development and operation of the system and general controls such as access controls. Most internal auditors will produce an annual report for the board on the effectiveness of the internal controls and risk management of the company which external auditors might read as part of their own risk assessment procedures.
Substantive procedures	As external auditors are primarily interested in internal audit's role as a control, the importance of internal audit as a source of substantive evidence will be less. However internal audit procedures may be a source of substantive evidence in particular areas, for example comparing supplier statements with the payables ledger. If the client has several sites, internal audit may have visited sites that external auditors will not have the chance to visit, and external audit may be able to place some reliance on the work done by internal audit on those sites.

4.1.3 Timing of liaison and co-ordination

All timing of internal audit work should be agreed as early as possible, and in particular how it co-ordinates with the external auditors' work. Liaison with the internal auditors should take place at regular intervals throughout the audit. Information on tests and conclusions should be passed both to and from internal auditors.

4.1.4 Evaluating specific work of the internal auditors

The ISA states 'in order for the external auditor to use specific work of the internal auditors, the external auditor shall evaluate and perform audit procedures on that work to determine its adequacy for the external auditor's purpose'.

The evaluation here will consider the scope of work and related audit programmes and whether the original assessment of the internal audit function remains appropriate.

Evaluation	
Training and proficiency	Have the internal auditors had sufficient and adequate technical training to carry out the work? Are the internal auditors proficient?
Supervision	Is the work properly supervised, reviewed and documented?
Evidence	Has sufficient, appropriate audit evidence been obtained by the internal auditors to reach a conclusion?
Conclusions	Are the conclusions reached appropriate, given the circumstances?
Reports	Are any reports produced by internal audit consistent with the result of the work performed?
Unusual matters	Have any unusual matters or exceptions arising and disclosed by internal audit been resolved properly?

The nature, timing and extent of the testing of the specific work of internal auditing will depend upon the external auditor's judgement of the risk and materiality of the area concerned, the preliminary assessment of internal auditing and the evaluation of specific work by internal auditing. Such tests may include examination of items already examined by internal auditors, examination of other similar items and observation of internal auditing procedures.

If the external auditors decide that the internal audit work is not adequate, they should extend their own procedures in order to obtain appropriate evidence.

Interactive question 7: Extensions plc [Difficulty level: Exam standard]

Extensions plc is a retailer of fashion accessories. It has a turnover of £54 million and 150 shops throughout the United Kingdom. It also has six regional warehouses from which the shops are supplied with goods.

The company has an internal audit department which is based at the company's head office in London. Internal auditors make regular visits to the shops and warehouses.

This is the first year that your firm has acted as auditor for Extensions plc. The partner in charge of the audit has expressed his opinion that the internal audit department might be able to assist the external audit team in carrying out its work.

Requirements

(a) State, with reasons, the information that you would require to make an assessment of the likely effectiveness and the relevance of the internal audit function.

(b) Describe four typical procedures that might be carried out by the internal auditors during their visits to the shops and warehouses, and on which you might wish to rely.

(c) Assuming that you intend to rely on the work of the internal audit department of Extensions plc, describe briefly the effect this will have on your audit of the company's financial statements.

See **Answer** at the end of this chapter.

4.2 Using the work of an expert

Definition

An **expert** is a person or firm possessing special skill, knowledge and experience in a particular field other than accounting and auditing.

Professional audit staff are highly trained and educated, but their experience and training is limited to accountancy and audit matters. In certain situations it will therefore be necessary to employ someone else with different expert knowledge.

Auditors have **sole responsibility** for their opinion, but may use the work of an expert. An expert may be engaged by:

- A client (management's expert) to provide **specialist advice** on a particular matter which affects the financial statements
- The auditors (auditor's expert) in order to obtain **sufficient audit evidence** regarding certain financial statement assertions

ISA 620 *Using the Work of an Auditor's Expert* defines an auditor's expert as someone who has expertise in a field other than accounting or auditing including expertise in such matters as:

- **Valuations of complex financial instruments and certain types of assets**, eg land and buildings, plant and machinery
- **Actuarial calculations of insurance or employee benefit liabilities**

- **Estimation of oil and gas reserves**
- **Valuation of environmental liabilities**
- **Interpretations of contracts, laws and regulations**
- **Analysis of complex or unusual tax compliance issues**

The ISA states that the auditor 'has sole responsibility for the audit opinion expressed, and that responsibility is not reduced by the auditor's use of the work of an auditor's expert'.

4.2.1 Determining the need to use the work of an expert

Considerations when deciding whether to use an auditor's expert may include:

- Whether management has used a management's expert in preparing the financial statements
- The nature and significance of the matter, including its complexity
- The risks of material misstatement in the matter
- The expected nature of procedures to respond to identified risks, including: the auditor's knowledge of and experience with the work of experts in relation to such matters; and
- The availability of alternative sources of audit evidence

When management has used a management's expert in preparing the financial statements, the auditor's decision on whether to use an auditor's expert may also be influenced by such factors as:

- The nature, scope and objectives of the management's expert's work
- Whether the management's expert is employed by the entity, or is a party engaged by it to provide relevant services
- The extent to which management can exercise control or influence over the work of the management's expert
- The management's expert's competence and capabilities
- Whether the management's expert is subject to technical performance standards or other professional or industry requirements
- Any controls within the entity over the management's expert's work

4.2.2 Competence, capabilities and objectivity of the auditor's expert

Experts used by the auditor must have the necessary competence (nature and level of expertise) capabilities (the time, resources and physical ability to exercise that competence) and objectivity (lack of bias, conflict of interest or the influence of others) for the auditor's purposes. In the case of external experts, the auditor must consider whether any interests or relationships are a potential threat to that expert's objectivity.

Information regarding the above qualities may come from a variety of sources, including:

- Personal experience with previous work of that expert
- Discussions with that expert
- Discussions with other auditors or others who are familiar with that expert's work
- Knowledge of that expert's qualifications, membership of a professional body or industry association, license to practice, or other forms of external recognition
- Published papers or books written by that expert
- The auditor's firm's quality control policies and procedures

The auditor will take into account whether the expert's work is subject to technical performance standards, other professional or industry requirements, ethical standards and other standards of professional bodies, or legislative requirements.

4.2.3 Agreement with the auditor's expert

The nature, scope and objectives of the auditor's expert's work will vary from one assignment to another and these must therefore be agreed between the auditor and the expert, whether the expert is internal or external.

The following circumstances indicate the need for the agreement to be in writing:

- The auditor's expert will have access to sensitive or confidential entity information
- The respective roles or responsibilities of the auditor and the auditor's expert are different from those normally expected
- Multi-jurisdictional legal or regulatory requirements apply
- The matter to which the auditor's expert's work relates is highly complex
- The auditor has not previously used work performed by that expert
- The greater the extent of the auditor's expert's work, and its significance in the context of the audit

The agreement between the auditor and the auditor's external expert may take the form of an engagement letter (as you have seen in your Assurance studies) although this is not the only form that the agreement may take. Where an engagement letter is used ISA 620 recommends that the following are included:

- Nature, scope and objectives of the auditor's external expert's work
- The respective roles and responsibilities of the auditor and the auditor's external expert
- Communications and reporting
- Confidentiality

4.2.4 Evaluating the adequacy of the auditor's expert's work

Auditors should assess whether the work of the expert is adequate for the auditor's purposes. In order to evaluate the adequacy the auditor may carry specific procedures such as:

- Inquiries of the auditor's expert
- Reviewing the auditor's expert's working papers and reports
- Corroborative procedures such as observing the expert's work and confirmation with third parties
- Discussion with another expert with relevant expertise
- Discussing the auditor's expert's report with management

Worked example: Valuation of a commercial building

An expert valuation of a commercial building could be compared to the value of other, similar commercial buildings in estate agent's windows or on the web.

The auditors do **not** have the expertise to judge the assumptions and methods used; these are the responsibility of the expert. However, the auditors should seek to obtain an understanding of these assumptions etc, to consider their reasonableness based on other audit evidence, knowledge of the business and so on.

This may involve discussion with both the client and the expert. Additional procedures (including use of another expert) may be necessary.

4.3 Other auditors (in a group situation)

When an audit firm audits a company that is a parent in a group of companies, they will be responsible for carrying out the audit on that parent company's individual financial statements and also the audit on that parent's group financial statements.

In respect of the group financial statements, the audit firm may or may not be the auditor for other companies in that group whose financial statements are consolidated into the group financial statements.

ISA 600 *Special Considerations – Audits of Group Financial Statements (Including the Work of Component Auditors)* provides guidance to the auditor of a group where one or more of the components of that group are audited by other auditors.

Definitions

Component is an entity whose financial information is included in the group financial statements.

Component auditors are auditors who perform work on financial information related to a component of the group audit.

Group engagement team are the auditors with responsibility for performing work on the consolidation process, communicating with component auditors and reporting on the group financial statements.

4.3.1 Responsibility

The group engagement partner is responsible for the audit opinion for the group, and for conducting the audit in accordance with legal and regulatory requirements. The auditor's report on the group financial statements should not therefore contain a reference to component auditors unless such a reference is required by law.

4.3.2 Understanding the Component Auditor

If a group engagement team is planning to request work on the financial information of a component from a component auditor, the team shall obtain an understanding of the following:

- Whether the component auditor understands and will comply with **ethical requirements** and can demonstrate **independence.**
- The component auditor's **professional competence.**
- Whether the group engagement team will be able to be involved in the work of the component auditor to the extent necessary to obtain **sufficient appropriate audit evidence.**
- Whether the component auditor operates in a regulatory environment that actively oversees auditors.

If a component auditor does not meet the independence requirements that are relevant to the group audit the group engagement team will need to obtain sufficient appropriate audit evidence relating to the financial information of the component without using the audit work of the component auditor.

4.3.3 Responding to Assessed Risks

ISA 600 states that 'the auditor is required to design and implement appropriate responses to address the assessed risks of material misstatement in the financial statements.' It is up to the group engagement team to determine the nature of the work to be done and whether it should be done by the group engagement team or by component auditors.

Where reliance is to be placed on the effective operation of group-wide controls at component level, these controls shall be tested, by either the group engagement team or by the component auditor.

4.3.4 Communication with the Component Auditor

The group engagement team will need to communicate its requirements, such as work to be performed, to the component auditor. Communication includes the following:

- Detail of the work to be performed and the use to be made of that work.
- The form and content of communication from the component auditor to the group engagement team
- Request for confirmation that the component auditor will cooperate with the group engagement team
- Ethical and independence requirements
- Materiality levels for the financial information of the component.

- Significant risks of fraud and error relating to the group that are relevant to the component auditor.
- A list of related parties and a request that the component auditor advises the group engagement team of any other related parties not on the list

The group engagement team will require the component auditor to communicate to them matters relevant to the conclusion on the group audit, including:

- Confirmation that the component auditor has complied with ethical, independence, and professional competence requirements
- Confirmation that the component auditor has complied with the group engagement team's requirements
- Financial information of the component audited by the component auditor
- Information on instances of non-compliance with laws or regulations
- A list of uncorrected misstatements
- Indicators of possible management bias
- Significant deficiencies in component internal control
- Significant matters communicated to those charged with governance including suspected fraud
- Any other matters relevant to the group audit
- Overall findings, conclusions or opinions

4.3.5 Evaluating the Sufficiency and Appropriateness of Audit Evidence Obtained

The group engagement team is responsible for evaluating communication from the component auditor and discussing any significant matters arising. On the basis of this the group engagement team will decide whether other documentation of the component auditor will need to be reviewed.

Where the work of the component auditor is deemed to be insufficient, the group engagement team will determine what additional procedures need to be performed, and by whom.

The group engagement team needs to ensure that sufficient appropriate audit evidence has been obtained by both its own procedures and those of the component auditor.

Where is has not been possible to obtain sufficient appropriate audit evidence the group engagement partner needs to evaluate the effect on the group audit opinion.

Interactive question 8: Using the work of other auditors

[Difficulty level: Exam standard]

You are the group auditor of Golden Holdings plc, a listed company, which has components in the UK and overseas, many of which are audited by other firms. All components are involved in the manufacture or distribution of metal goods and have the same accounting period as Golden Holdings plc.

Outline why you would wish to review the work of the auditors of components not audited by your firm and detail the work you would carry out in that review.

5 Audit of accounting estimates

Section overview

- Financial statements contain many estimates
- These estimates are often made when there are uncertainties about the outcome of events and involve the use of judgement
- As a result the risk of material misstatements is higher where estimates are involved

5.1 The nature of estimates

Right from the start of your accounting studies you will be aware of some of the main types of estimates. Examples include:

- Allowances for receivables
- Allowances to reduce inventories to net realisable value
- Useful lives for depreciation of non-current assets
- Warranty provisions
- Provisions for losses on lawsuits

The risk of misstatement in these areas is obvious. If management intended to overstate profits, for example, they are much more likely to attempt to reduce the amount of the allowance for receivables than, say, to omit the last week's worth of supplier invoices received in the financial year.

5.2 The audit approach

ISA 540 *Auditing Accounting Estimates, Including Fair Value Accounting Estimates and Related Disclosures* emphasises the basic requirement to obtain **sufficient appropriate audit evidence.** The standard goes on to require the auditor to obtain an understanding of the following:

- Financial reporting framework applicable to accounting estimates
- How management identifies transactions, events and conditions that give rise to accounting estimates
- How management makes the accounting estimates and on what data they are based. This includes consideration of
  - Method used in making the accounting estimate
  - Relevant controls
  - Whether management has used an expert
  - The assumptions underlying the accounting estimates
  - Whether there has been or ought to have been a change from the prior period in the methods and, if so, why; and
  - Whether and, if so, how management has assessed the effect of estimation uncertainty

5.3 Evaluation of results

The auditor must assess the reasonableness of estimates in the light of:

- The auditor's understanding of the entity and its environment
- Whether the estimates are consistent with other evidence obtained during the audit

Interactive question 9: Estimated allowances [Difficulty level: standard]

Explain how the auditor would approach the audit of an allowance for receivables.

6 Practical issues

Section overview

- The audit strategy will also address practical issues such as audit timing, staffing and location.

6.1 The audit team

As part of the audit planning process, the right team will need to be selected:

This will depend on matching the need for:

- Experience
- Specialist knowledge
- Ensuring that work is done at the right level

with the risks associated with the audit.

As discussed in Chapter 5, for every engagement there will be an engagement partner who takes overall responsibility for the engagement and who has specific responsibility for ensuring the firm and the team's:

- Competence
- Objectivity

and for:

- Approving the audit strategy
- Communicating his or her knowledge of the client to the audit team
- Ensuring that staff are briefed and supervised appropriately
- Ensuring appropriate reviews are carried out of staff's work
- Reviewing the financial statements, the key areas and any working papers not otherwise reviewed.

There should normally be at least one other person involved on the audit to review the work done.

Beyond this the precise make-up of the team will depend on the scale of the engagement and the different roles can be filled by people with different levels of experience within the firm.

However, most engagements will have a 'senior' or 'in charge' responsible for the day-to-day running of the audit and supervising assistants.

There may well be a 'manager' or 'supervisor' who has more responsibilities for the administration, planning and review of the engagement and would be expected to do less of the detailed testing work than the senior.

Finally there are the assistants who, depending on their experience will take on the execution of the more detailed audit tasks.

The audit strategy should make clear who is responsible for which aspects of the audit, and should strike the difficult balance between:

- Ensuring each member of the team has sufficient experience for the job in hand
- Setting new challenges so that experience can be gained, and
- Cost

6.2 Budgets and deadlines

Audit firms, like any business, are in business to make a profit. Whilst the pursuit of profit must not take precedence over professional and quality considerations, nevertheless the audit plan should make it perfectly clear:

- When the deadline is
- How much the budget is

6.3 Interim and final audits

Typically much of the systems assessment work and tests of details on the profit and loss account, will be carried out at the interim stage, with greater focus on the balance sheet at a final audit.

However, think about a number of factors here:

- What about the income statement for the last couple of months of the year?
- If the auditors are relying on controls, were they effective in the period between the interim audit and the year end?
- If the auditors have tested inventory, or receivables at the interim stage, are they happy with the 'roll forward' to the year end?

6.4 Location

As hinted at above, the location that the audit work takes place at will depend on the nature of the client and the risk assessment. Some clients will only have one location, in which case the audit will take place at that location. Other clients may have several locations, and the auditors will have to make judgements about which locations are more risky than others and need the auditor to visit them. It may be necessary to attend all locations that a client has at some stage during the audit.

6.5 Nature of evidence

It will be important to address the practical issue of what sources of evidence the audit firm expects to obtain during the audit. You learnt about the quality of audit evidence in your Assurance Study Manual. Information generated by the client is never as good quality as information generated by the auditor or from third parties. The audit strategy should set out where information should be sought from third parties (such as in respect of receivables or confirmation of a loan).

Summary and Self-test

Summary

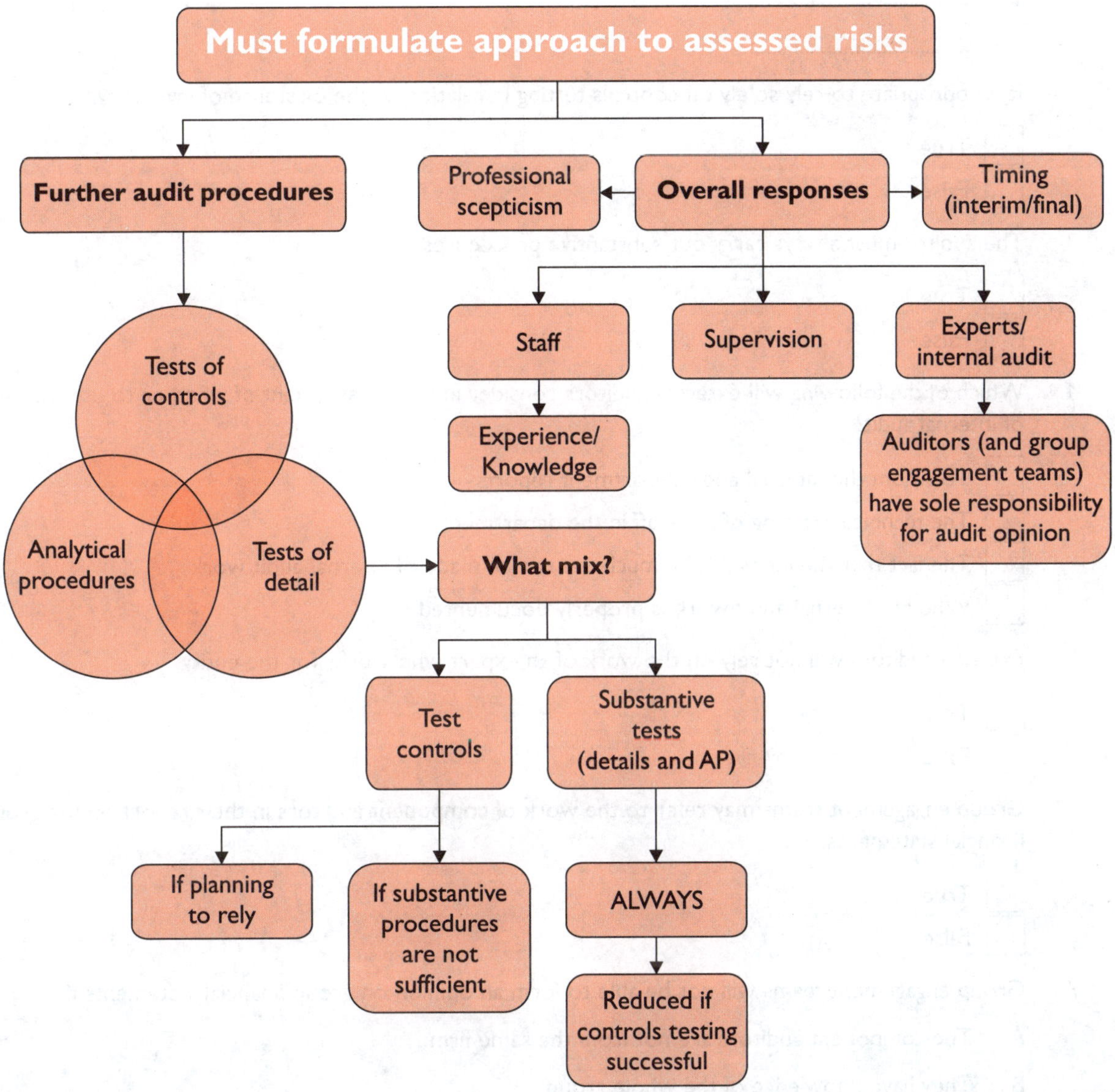

Must formulate approach to assessed risks
Further audit procedures
Professional scepticism
Overall responses
Timing (interim/final)
Tests of controls
Analytical procedures
Tests of detail
Staff
Supervision
Experts/ internal audit
Experience/ Knowledge
Auditors (and group engagement teams) have sole responsibility for audit opinion
What mix?
Test controls
Substantive tests (details and AP)
If planning to rely
If substantive procedures are not sufficient
ALWAYS
Reduced if controls testing successful

Self-test

Answer the following questions.

1 The three sources of audit confidence are:

1 ....

2 ....

3 ....

2 It is appropriate to rely solely on controls testing in relation to the existence of inventory.

☐ True

☐ False

3 The auditor must always carry out substantive procedures.

☐ True

☐ False

4 Which of the following will external auditors consider in their assessment of whether to use the work of internal audit?

☐ To whom the internal audit department reports

☐ The technical training of the staff in the department

☐ The fact that the fee will fall if much use can be made of internal audit work

☐ Whether internal audit work is properly documented

5 External auditors will not rely on the work of an expert who works for the entity.

☐ True

☐ False

6 Group engagement teams may refer to the work of component auditors in their report on the group financial statements.

☐ True

☐ False

7 Group engagement teams will not be able to form an opinion on group financial statements if:

A The component auditors are not from the same firm

B They have knowledge of the whole group

C The component auditors do not carry out all the procedures as specified by the group engagement team

D The portion of the financial statements they do not audit is material

8 The minimum ideal number of staff used in an audit is:

A 1
B 2
C 3
D 4

Exam-style question

9 Gasoleum Ltd

Your firm is the auditor of Gasoleum Ltd which operates 15 petrol stations in and around London. You are the senior in charge of the audit for the year ending 31 July 20X7 and are engaged on the audit planning.

Most of the company's sites are long-established and, as well as supplying fuel, oil, air and water, have a car wash and a shop.

Over the last few years, due to the intense price competition in petrol retailing, the shops have been expanded into mini-markets with a wide range of motor accessories, food, drinks and household products. They also now sell National Lottery tickets.

Point-of-sale PCs are installed in all the petrol stations, linked on-line via a network to the computer at head office. Sales and inventory data are input direct from the PCs.

The company has an internal auditor, whose principal function is to monitor continuously and test the operation of internal controls throughout the organisation. The internal auditor is also responsible for co-ordinating the year end inventory count.

Requirements

Prepare notes for a planning meeting with the audit partner which

(a) Identify, from the situation outlined above, circumstances particular to Gasoleum Ltd that should be taken into account when planning the audit, explaining clearly why these matters should be taken into account. **(6 marks)**

(b) Describe the extent to which the work performed by the internal auditor may affect your planning, and the factors that could limit the use you may wish to make of his work. **(6 marks)**

(12 marks)

Now, go back to the Learning Objectives in the Introduction. If you are satisfied that you have achieved these objectives, please tick them off.

Technical reference

1 Responding to the risk assessment

• Overall responses	ISA 330
• Responses to risks of material misstatement at the assertion level	ISA 330

2 Reliance on controls

ISA 330

3 Substantive approach

ISA 330

4 Reliance on the work of others

ISA 230
ISA 501
ISA 505
ISA 540

• Internal audit	ISA 610
• Experts	ISA 620
• Other auditors	ISA 600

5 Audit of accounting estimates

ISA 540

Answers to Interactive questions

Answer to Interactive question 1

The factors are:

- The approach that has been taken in previous years
- Whether a substantive approach would be more effective
- The results of walk-through tests on the systems (that is, do the systems operate as the auditor has been lead to believe, if so, it may be possible to rely on internal controls)
- The results of preliminary evaluations of the effectiveness of the controls
- Improvements made to the system of control (perhaps as a result of a management letter in prior years)

Answer to Interactive question 2

The conditions are as follows:

- Whether the controls have operated throughout the year
- Whether the control has been evidenced and tested
- Whether reliance on the control assists audit objectives, that is, whether it is relevant to the validity of a financial statement assertion, such as that sales are complete
- Whether it is cost-effective to test controls
- Whether the results of tests of controls are satisfactory

Answer to Interactive question 3

(a) **Supervisor's assumptions**

Objectives and limitations

Due to inherent limitations (including human error/misunderstanding, collusion and override), an internal control system can only provide reasonable confidence that internal control objectives (including completeness, accuracy and validity) are met.

(i) **Completeness**

To ensure that all workers who should be paid are included on the payroll

– Payroll expense could be reconciled to production output records, and

– Management could review exception reports of employees having personnel records but not included on the payroll.

However,

Cost/benefit

The expense of setting up computerised personnel records may outweigh the benefit to the company. (Risk is of over payment as employees entitled to pay are likely to bring non-payment to management's attention promptly!)

Changes in conditions

A reduction in the ratio of production to support staff may limit the usefulness of production output records as a basis of comparison.

(ii) **Accuracy**

To prevent errors in payroll deductions

- Calculations of PAYE, NICs etc can be checked prior to processing, and
- Non-statutory deductions (eg pension contributions, union subscriptions) should require prior authorisation in writing.

However,

Human error/misunderstanding

Errors in deductions may not be detected, due to fatigue, distraction, misjudgement or misinterpretation.

Non-routine transactions

Systematic checking procedures may be directed at routine deductions (eg PAYE) rather than non-routine transactions (eg give as you earn, maintenance payments).

(iii) **Validity**

To ensure that employees are only paid for work done

- Hours worked per time sheets (or clock cards) can be approved by a departmental manager (or supervisor), and
- The duties of payroll preparation and payment should be segregated.

However,

Abuse or override

Authorisation could be given for a new employee to be added to the payroll without the proper checks being carried out by the authoriser.

Collusion

The person responsible for paying wages could collude with the person responsible for accounting for wages to perpetrate and conceal a theft of wages.

(b) **Internal control terminology**

(i) **Segregation of duties**

Meaning

Segregation of duties is a factor reflected in the control environment (the overall attitude, awareness and actions of management regarding internal controls in the entity).

If one person has responsibility for the recording and processing of a complete transaction, he may also have the power to falsify the records or to misappropriate money or assets without being discovered.

Separation of these responsibilities will reduce the risk of intentional or unintentional errors occurring.

The functions that should normally be separated include authorisation, execution, custody and recording.

Examples

- Calculations of PAYE and NIC deductions should be reviewed and authorised by the payroll supervisor who is not actually involved in performing the calculations.
- Unclaimed wages should be kept by someone (eg the cashier) other than the person responsible for recording payroll entries, otherwise there could be a temptation to falsify the figures and pocket some of the wages.

(ii) **Approval and control of documents**

Meaning

Approval and control of documents is a specific control procedure (aimed at preventing or detecting and correcting errors).

Approval is concerned with ensuring that transactions are properly authorised prior to execution.

Control of documents is aimed at ensuring that all, and only valid transactions, are promptly recorded.

Examples

– Overtime pay should be approved by a manager or director prior to payroll preparation, to ensure that employees are paid at authorised rates.

– Clock cards should be batched and control totals established (eg number of cards, total hours worked, hash total of employee number) prior to submission to payroll department, to prevent (or detect for early investigation) any omissions (or unauthorised insertions).

– The numerical sequence of forms for new joiners should be checked periodically to detect omissions (or unauthorised insertions).

Answer to Interactive question 4

Full substantive testing will be used when:

- The auditors' initial assessment is that controls are not strong
- There is a lack of evidence that controls are in operation
- The controls are tested and results show that the controls are not strong
- It is not cost-effective to test controls

Answer to Interactive question 5

(a)

Analytical procedures	Possible reasons for change
• Analyse revenue per product type by month.	A difference in the rate of increase would indicate a switch from one product to the other. Seasonal variations are expected as Glowvine is largely a winter product and Eau Vital a summer product.
• Analyse gross profit per product type by month.	GP margin has increased from 55.5% to 59.1%. The higher margin indicates a move from Glowvine to Eau Vital (possibly due to a mild winter in 20X5/X6).
• Analyse cost of goods sold per product type by month.	Cost of goods sold only increased by 60.6%, while revenue increased by almost 75%. Again, a possible reason could be the switch from one product to the other. It does seem a disproportionately small increase, especially as royalties are included in cost of goods sold and remain constant per bottle sold, regardless of product. However, recycling of glass bottle returns could account for the slower rate of increase.

Analytical procedures	Possible reasons for change
• Analyse distribution and administrative costs into:	These have increased by 153%, contributing to the fall in net profit margin from 43% to 41%. The increase in these costs could have been caused by:
– Administrative cost (especially deposit scheme)	• Implementation of the deposit scheme (unlikely to account for the whole increase as not operational for the whole year)
– Advertising costs	• Increased advertising costs to promote the deposit scheme and "environment friendly" nature of the products (this could also have contributed to the increase in revenue)
– Transport costs	• Increased transport costs in proportion to the 75% increase in revenue
– Labour costs	• Increased labour costs, again in proportion to the rise in revenue
• Analysis of nature, valuation and consistency of treatment of closing inventories. Compare with inventories held at end of previous years. The disproportionately smaller increase in cost of goods sold could be caused by an error in the counting or valuation of closing inventories, causing them to be overstated and thus cost of goods sold reduced.	The disproportionately smaller increase in cost of goods sold could be caused by an error in the counting or valuation of closing inventories, causing them to be overstated and thus cost of goods sold reduced.

(b) **Impact of deposit scheme on audit of liabilities**

Liabilities at the 20X6 year end will have increased, as this is the first year in which the scheme has been implemented. This should be evident in analytical procedures on sundry payables.

The amount may be material as the number of bottles sold and not returned per annum could be high.

It is necessary to ascertain and evaluate the client's procedure for recording

(i) The number of bottles (or cases) sold
(ii) The number of bottles returned
(iii) The number outstanding.

As this is the first year of the scheme there will be no opening liability to provide added assurance.

Consideration should be given to the length of time the client intends to keep the provision in place. It may be that, each year, the previous year's provision can be written back.

Because of the uncertainty in calculating the liability required and the fact that the final figure may rest on an estimate of the number of bottles likely to be returned, the auditor's main concern will be that liabilities are not understated.

The auditor therefore needs to be satisfied that returns are recorded with reasonable accuracy.

Records of returns will be received from retailers (mainly supermarkets and off-licences) and the auditor will need to be satisfied that the client can reasonably rely on these records. Since the retailers will be requesting a refund of money paid by them with the returns, there is a risk that the number of returns may be overstated.

In summary, the principal impact on the audit of liabilities will be

(i) An additional year end liability in 20X6
(ii) Uncertainty in the calculation of the liability, and therefore
(iii) The risk that this liability may be understated.

Answer to Interactive question 6

- The objectivity of the department, including its freedom from conflicting responsibilities and the level of management it reports to. In this case, you know that Mr Gnome reports directly to the board of directors, so the department has an important status in the company. You would also consider whether there is any limitation on the assignments carried out, and to what extent recommendations are acted upon by management.
- The technical competence of the people carrying out the work. In this case it would be necessary to inquire about the competence of Mr Gnome; for example, is he a qualified accountant? It would also be necessary to identify the other members of the internal audit team (if there are any) and assess their competence as well.
- The application of due professional care. The external auditors should review the work carried out by the internal auditors to check that it was documented in the first place, and to assess whether it was planned and whether there is evidence of its being supervised and reviewed.
- Communication with external audit. You would need to enquire what arrangements have been put in place to enable internal audit to communicate freely and effectively with external audit.

Answer to Interactive question 7

(a)

Information	Reasons
• The organisational status and reporting responsibilities of the internal auditor and any constraints and restrictions thereon.	• The degree of objectivity is increased when internal audit – Is free to plan and carry out its work and communicate fully with the external auditor – Has access to the highest level of management
• Areas of responsibility assigned by management to internal audit, such as review of – Accounting systems and internal controls – Implementation of corporate plans	• Not all areas in which internal audit may operate will be relevant to the external auditor. (Relevant) (Not relevant)
• Routine tasks carried out by internal audit staff such as authorisation of petty cash reimbursements.	• In these respects staff are not functioning as internal audit (simply as an internal control).
• Internal auditor's formal terms of reference.	• Internal auditor's role will be most relevant where it – Has a bearing on the financial statements – Involves a specialisation
• Internal audit documentation such as an audit manual and audit plans.	• It is more likely that due professional care is being exercised where the work of internal audit is properly planned, controlled, recorded and reviewed.
• Professional membership and practical experience (including computer auditing skills) of internal audit staff.	• Unless internal audit is technically competent it is inappropriate to place reliance on it.
• Internal audit reports generated and feedback thereon.	• How the company responds to internal audit findings may be regarded as a measure of the department's effectiveness.

Information	Reasons
• Number of staff, computer facilities and any other resources available to internal audit.	• The effectiveness of internal audit (and hence the reliance placed thereon) will be limited if the department is under-resourced.

(b) Typical procedures (**four** only)

(i) **Inspection of tangible non-current assets**

Assets seen at the warehouses (eg delivery vehicle fleet) should be noted and subsequently agreed to the fixed asset register maintained at head office (HO). Assets recorded in the register (eg shop fixtures and fittings) should be selected for inspection prior to visits to ensure their existence.

(ii) **Attendance at inventory counts**

Periodic counts (eg monthly) should be attended

– On a rotational basis
– At warehouses and larger shops

to ensure adherence to the company's procedures. Test counts should be made to confirm the accuracy and completeness of the inventory counts.

(iii) **Cash**

Cash counts should be carried out on cash register takings (and petty cash floats) whenever shops (and warehouses) are visited on a 'surprise' basis.

(iv) **Goods despatch**

Internal control procedures should be observed to be in operation, for example, to ensure that all despatches are documented and destined for the company's retail outlets.

(v) **Employee verification**

Payroll procedures are likely to be carried out at HO, warehouses and shops informing HO on a weekly basis of hours worked by employees, illness and holiday etc. However, new employees, especially in the shops (and probably also in the warehouses) will be recruited locally and their details notified to HO.

Internal audit will be able to select a sample of employees from HO records and ensure on their visits to shops and warehouses that these represent *bona fide* employees.

(c) **Effect on audit**

(i) **Systems documentation**

The accuracy of systems documentation which has been prepared by internal audit need only be confirmed using 'walk-through tests'. This saves time (if the systems documentation is correct) since only copies will be required for the audit file.

(ii) **Tests of controls**

The level of independent testing (ie by the external auditor) can be reduced where controls have been satisfactorily tested by internal audit, especially if error rates are found to be similar. In particular, attendance at stocktaking at the year end may be limited to those locations with the highest stockholdings.

(iii) **Substantive procedures**

Internal audit's evidence (eg concerning the existence of tangible non-current assets) will reduce sample sizes for year end verification work. Substantive procedures may also be reduced where the internal audit checks reconciliations (eg of suppliers' statements to ledger balances, receivables and payables control accounts and bank reconciliations).

Answer to Interactive question 8

Reasons for reviewing the work of other auditors

The main consideration which concerns the audit of all group accounts is that the parent company's auditors are responsible to the members of that company for the audit opinion on the whole of the group financial statements.

It may be stated (in the notes to the financial statements) that the financial statements of certain components have been audited by other firms, but this does not absolve the parent company auditors from any of their responsibilities.

The auditors of a parent company have to report to its members on the truth and fairness of the view given by the financial statements of the company and its components dealt with in the group financial statements. The auditors should have powers to obtain such information and explanations as they reasonably require from the components and their auditors, or from the parent company in the case of overseas components, in order that they can discharge their responsibilities as parent company auditors.

The auditing standard ISA 600 clarifies how the group engagement team can carry out a review of the audits of components in order to satisfy themselves that, with the inclusion of figures not audited by themselves, the group financial statements give a true and fair view.

The scope, standard and independence of the work carried out by the auditors of components (the component auditors) are the most important matters which need to be examined by the group engagement team before relying on financial statements not audited by them. The group engagement team need to be satisfied that all material areas of the financial statements of components have been audited satisfactorily and in a manner compatible with that of the group engagement team's requirements. .

Work to be carried out by group engagement team in reviewing the component auditors' work

(i) Before commencing the audit the group engagement team needs to provide instructions to the component auditor in the form of an engagement letter which should include the following matters relating to planning the audit work:

- Confirmation that the component auditor will cooperate with the group engagement team
- Timetable for completing the audit
- Dates of planned visits
- Key contacts
- Work to be performed by the component auditor
- Ethical requirements
- Component materiality levelsDetails of related parties
- Work to be performed on intra-group transactions
- Guidance on statutory reporting responsibilities
- Specific instructions for a subsequent events review where required

(ii) Carry out a detailed review of the component auditors' working papers on each component whose results materially affect the view given by the group financial statements. This review will enable the group engagement team to ascertain whether (*inter alia*):

- An up-to-date permanent file exists with details of the nature of the component's business, its staff organisation, its accounting records, previous year's financial statements and copies of important legal documents.
- The systems examination has been properly completed, documented and reported on to management after discussion.
- Tests of controls and substantive procedures have been properly and appropriately carried out, and audit programmes properly completed and signed.
- All other working papers are comprehensive and explicit.
- The overall review of the financial statements has been adequately carried out, and adequate use of analytical procedures has been undertaken throughout the audit.

CHAPTER 10

- The financial statements agree in all respects with the accounting records and comply with all relevant legal requirements and accounting standards.
- Minutes of board and general meetings have been scrutinised and important matters noted.
- The audit work has been carried out in accordance with approved auditing standards.
- The financial statements agree in all respects with the accounting records and comply with all relevant legal and professional requirements.
- The audit work has been properly reviewed within the firm of auditors and any laid-down quality control procedures adhered to.
- Any points requiring discussion with the parent company's management have been noted and brought to the group engagement team's' attention (including any matters which might warrant a qualification in the audit report on the component company's financial statements).
- Adequate audit evidence has been obtained to form a basis for the audit opinion on both the components' financial statements and those of the group.

If the group engagement team are not satisfied as a result of the above review, they should arrange for further audit work to be carried out either by the component auditors on their behalf, or jointly with them. The component auditors are fully responsible for their own work; any additional tests are those required for the purpose of the audit of the group financial statements.

Answer to Interactive question 9

Audit approach

- Review the requirements of the appropriate financial reporting framework for allowances for receivables
- Discuss with management how the allowance has been calculated
- Obtain a breakdown of the allowance, agree balances to the receivables ledger and reperform calculations
- Compare actual receivables written off in prior periods with previous estimates.
- Ascertain who is responsible for reviewing and approving the allowance.
- Obtain an aged listing of receivables as at the reporting date and identify overdue amounts and review correspondence relating to these accounts and arrive at an independent estimate of the allowance required.
- Compare this with management's estimate
- Review cash received from customers after the reporting date up to the date of the auditor's report to identify whether any receivables balances that appeared to be doubtful have subsequently been settled.

Answers to Self-test

1 1 Tests of controls
  2 Analytical procedures
  3 Tests of details

2 False

3 True

4 To whom they report

Their technical training

Whether internal audit work is properly documented

5 False

6 False

7 C

8 B (one to carry out the work and another to review it)

Exam-style question

9 **Notes for a planning meeting**

(a)

Circumstance	Why taken into account
• Multiple business locations.	• Increases inherent risk (eg if the organisational structure is loose and difficult to manage).
• Intense price competition.	• May lead to uneconomic price discounting, possibly threatening viability of business.
• Recent expansion of outlets into minimarkets.	• Increases complexity of business and may lead to loss of management control.
• Perishable nature and limited shelf-life of food and drinks inventories.	• Increase risk of overstatement of inventory values.
• Large volume of cash transactions.	• Increases risk of incomplete income recording.
• Nature of the business (garage environment).	• Increases risk of loss of inventories and cash due to theft or staff pilferage. • May limit effectiveness of physical security controls (eg over access to terminals).
• Recent introduction of sales of National Lottery tickets.	• Increases inherent risk (eg the risk of loss to Gasoleum Ltd if incorrect amounts are paid out on winning tickets).
• Direct input via PCs at branches.	• Increases risk of misstatement, as batch controls will not be feasible and scope for other input controls may be limited.
• Small number of staff at each location (eg one or two).	• Limits scope for segregation of duties within branches and therefore increases control risk.
• Branch-based nature of business.	• Limits effectiveness of management control over activities of individual branches thereby increasing control risk.
• Use of part-time staff and high staff turnover.	• May inhibit effectiveness of controls within branches.

(b) **Effect of work of internal auditor on audit planning**

(i) The internal auditor's identification and documentation of areas of weakness will give direction to areas requiring increased substantive procedures.

(ii) Work of the internal auditor may assist in selection of branches for audit visits, (eg where control failures have occurred).

(iii) The internal auditor may attend year end inventory counts at one or more branches, potentially reducing the number of branches to be visited by us.

(iv) Work performed by the internal auditor may provide evidence to confirm operation of control procedures, on which we may seek to rely to reduce the extent of our own procedures.

(v) Documentation of systems and controls by the internal auditor, including changes due to the National Lottery, may reduce extent of our planning visits, as walk-through checks may be sufficient to confirm systems documentation.

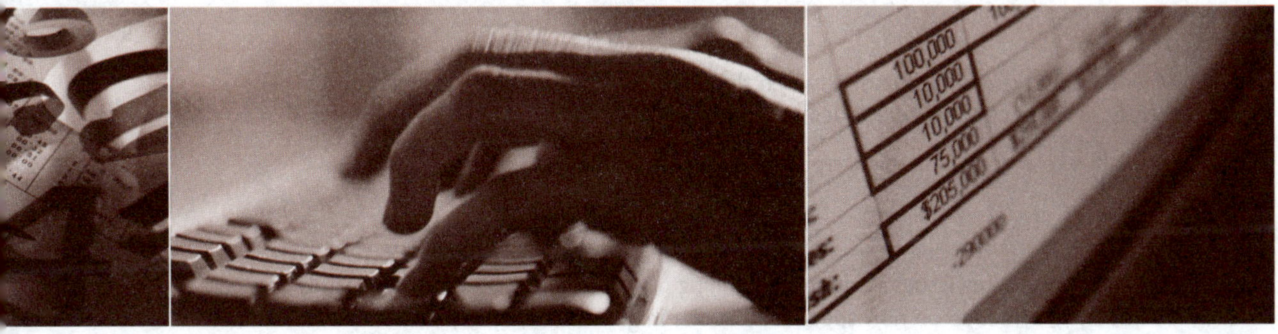

chapter 11

Audits of different types of entity

Introduction

Learning objective

Tick off

- To understand the differences between the audit of non-specialised entities and other entities, such as specialised entities or not-for-profit entities

Specific syllabus references for this chapter are: 3m, n, o.

Syllabus links

You have covered the key issues relating to planning non-specialised audits in this Study Manual. You covered obtaining evidence on non-specialised audits in greater detail in your Assurance studies.

Examination context

Complex auditing requirements relating to specialised entities are not examinable.

In the assessment, candidates may be required to:

- Discuss the differences between the audit of a non-specialised profit oriented entity and the audit of a given specialised profit oriented entity
- Discuss the differences between the audit of a non-specialised profit oriented entity and the audit of a given not-for-profit entity
- Specify and explain the steps necessary to plan, perform and conclude and report on the audit of the financial statements of a non-specialised profit oriented entity in accordance with the terms of the engagement including appropriate auditing standards

1 Non-specialised and specialised entities

Section overview

- The majority of audits relate to non-specialised profit orientated entities.
- The standard audit features outlined in this manual and the Assurance manual apply to this type of entity.
- Some entities are 'special' in some way, for example:
  - The entity is subject to extra regulations, such as banks or insurers, or charities (note that we shall look in particular at not-for-profit entities below)
  - The entity is subject to professional rules, such as solicitors
- Such entities may be subject to special auditing guidance, all of which is outside the scope of your syllabus.
- It is important to note that many of these entities require a 'normal' statutory audit as well as any additional requirements upon them.
- In which case, the auditors need to assess the particular risks associated with the specialised entities which will cause any differences in audit approach.

Many audits undertaken in the UK relate to non-specialised profit-making entities (that is a 'normal' company operating for profit. For example, a manufacturing company, a service company, a retail company). The audit procedures outlined in this Study Manual so far and in your Assurance manual all relate to this type of entity, and the majority of questions in your paper are likely to be set in this context. However, some entities are 'special' in some way, for example, they are subject to extra laws and regulations (for example, banks or insurers) or they are subject to particular professional rules, such as solicitors. Such entities may or may not require a statutory audit. As always the auditor must be aware of the particular risks associated with the entity in order to plan and conduct the audit. .

Specialised entities are often subject to particular requirements that pose additional factors for auditors. For example, under their professional rules, solicitors require a 'solicitors' accounts rules audit'. Some specialised entities are subject to special accounting and auditing guidance, which adds detail to the audit, in addition to the normal statutory audit that is being carried out. Such specialised guidance is beyond the scope of your syllabus. You should simply be aware that audits of such specialised entities will have special requirements in addition to normal audit requirements that makes auditing them more complex.

2 Not-for-profit entities

Section overview

- There are various types of organisations which do not exist for the purpose of maximising shareholder wealth, which may require an audit.
- The audit risks associated with not-for-profit organisations may well be different from other entities.
- Cash may be significant in small not-for-profit charities and controls are likely to be limited. Income may well be a risk area, particularly where money is donated or raised informally.
- Obtaining audit evidence may be a problem, particularly where small charities have informal arrangements and there might be limitations on the scope of the audit.
- In all not-for-profit audits it will be necessary to ensure accounting policies used are appropriate.
- The nature of the report will depend on statutory and entity requirements, but it should conform to ISA 700 criteria.
- The public sector comprises a large number of varied not-for-profit organisations, and also private companies which are profit oriented, running (outsourced) public services.

The key objective of most companies is to manage the shareholders' investments well. In a large majority of cases, 'manage the shareholders' investment' means 'create a profit', as this will create returns to the shareholders in the terms of dividends or growth in the capital value of the share. However, some companies and other entities do not operate for the purpose of making profit but have other objectives. Examples include charities and organisations in the public sector.

Many of these organisations are legislated for and the Acts which relate to them may specify how they are to report their results. Some of the organisations mentioned above may be companies (often companies limited by guarantee) and so are required to prepare financial statements and have them audited under companies legislation.

Where a statutory audit is required, the auditors will be required to produce the statutory audit opinion concerning the truth and fairness of financial statements.

Where a statutory audit is not required, it is possible that the organisation might have one anyway for the benefit of interested stakeholders, such as the public or people who give to a charity.

It is also possible that such entities will have special, additional requirements of an audit. These may be required by a Regulator, or by the constitution of the organisation. For example, a charity's constitution may require an audit of whether the charity is operating in accordance with its charitable purpose.

An audit of a not-for-profit organisation may vary from a 'for-profit audit' due to:

- Its objectives and the impact on operations and reporting
- The purpose an audit is required

When carrying out an audit of a not-for-profit organisation, it is vital that the auditor establishes:

- Whether a statutory audit is required
- If not, what the objectives of the engagement are
- What the engagement is to report on, and
- To whom the report should be addressed, and
- What form the report should take

2.1 Charities

Charities are regulated under the Charities Act 2006. This sets out what a charity is and outlines how they are regulated. The charities' regulator is the Charity Commission.

Definition

Charity: An institution which:

- Is established for charitable purposes **only** and
- Falls to be subject to the control of the High Court in the exercise of its jurisdiction with respect to charities

The Charities Act 2006 sets out twelve charitable purposes:

- Prevention or relief of poverty
- Advancement of one or more of the following:
  - Education
  - Religion
  - Health/saving lives
  - Citizenship/community development
  - Arts/culture/heritage/science
  - Amateur sport
  - Human rights/conflict resolution/promotion of religious or racial harmony/equality/diversity
  - Environmental protection/improvement
  - Animal welfare

- The relief of those in need by reason of youth, age, ill-health, disability, financial hardship or other disadvantage
- The promotion of the efficiency of the armed forces of the Crown, the police, fire and rescue or ambulance services

There is a Charities Statement of Recommended Practice (SORP) 2005 outlining what a charity's accounts should comprise. It suggests:

- A **statement of financial activities** (SOFA) that shows all resources made available to the charity and all expenditure incurred and reconciles all changes in its funds
- Where the charity is required to prepare accounts in accordance with the Companies Act, or similar legislation, or where the governing instrument so requires, a **summary income and expenditure account** (in addition to the SOFA) in certain circumstances
- A **balance sheet** that shows the assets, liabilities and funds of the charity. The balance sheet (or its notes) should also explain, in general terms, how the funds may, because of restrictions imposed by donors, be utilised
- A **cash flow statement**, where required by accounting standards
- **Notes**

The financial thresholds for determining whether charity accounts require auditing are fairly complex, but in general terms for years ending on or after 1 April 2009 unincorporated charities will need an audit if gross income is more than:

- £500,000 or
- £250,000 and total assets are more than £3.26m

All charities with a gross income of more than £25,000 are required to send a copy of their accounts to the Charity Commission.

Charities with a gross income of between £25,000 and £500,000 are required to have an independent verification of their financial statements. Where gross income is more than £250,000 the independent examination must be by a member of an approved professional organisation (for example a qualified accountant).

A charity's governing document may contain specific provisions about audit requirements. In such cases the charity must follow the higher standard of scrutiny required by either the statutory framework or governing document.

The verification process is a less onerous form of scrutiny than an audit and correspondingly gives a lower level of assurance. The examiner is not required to give an opinion as to whether the accounts show a true and fair view. Instead he must report whether or not any matter has come to his attention indicating that:

- Proper accounting records have not been kept
- The accounts do not comply with such records
- The accounts fail to comply with relevant Regulations

In addition, if such matters have become apparent, the report should include details of:

- Material expenditure or actions contrary to the trusts of the charity
- Failure to provide information or explanations to which the examiner is entitled
- Evidence that the accounts prepared on an accruals basis are materially inconsistent with the trustees' annual report.

In order to produce this report, the verifier should:

- Carry out procedures to be satisfied the charity qualifies for this independent verification
- Agree a timetable for the verification
- Obtain an understanding of the charity and its environment

- Record the examination procedures carried out and any matters important to support the statements made in the report
- Compare the accounts of the charity with the charity's accounting records in sufficient detail to be able to decide the accounts are in accordance with the records
- Review the accounting records
- Carry out analytical procedures to identify unusual items in the accounts
- Carry out detailed procedures as judged necessary
- Consider whether accounting policies are reasonable
- Enquire about subsequent events
- Consider if the Trustee's report is consistent with the accounts
- Review the evidence obtained

2.1.1 Planning

When planning the audit of a charity, the auditors should particularly consider the following:

- The **scope** of the audit
- Recent **recommendations** of the **Charity Commissioners** or the other regulatory bodies
- The **acceptability of accounting policies** adopted
- **Changes in circumstances** in the sector in which the charity operates
- **Past experience** of the effectiveness of the charity's accounting system
- **Key audit areas**
- The **amount of detail included** in the financial statements on which the auditors are required to report

In order to identify the key audit areas, the auditors will have to consider audit risk.

There are certain risks applicable to charities that might not necessarily be applicable to other companies. The auditors should consider the following:

Problem	Key factors
Inherent risk	• The complexity and extent of regulation • The significance of donations and cash receipts • Difficulties of the charity in establishing ownership and timing of voluntary income where funds are raised by non-controlled bodies • Lack of predictable income or precisely identifiable relationship between expenditure and income • Uncertainty of future income • Restrictions imposed by the objectives and powers given by charities' governing documents • The importance of restricted funds (funds which the company is only allowed to put to a specific purpose) • The extent and nature of trading activities must be compatible with the entity's charitable status • The complexity of tax rules (whether Income, Capital, Value Added or local rates) relating to charities • The sensitivity of certain key statistics, such as the proportion of resources used in administration • The need to maintain adequate resources for future expenditure while avoiding the build up of reserves which could appear excessive

Problem	Key factors
Control risk	• The amount of time committed by trustees to the charity's affairs • The skills and qualifications of individual trustees • The frequency and regularity of trustee meetings • The form and content of trustee meetings • The independence of trustees from each other • The division of duties between trustees • The degree of involvement in, or supervision of, the charity's transactions on the part of individual trustees
Control environment	• A recognised plan of the charity's structure showing clearly the areas of responsibility and lines of authority and reporting • Segregation of duties • Supervision by trustees of activities of staff where segregation of duties is not practical • Competence, training and qualification of paid staff and any volunteers appropriate to the tasks they have to perform • Involvement of the trustees in the recruitment, appointment and supervision of senior executives • Access of trustees to independent professional advice where necessary • Budgetary controls in the form of estimates of income and expenditure for each financial year and comparison of actual results with the estimates on a regular basis • Communication of results of such reviews to the trustees on a regular basis

2.1.2 Internal controls

Small charities in particular will generally suffer from internal control weaknesses common to small enterprises, such as **lack of segregation of duties** and use of **unqualified staff**. Shortcomings may arise from the staff's lack of training and also, if they are volunteers, from their attitude, in that they may resent formal procedures.

The auditors will have to consider particularly carefully whether they will be able to obtain adequate assurance that the accounting records do reflect all the transactions of the enterprise and bear in mind whether there are any related statutory reporting requirements.

The following sorts of internal control might be typical of a number of charities.

Cash donations	
Source	**Examples of controls**
Collecting boxes and tins	• Numerical control over boxes and tins • Satisfactory sealing of boxes and tins so that any opening prior to recording cash is apparent • Regular collection and recording of proceeds from collecting boxes • Dual control over counting and recording of proceeds
Postal receipts	• Unopened mail kept securely • Dual control over the opening of mail • Immediate recording of donations on opening of mail or receipt • Agreement of bank paying-in slips to record of receipts by an independent person

Other donations	
Source	**Examples of controls**
Gift aid	• Regular checks and follow-up procedures to ensure due amounts are received • Regular checks to ensure all tax repayments have been obtained
Legacies	• Comprehensive correspondence files maintained in respect of each legacy • Regular reports and follow-up procedures undertaken in respect of outstanding legacies
Donations in kind	• In the case of charity shops, separation of recording, storage and sale of inventory

Other income	
Source	**Examples of controls**
Fund-raising activities	• Records maintained for each fund-raising event • Other appropriate controls maintained over receipts • Controls maintained over expenses as for administrative expenses
Central and local government grants and loans	• Regular checks that all sources of income or funds are fully utilised and appropriate claims made • Ensuring income or funds are correctly applied

Use of resources	
Resource	**Examples of controls**
Restricted funds	• Separate records maintained of relevant revenue, expenditure and assets • Terms controlling application of fund • Oversight of application of fund monies by independent personnel or trustees
Grants to beneficiaries	• Records maintained, as appropriate, of requests for material grants received and their treatment • Appropriate checks made on applications and applicants for grants, and that amounts paid are *intra vires*
	• Records maintained of all grant decisions, checking that proper authority exists, that adequate documentation is presented to decision-making meetings, and that any conflicts of interest are recorded • Control to ensure grants made are properly spent by the recipient for the specified purpose, for example requirements for returns with supporting documentation or auditors' reports concerning expenditure, or monitoring visits

Conversely, large charities might have very strong controls and the auditors may find that they are able to rely on them to a great extent. Remember, however, that while relying on controls might be acceptable in order to determine whether the financial statements give a true and fair view, it might not be acceptable to meet any special additional auditing requirements that the charity has.

2.1.3 Substantive procedures

When designing substantive procedures for charities the auditors should give special attention to the possibility of:

- **Understatement or incompleteness** of the **recording of all income** including gifts in kind, cash donations, and legacies
- **Overstatement of cash grants or expenses**
- **Misanalysis** or misuse in the application of funds (such as restricted funds which the charity might only be able to use for specific purposes)
- **Misstatement** or omission of **assets** including donated properties and investments
- The existence of **restricted or uncontrollable funds** in foreign or independent branches

Completeness of income can be a particularly problematic area. Areas auditors may check:

- Loss of income through fraud
- Recognition of income from professional fund raisers
- Recognition of income from branches, associates or subsidiaries
- Income from informal fund-raising groups
- Income from grants

2.1.4 Overall review

The auditors must consider carefully whether the **accounting policies** adopted are **appropriate** to the activities, constitution and objectives of the charity, and are consistently applied, and whether the financial statements adequately disclose these policies and fairly present the state of affairs and the results for the accounting period.

In particular, the auditors should consider the basis of disclosing income from fund-raising activities (for example net or gross), accounting for income and expenses (accruals or cash), the capitalising of expenditure on non-current assets, apportioning administrative expenditure, and recognising income from donations and legacies.

Charities without significant endowments or accumulated funds will often be dependent upon future income from voluntary sources. In these circumstances auditors may question whether a going concern basis of accounting is appropriate.

2.1.5 Reporting

On not-for-profit audits where a statutory audit report is required, the auditors should issue the standard audit report which we will consider in Chapter 13. They should also consider whether any additional statutory requirements fall on the audit report.

Where an association or charity is having an audit for the benefit of its members or trustees, the standard audit report may not be required or appropriate. The auditor should bear in mind the objectives of the audit and make suitable references in the audit report. However, the ISA 700 format will still be relevant. The auditor should ensure that he makes the following matters clear:

- The addressees of the report
- What the report relates to
- The scope of the engagement
- The respective responsibilities of auditors and management/trustees/directors
- The work done
- The opinion formed

The points made above are general points. Remember that not all clubs and charities will be the same. If you have a question in the exam relating to a charity, apply this general knowledge to the specifics given in the question and be **logical** when formulating your answer.

Worked example: Charity

Headington Hospice Co is a small, local charity which operates a small children's hospice and two charity shops which raise money for the ongoing work of the hospice. The hospice receives grants from the health authority, sponsorship from some local businesses, receives income from the charity shops which are entirely voluntarily operated and receives donations from individuals. It employs three nurses, a part-time hospice manager and an accountant donates his time to keep the books and produce the annual accounts. As the company's turnover falls below the exemption limit, it is not required to have an audit by law, but the terms of its constitution require that an audit of the accounts is required for the benefit of the trustees that gives an opinion as to whether the financial statements give a true and fair view and to whether the charity is meeting its objectives, as set out in the constitutional document.

The scope of this audit is therefore two-fold. The auditors are to report on the truth and fairness of the financial statement for the benefit of the trustees and also on whether the charity is meeting its objectives. The auditors should therefore establish what the objectives of the charity are, and consider whether the objectives are being met.

The auditors should consider whether any recommendations of the Charity Commissioners apply to Headington Hospice. It is unlikely that there have been any substantial changes in the sector in which it works.

In terms of audit approach, the auditor will need to devote attention to cash receipts and income, as the Hospice receives donations from the public and also receives cash income from the charity shops. The auditors will need to determine if there is a good control system in place and whether they feel that they can place reliance on it.

In terms of substantive procedures, in particular, it will be necessary to consider non-current assets, to determine whether the premises the hospice and charity shops should be included on the balance sheet of the charity. The auditor will also need to assess the nature of the grants received from the health authority to determine how they should be accounted for. These things should all be considered as part of the accounting policy review. The auditor should also be aware of issues such as depreciation during this review, as the hospice may own specialised medical equipment which makes such issues complex.

Another matter which the auditor must consider is the issue of going concern. This will include an assessment of the sponsorship deals which the charity has in place and any consideration of future sponsorship. The grant position must also be considered, as must the likelihood of future donations. The auditors should also consider matters such as personnel, for example, whether any existing arrangements with doctors' practices will continue in existence.

The issues relating to cash donations and grants will be particularly relevant.

Particular matters which might be an issue at Headington Hospice are:

- Completeness of cash income from various sources
- Accounting for the grants from the local authority

Interactive question 1: Links Famine Relief [Difficulty level: Exam standard]

You have recently been appointed to audit Links Famine Relief, a small registered charity which receives donations from individuals to provide food in worldwide famine areas.

The charity is run by a voluntary management committee, which has monthly meetings, and it employs the following full-time staff:

(a) A director, Mr Roberts, who suggests fund raising activities and payments for relief of famine, and implements the policies adopted by the management committee; and

(b) A secretary (and bookkeeper), Mrs Beech, who deals with correspondence and keeps the accounting records.

Links Famine Relief is required by its constitution to have an annual external audit of its financial statements.

You are planning the audit of income of the charity for the year ended 5 April 20X7 and are considering the controls which should be exercised over income.

The previous year's accounts, to 5 April 20X6 (which have been audited by another firm) show the following income.

	£	£
Gifts under non-taxing arrangements		15,335
Tax reclaimed on gifts under non-taxing arrangements		4,325
		19,660
Postal donations		63,452
Autumn Fair		2,671
Other income		
Legacies	7,538	
Bank deposit account interest	2,774	
		10,312
		96,095

Notes

(a) Income from gifts under non-taxing arrangements is stated net. Each person who pays by gift aid has filled in a special tax form, which is kept by the secretary, Mrs Beech.

(b) All gifts under non-taxing arrangements are paid by banker's order – they are credited directly to the charity's bank account from the donor's bank. Donors make their payments by gift aid either monthly or annually.

(c) The tax reclaimed on these gifts is 28.2% (22/78) of the net value of the gifts, and relates to income received during the year – as the tax is received after the year-end, an appropriate amount recoverable is included in the balance sheet. The treasurer, who is a voluntary (unpaid) member of the management committee, completes the form for reclaiming the income tax, using the special tax forms (in (a) above) and checks to the full-time secretary's records that each donor has made the full payment in the year required by the arrangement.

(d) Donations received through the post are dealt with by Mrs Beech. These donations are either cheques or cash (bank notes and coins). Mrs Beech prepares a daily list of donations received, which lists the cheques received and total cash (divided between the different denominations of bank note and coin). The total on this form is recorded in the cash book. She then prepares a paying-in slip and banks these donations daily. When there is a special fund-raising campaign, Mrs Beech receives help in dealing with these donations from voluntary members of the management committee.

(e) The Autumn Fair takes place every year on a Saturday in October – members of the management committee and other supporters of the charity give items to sell (for example food, garden plants, clothing) – a charge is made for entrance to the fair and coffee and biscuits are available at a small charge. At the end of the fair, Mrs Beech collects the takings from each of the stalls, and she banks them the following Monday.

(f) Legacies are received irregularly, and are usually sent directly to the director of the charity, who gives them to Mrs Beech for banking – they are stated separately on the daily bankings form (in (d) above).

(g) Bank deposit account interest is paid gross of income tax by the bank, as the Links Famine Relief is a charity.

Requirement

List and briefly describe the work you would carry out on the audit of income of the charity, the controls you would expect to see in operation and the problems you may experience for the following sources of income, as detailed in the income statement above.

(a) Gifts under non-taxing arrangements
(b) Tax reclaimed on gifts made under non-taxing arrangements
(c) Donations received through the post
(d) Autumn Fair

See **Answer** at the end of this chapter.

2.2 Public sector

The following provides a brief introduction to public sector auditing and some of the concepts used in the audit of public sector entities. You are only required to have knowledge of how audit of public sector entities differs from the audit of non-specialised entities. In depth knowledge of the working of the public sector, the operation of the NAO (National Audit Office) and the Audit Commission and the content of GIAS (Government Internal Audit Standards) is not required.

The public sector comprises a great variety of organisations including central and local government. It also includes private companies which are profit orientated, running outsourced public services. Auditing by an independent external auditor is important, in order to provide external accountability to the community at large. For example, local authorities which provide many local services such as schools will be subject to an audit of their financial statements, as will the NHS Trust that runs local hospitals. Audit helps to ensure that:

- Public funds have been spent on proper, authorised purposes and legally within statutory powers.
- Organisations install and operate controls to limit the possibility of corrupt practice, fraud and poor administration.

The manner in which the auditors conduct their work is affected by auditing standards and other regulatory influences including:

- Specific statutory requirements
- Requirements of the sponsoring (or funding) department
- Contractual requirements contained in terms of engagement.

Organisations in the public sector are often subject to a high degree of regulation. The nature of regulation affecting public sector bodies ranges from statutory to detailed administrative requirements.

In England, the National Audit Office and the Audit Commission are public sector organisations specialising in public sector audit work. These or similar bodies cover Northern Ireland, Scotland and Wales.

2.2.1 Principles of audit in the public sector

The purpose of audit in the public sector is accountability. It helps ensure that public money is spent wisely and handled with integrity. Audit in the public sector is not just an exercise in checking what has happened in the past, but making recommendations for future good practice.

The Public Audit Forum (a representative of four major public audit associations in the UK) sets out three key principles of audit in the public sector:

- **Independence** of public sector auditors from organisations being audited
- The wide **scope** of audit in the public sector (see below)
- The ability of public sector auditors to **make their results available** to the public and democratically appointed officials.

The wide scope of audit in the public sector is an important issue and one in which it differs from the statutory 'private' companies audit we have focused on thus far in your studies. A public sector audit covers not only the audit of financial statements, and internal control systems if required, but also covers the issues of regularity, propriety and value for money.

Regularity

In a public sector audit, auditors must ensure that the transactions carried out by the organisation are **in accordance with the legislation that governs those transactions**, or the regulations issued by Parliament or HM Treasury in relation to that organisation.

Propriety

This concept is linked to the expectations of the public or the authority which sets up the organisation being audited, that is, auditors must ensure that transactions and business are **being carried out in the way that they should be**, that is ethically, with integrity and according to any existing standards of conduct.

Value for money

Finally, in a public sector audit it is critical to ensure that that **best use is being made of resources** (money raised from the public through taxation) in providing the service. Public sector audits therefore include evaluations of the economy (spend less), efficiency (spend well) and effectiveness (spend wisely) of use of public resources.

2.2.2 The Committee of Public Accounts

The Committee of Public Accounts is an all-party committee appointed by the House of Commons to examine public expenditure to ensure that it achieves value for money. The Commons itself decides how public money is spent on an annual basis.

2.2.3 The National Audit Office

The head of the National Audit Office is the Comptroller and Auditor General (C&AG) who is responsible for auditing the accounts of all government departments (such as the Department for Work and Pensions) and non-departmental government agencies (such as the Passport Agency) and reporting the results to Parliament. In practice this responsibility is delegated to the National Audit Office (NAO).

The NAO ensures that the public sector is accountable. The C&AG can report to Parliament on the way that public money is spent by central government. Evidence from reports produced by the C&AG may be used by The Committee of Public Accounts to make recommendations to Government. The C&AG is appointed by the Queen, on the advice of the prime minister, and is accountable to The Committee of Public Accounts.

Accounting officers are normally the most senior officials in a public sector entity with a personal responsibility for the propriety and regularity of the public finances for which he or she is answerable; for the keeping of proper accounts; for prudent and economical administration; for the avoidance of waste and extravagance; and for the efficient and effective use of all the available resources (HM Treasury definition). Accounting officers may be called to give evidence before The Committee of Public Accounts on the basis of reports by the C&AG.

2.2.4 Audit Commission

The Audit Commission exists to ensure that public money is spent economically, efficiently and effectively in local government, housing, health, criminal justice and the fire and rescue services. It has a Code of Audit Practice. One of its roles is to appoint auditors to local government and health providers (for example, local authorities and NHS Trusts as outlined above). Usually the auditors are employees of the Audit Commission but the Audit Commission may also appoint approved firms to carry out such audits.

The Audit Commission is audited by the NAO.

2.2.5 Audit of government grants

Government grants, such as enterprise development schemes, are issued in response to certain criteria, such as a need to improve employment in disadvantaged areas. It is important that such grant schemes are audited to ensure that the criteria for the grants are being met, that the schemes operate well and whether the government department responsible for the grant is managing it and ensuring its effectiveness.

The NAO audits the regional grant scheme in England, whilst the Audit Commission audits local government grants.

2.2.6 International Standards on Auditing

The International Standards on Auditing apply to audit work undertaken in the public sector. A number of standards finish with a section on the 'Public Sector Perspective' which highlight some of the different considerations that apply in the audit of entities in the public sector. Some examples are given below:

- ISA 315 *Identifying and Assessing the Risks of Material Misstatement through Understanding the Entity and its Environment.*

  When carrying out audits of public sector entities, the auditor takes into account the legislative framework and any other relevant regulations, ordinances or ministerial directives that affect the audit mandate and other special auditing requirements.

- ISA 520 *Analytical Procedures*

  The relationships between individual financial statement items traditionally considered in the audit of business entities may not always be appropriate in the audit of governments or other non-business public sector entities: for example, in many such public sector entities there is often little direct relationship between revenues and expenditures.

  In the public sector industry data or statistics for comparative purposes may not be available.

- ISA 570 *Going Concern*

  The appropriateness of the use of the going concern assumption in the preparation of the financial statements is generally not in question when auditing either a central government or those public sector entities having arrangements backed by central government. However where such arrangements do not exist, or where central government funding of the entity may be withdrawn and the existence of the entity may be at risk, this ISA will provide useful guidance. As governments privatise government entities, going concern issues will become increasingly relevant to the public sector.

2.2.7 Internal audit

Many government departments are required by statute to have internal auditors. Internal audit is an independent, objective assurance and consulting activity designed to add value and improve an organisation's operations. It helps an organisation accomplish its objectives by bringing a systematic, disciplined approach to evaluate and improve the effectiveness of risk management, control and governance processes.

There is a code of ethics for internal auditors in central government. There are four key principles and rules of conduct covering:

- Integrity
- Objectivity
- Competency
- Confidentiality

The Government has also issued Government Internal Audit Standards (GIAS) to facilitate the work of internal auditors in the public sector. GIAS are mandatory for all central government departments and are supported by good practice guides.

GIAS are grouped under the general headings of attribute standards and performance standards. The Attribute Standards address the characteristics of organisations and parties performing internal audit activities. The Performance Standards describe the nature of internal audit activities and provide quality criteria against which the performance of these services can be evaluated.

These are briefly described below:

Government Internal Audit Standards	
Attribute standards	
1	Purpose, authority and responsibility. The purpose, authority and responsibility of the internal audit activity must be formally defined
2	Independence and objectivity. The internal audit activity must be independent, and internal auditors must be objective in performing their work.
3	Proficiency and due professional care. Engagements must be performed with proficiency and due professional care.
4	Quality assurance and improvement programme. The chief audit executive must develop and maintain a quality assurance and improvement programme that covers all aspects of the internal audit activity.

Government Internal Audit Standards	
Performance standards	
5	Managing the internal audit activity. The chief audit executive must effectively manage the internal audit activity to ensure it adds value to the organisation.
6	Nature of work. The internal audit activity must evaluate and contribute to the improvement of governance, risk management and control processes, using a systematic and disciplined approach.
7	Engagement planning. Internal auditors must develop and document a plan for each engagement, including the engagement's objectives, scope, timing and resource allocations.
8	Performing the engagement. Internal auditors must identify, analyse, evaluate and document sufficient information to achieve the engagement's objectives.
9	Communicating results. Internal auditors must communicate the engagement results.
10	Monitoring progress. The chief audit executive must establish and maintain a system to monitor the disposition of results communicated to management.
11	Resolution of senior management's acceptance of risks. When the chief audit executive believes that senior management has accepted a level of residual risk that may be unacceptable to the organisation, the chief audit executive must discuss the matter with senior management. If the decision regarding residual risk is not resolved, the chief audit executive must report the matter to the board for resolution.

Summary and Self-test

Summary

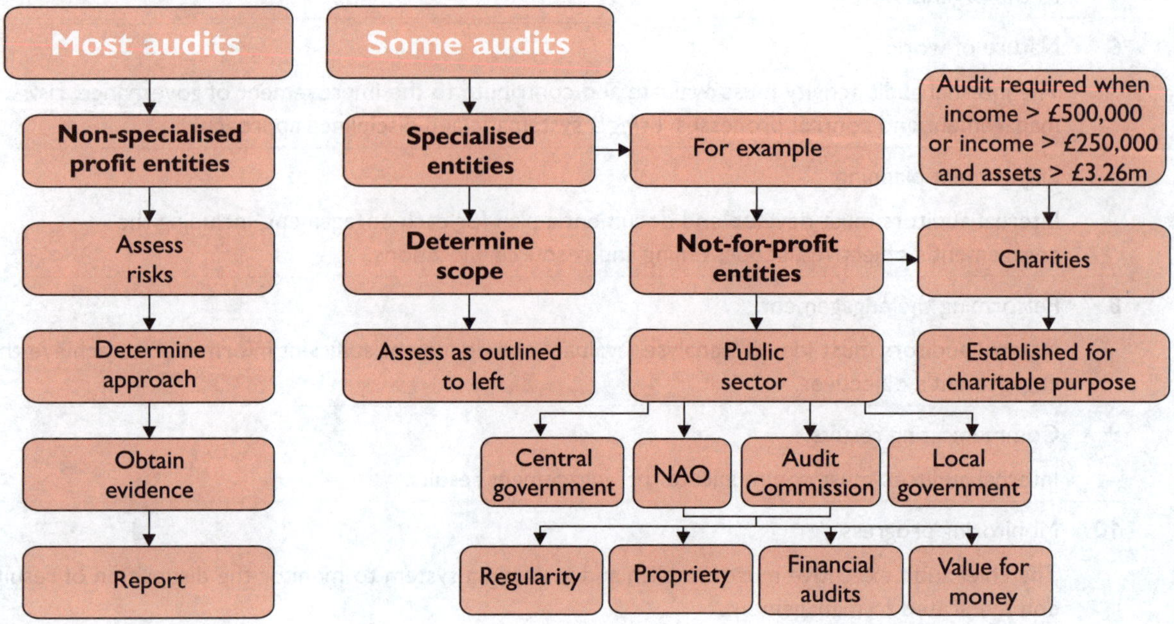

Self-test

Answer the following questions.

1 Which of the following might require a specialist audit and why?

- ☐ Care Share Ltd, a charity limited by guarantee
- ☐ Pytox plc, a listed parent of a group of manufacturing companies
- ☐ Loyds plc, a bank
- ☐ Allied Insurance Company plc, an insurer
- ☐ Linens Ltd, a retail company

2 Will an audit report for a charity have to conform to IAS 700 criteria?

3 What is NAO?

4 Help the Kids Ltd, a registered charity, has income of £150,000 and assets of £750,000. It is required to have an audit of its financial statements.

- ☐ True
- ☐ False

5 What four issues are likely to fall within the scope of a public audit?

(1) ....
(2) ....
(3) ....
(4) ....

Exam-style question

6 You have been appointed the auditor of Safe Haven which has a year end of 31 May. Safe Haven is a small registered charity based in a small town in Warshire. The organisation provides shelter for abandoned dogs and puppies with the aim of finding new homes for as many as possible.

The charity is managed by a voluntary committee, including a Chairman (Alun Jenkins), a Treasurer (Gordon Brand) and a Secretary (Amanda Jones). Appointment is by annual election by the committee each year however Alun, Gordon and Amanda have held their posts for a number of years as other committee members feel unable to give the required time commitment.

Safe Haven also employs a number of paid employees. The shelter is managed by John and Jane Sheldon, who are husband and wife. There is a kennel maid and a part time bookkeeper. In addition a number of unpaid volunteers help out at the shelter as and when they are needed depending on the number of animals at the centre at a particular point in time.

The main sources of income are as follows:

- **Charity shop**
  This is run by a full time manager, assisted by a team of volunteers. Members of the public make donations (primarily clothes and toys) which are then sold in the shop. All transactions are in cash. The shop does not accept cheques or credit cards. The transactions are recorded by the till, with completed till rolls being passed on to the bookkeeper.

- **Collections**
  Volunteers make house to house calls on a regular basis. In addition, on Saturday mornings volunteers make collections in three local town centres. All cash is counted by the volunteers, and returned to the bookkeeper with a receipt confirming the amount.

- **Dog Show**
  Each year on 1st June, a Peace Festival is held in the town. As part of this event Safe Haven organise a dog show. Any member of the public can enter their dog by completing an entry form which can be obtained from the shop.

  Tickets to see the show can be purchased up to two weeks in advance from the shop or can be purchased on the day at the Festival. In recent years the show has been a great success although two years ago it had to be cancelled due to bad weather.

  T-shirts can also be purchased from a stall manned by volunteers.

- **Sponsorship**
  Safe Haven is sponsored by a local pet supplies company. The company makes an annual donation and provides prizes for the winners of the dog show. In return for this their services are advertised in the event programme and their logo is printed on the T shirts.

The main expenses are as follows:

- **Rent, rates, heat and light**
  Both the shelter and the shop are rented properties. These expenses are all paid by monthly direct debit.

- **Employee costs**
  John and Jane Sheldon and the shop manager are salaried. They are paid directly into their bank accounts on a monthly basis. The kennel maid and the bookkeeper are paid by the hour. They are paid by cheque on a weekly basis.

- **Vet bills**
  The local vet provides his time free but any medicines etc do need to be paid for. Payments are made by cheque on receipt of the invoice.

- **Printing costs**
  Leaflets are produced to support fund raising campaigns. The most significant element of this cost is the dog show programme which outlines the timetable of events. The programmes are printed and delivered to Safe Haven in May. The printer invoices at the time of delivery.

The accounts are maintained by the bookkeeper on a computerised spreadsheet. Occasionally, the treasurer may also assist with the preparation of accounting information at particularly busy times in the year, for example, immediately after the dog show.

Requirements

(a) List the factors specific to the audit of a charity which would affect inherent and control risk.

(b) As the auditor of Safe Haven discuss the key planning issues based on the above scenario.

(c) Outline the audit work you would plan to perform in respect of the following expenses:

(i) Rent, rates, light and heat
(ii) Employee costs
(iii) Vet bills
(iv) Printing costs. **(20 marks)**

Now, go back to the Learning Objectives in the Introduction. If you are satisfied you have achieved these objectives, please tick them off.

Technical reference

1 Non-specialised and specialised entities	**n/a**
2 Not-for-profit entities	**Charities SORP**

Answer to Interactive question

Answer to Interactive question 1

The audit consideration in relation to the various sources of income of the Links Famine Relief charity would be as follows.

(a) **Gifts made under non-taxing arrangements**

This type of income should not present any particular audit problem as the donations are made by banker's order direct to the charity's bank account and so it would be difficult for such income to be 'intercepted' and misappropriated.

Specific tests required would be as follows.

(i) Check a sample of receipts from the bank statements to the cash book to ensure that the income has been properly recorded.

(ii) Check a sample of the receipts to the special tax forms to ensure that the full amount due has been received.

Any discrepancies revealed by either of the above tests should be followed up with Mrs Beech.

(b) **Tax reclaimed on gifts made under non-taxing arrangements**

Once again this income should not pose any particular audit problems. The auditors should check the claim form submitted to the tax authorities.

(c) **Donations received through the post**

There is a serious problem here as the nature of this income is not predictable and also because of the lack of internal check with Mrs Beech being almost entirely responsible for the receipt of these monies, the recording of the income and the banking of the cash and cheques received. The auditors may ultimately have to express a qualified opinion relating to the uncertainty surrounding the completeness of income of this type.

Notwithstanding the above reservations, specific audit tests required would be as follows.

(i) Check the details on the daily listings of donations received to the cash book, bank statements and paying-in slips, ensuring that the details agree in all respects and that there is no evidence of any delay in the banking of this income.

(ii) Check the donations received by reference to any correspondence which may have been received with the cheques or cash.

(iii) Consider whether the level of income appears reasonable in comparison with previous years and in the light of any special appeals that the charity is known to have made during the course of the year.

(iv) Carry out, with permission of the management committee, surprise checks to vouch the completeness and accuracy of the procedures relating to this source of income.

(d) **Autumn Fair**

Once again there is a potential problem here because of the level of responsibility vested in one person, namely Mrs Beech.

Specific work required would be as follows.

(i) Attend the event to observe the proper application of laid down procedures and count the cash at the end of the day.

(ii) Check any records maintained by individual stallholders to the summary prepared by Mrs Beech.

(iii) Check the vouchers supporting any expenditure deducted from the proceeds in order to arrive at the net bankings.

(iv) Agree the summary prepared by Mrs Beech to the entry in the cash book and on the bank statement.

Answers to Self-test

1
- Care Share Ltd might have additional Charity Commissioner requirements
- Loyds plc is likely to have additional banking requirements
- Allied Insurance Company plc is likely to have additional insurance requirements

2 Only if the charity requires a statutory audit.

3 The National Audit Office (NAO) is an independent body which scrutinises public spending on behalf of Parliament. It is responsible for auditing the accounts of central government departments and other public bodies.

4 False. Help the Kids Ltd would only be required to have an audit if its income was over £500,000 and its assets were greater than £2.8m.

5 (1) Audit of financial statements
(2) Regularity
(3) Propriety
(4) Value for money

6 (a) The following factors would be relevant:

Inherent risk

(i) The extent of regulation depending on the specific nature of the charity
(ii) The significance of donations and cash receipts
(iii) The extent of credit card and internet donations
(iv) The valuation of gifts of assets
(v) Lack of predictable income
(vi) Lack of direct relationship between income and expenditure
(vii) The sensitivity of issues including the proportion of resources used in admin and fund raising

Control risk

(i) The time committed by trustees to the charity's affairs
(ii) The skills and qualifications of the individual trustees
(iii) The frequency, form and content of trustee meetings
(iv) The division of duties between trustees
(v) The supervision by the trustees of volunteers

(b) Planning issues for Safe Haven would be as follows:

Completeness of income

Overall this risk is high due to the following factors: the majority of the income is generated in cash, there are numerous different sources of income, and a wide range of people have access to the asset itself due to the use of volunteers.

Looking at each source of income in turn the following points are relevant:

Charity shop

Whilst till receipts can be agreed to cash received this does not guarantee that all sales have been put through the till. The main problem here is that it may be difficult to establish an expected relationship between 'sales' and 'cost of sales'. Items sold are donated by the public so much will depend on how these items are valued by the charity.

Street collections

Reconciliations can be performed between cash collected and the receipts submitted by the volunteers to determine accurate recording. Completeness of income, however, will depend largely on the integrity of the volunteers and the overall controls put in place by the charity. In this instance risk is increased by the unpredictable nature of this source of income and the fact that the collection boxes are not sealed. Those responsible for collecting the cash are also responsible for opening the boxes and counting the cash before handing it over to the bookkeeper. This increases the risk of misappropriation.

Dog show tickets and T-shirts sales

Completeness of income in respect of these sources of revenue is still a concern due to the cash nature of these transactions but more reliable evidence should be available. Revenue generated from ticket sales can be reconciled to the number of tickets sold. This assumes that the charity exercises some control over the issue of tickets for example, tickets are numbered so that it is possible to determine the number sold.

For the T-shirt sales it should be possible to validate the income by comparing the number of items sold with the revenue generated. This depends on the charity adopting very simple stock control.

Sponsorship

Completeness should not be an issue here as the amount involved is predetermined and is likely to be paid by cheque or by bank transfer.

Controls

In addition to the specific control issue mentioned above the assessment of the overall control environment will be essential at the planning stage of the audit. As there are concerns about the completeness of income the control environment will provide key evidence about the integrity of the revenue balance.

The auditor will need to consider the ability of the committee to run the organisation effectively. The information suggests that the three main committee members are responsible for the majority of the management so it will be important to determine their respective skills and whether they are able to devote sufficient time.

The ability of the bookkeeper will also need to be established in particular the possible lack of segregation of duties and the fact that the job is currently only done on a part time basis. It may be that records are not being maintained as they should be due to the limited number of hours being worked by that individual. This is emphasised by the fact that the Treasurer is sometimes required to help out.

Accounting Treatment

At the planning stage the accounting policies of the charity will need to be reviewed to ensure that they are appropriate and consistent. In particular the point at which income is recognised will need to be established together with any related costs. This is relevant to the income generated from the sale of tickets for the annual dog show. Tickets are available in the last two weeks in May, that is, the last two weeks before the year end and the main cost involved in the show, being the printing of the show programme is also incurred and invoiced in May. The show itself takes place in June.

In respect of the ticket sales made in May it could be argued that this income should not be recognised until the show takes place as it is only earned at this point. However, if the proceeds are non-returnable irrespective of whether the show takes place or not it could be argued that it represents a donation which can be recognised on receipt.

In respect of the programme costs the treatment is a little clearer. These should be provided for at the end of the year even though they relate to an activity which will take place after the year end. Per FRS 12 there is an obligation to pay for the programmes as a result of a past event that is, the printing company have produced and delivered the programmes.

Evidence

At the planning stage the overall strategy to adopt will need to be determined. In this case it is likely that a controls based approach will be adopted (as completeness of income is one of the key risks) supported by substantive testing, the extent of which will depend on the results of the tests of controls. The use of analytical review will be more limited due to the lack of predictive patterns in relation to many aspects of the organisation and the lack of relationships between account balances.

(c) The audit plan would include the following:

Rent, rates, light and heat

(i) Agree total rent/rates for the year to the lease/ annual bill

(ii) Check direct debit amounts in the cash book/bank statement

(iii) Compare the cost of heat and light for this year and the previous year and follow up if there are any major differences

(iv) Look at the date on the last utility bill to determine the need for any prepayment or accrual adjustment.

Employee costs

(i) For salaried staff check annual salary to personnel details/contract of employment.

(ii) For the bookkeeper and the kennel maid review the controls over the recording of hours worked and check the hourly rates applied to personnel details/contracts of employment.

(iii) Check a sample of standing data used to process the payroll.

(iv) Recalculate a sample of monthly calculations to ensure that deductions are being made correctly.

(v) Review controls over the weekly authorisation of pay checks and monthly bank transfers.

Vet bills

(i) Confirm with the vet that he has given his time for free.

(ii) Compare the total vet bill for this year and last year and calculate a 'cost per animal rescued' if possible.

(iii) Trace a sample of entries made in the cash book in respect of vet fees back to the original invoice to confirm that the cost is in respect of this.

(iv) Review invoices received after the year end to ensure that any necessary accruals have been recognised.

Printing costs

(i) Obtain the printers' invoice and check that a provision has been included in the accounts at the year end for an amount matching that on the invoice.

(ii) Confirm that the programmes have been received.

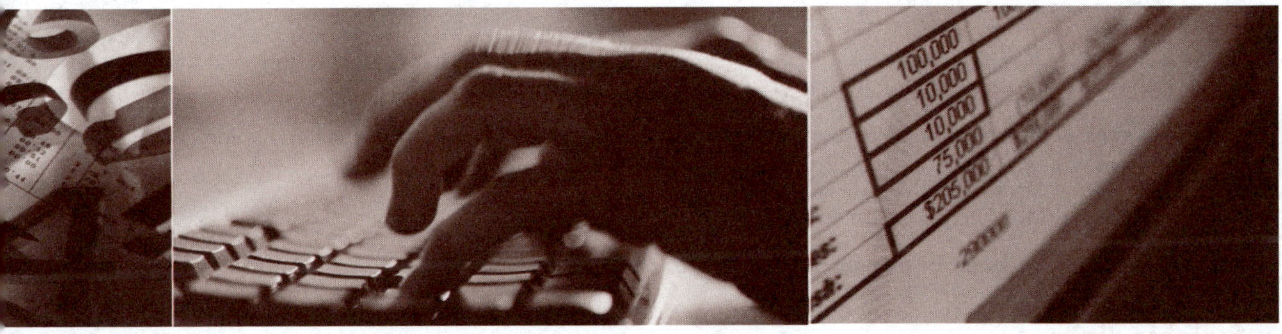

chapter 12

Audit completion

Introduction

Learning objectives

Tick off

- Understand the processes that auditors carry out at the end of the audit ☐
- Be aware of the procedures that are carried out in respect of subsequent events and going concern ☐
- Be able to draw conclusions on audit matters ☐

Specific syllabus references for this chapter are: 4a, b, c, f, g.

Syllabus links

You will have considered the issue of going concern in Accounting.

Examination context

The reviews carried out at the end of the audit, such as going concern and subsequent events reviews are extremely important so could easily be examined in a short form or a long form question in the exam.

Candidates will be able to conclude and report on assurance engagements in accordance with the terms of the engagements and appropriate standards.

In the assessment, candidates may be required to:

- Describe the nature and timing of specific procedures designed to identify subsequent events that may require adjustment or disclosure in relation to the matters being reported on
- Evaluate, quantitatively and qualitatively (including the use of analytical procedures), the results and conclusions obtained from assurance tests and procedures
- Draw conclusions on the ability to report on an assurance engagement which are consistent with the results of assurance work
- Judge when to refer reporting matters for specialist help
- Draw conclusions on the ability to report on an audit engagement, including the opinion for a statutory audit, which are consistent with the results of audit work

1 Introduction

Section overview

- Although completion should in theory be simple if the audit has been well-planned and executed, there are a number of aspects to it which can make it complex.

There are three phases to the audit:

- Planning
- Evidence gathering
- Completion

In the theory, the completion phase should be relatively smooth:

- If the work has been well planned
- If the staff have been well briefed and well trained
- If the staff execute the plan efficiently and to time

All the partner has to do is review the file, come to a decision about the final issues demanding professional judgement and sign off the accounts. However, there are lots of components to the completion phase.

The fact is that if the various procedures and other activities which make up the completion phase are not accomplished efficiently and to time, almost everything else is wasted. Budget overruns and underrecovery also tend to happen if closedown is not managed well.

This chapter talks in terms of audit, due to the auditing standards covered in it, but similar procedures might be carried out as part of a review.

2 Objective

Section overview

- The partner needs to consider:
  - The financial statements
  - The work done to support the audit opinion

Remember the possible cost of getting the audit opinion wrong:

- If someone can demonstrate that the auditor owed them a duty of care and they suffered loss by relying on the financial statements, they could sue the auditor.

- As a member of the ICAEW the auditor could also face disciplinary proceedings, fines and penalties.

Making sure the appropriate opinion is given is therefore important.

There are two components of the completion phase:

- The financial statements themselves; and
- The work which has been done to support the opinion

2.1 The financial statements

When considering the financial statements at the completion stage, the partner responsible for signing the audit report is interested in the answers to three questions:

- Do the financial statements comply with the provisions of the Companies Act 2006?
- Do the financial statements make sense?
- Has the audit report been drafted properly? (We will look at this in Chapter 13.)

We will consider the first two questions in the next section of this chapter.

2.2 The work done to support the opinion

Your review of the work done has four aspects to it:

- Whether the work done was in-line with the audit plan
- Whether the right work has been done (perhaps the plan needed to be flexed in the light of conditions actually encountered by the client)
- Whether enough work has been done
- The issues arising

3 Financial statement review

Section overview

- The important questions are:
  - Do the financial statements comply with the law and regulations (which will be tested using a disclosure checklist)
  - Do the financial statements make sense (which will be tested by analytical procedures)

3.1 Do the financial statements comply with the Companies Act 2006?

Determining this ought to be relatively simple – every firm should use a checklist to ensure that the financial statements comply with the disclosure requirements of the Companies Act and relevant accounting standards. Such checklists usually form a part of the 'audit packs' which firms use.

To some extent the job has been made easier by the widespread use of accounts production software, but software is only as good as the people writing it, installing it and using it.

For example:

- If directors' emoluments are not coded to the right account in the chart of accounts they will not be disclosed properly in the financial statements
- If the client has a material accounting policy which is not in the 'standard list' in the template on which the financial statements are based, it will not appear in the accounting policies note unless you add it.

Checklisting the accounts, therefore is still a good idea.

As you know from your other studies, the nature of financial statements these days is incredibly complex. For UK companies be aware that:

- There are a large number of financial reporting standards – either UK or International – applicable to financial statements
- The Companies Act itself is a substantial document which determines the format to be used in financial statements and the disclosures to be made on the face of the primary statements and in the supporting notes
- The directors' report and other information released with the financial statements, need to be consistent with the financial statements so the auditor must read that information and resolve any inconsistencies.

3.2 Do the financial statements make sense?

We have considered the techniques required to carry out analytical procedures as part of the risk assessment process at the planning stage and as a substantive procedure.

Analytical procedures **must** also be used in the overall review at the end of the audit to assist the auditor when forming an overall conclusion as to whether the financial statements are consistent with the auditor's understanding of the entity.

The steps for carrying out analytical procedures at this stage of the audit are very similar to those used as part of the risk assessment process at the planning stage, but they happen in a rather different way

- Interpretation
- Investigation
- Corroboration

3.2.1 Interpretation

The person carrying out the analytical procedures, reads through the financial statements and interprets them, considering the absolute figures themselves and relevant ratios.

3.2.2 Investigation

When analytical procedures are used as risk assessment procedures or as a substantive procedure, the aim is to identify potential problems. The problems are then investigated during fieldwork by making enquiries and gathering audit evidence.

At the completion stage the reviewer will expect to find the answers to the issues raised by the review on the audit file.

3.2.3 Corroboration

Should those answers not be on the file, further work will need to be done.

From a practical point of view it is worth remembering the following:

- For the smaller client the working papers supporting the final analytical procedures may well be simply an update of the work done at the planning stage.
- For the larger client the review becomes a much more specific exercise.
- The financial statements used for the analytical procedures need to incorporate any adjustments made as a result of the audit.
- Any problems identified by the procedures, which indicate that the financial statements should to be amended, need to be actioned.

4 Other matters

Section overview

- The auditor needs to:
  - Evaluate discovered errors
  - Ensure opening balance and comparatives are correct
  - Review whenever the going concern basis of the financial statements is appropriate
  - Review subsequent events
  - Obtain necessary management representations

At the completion stage the reviewer has to consider the issues which have been raised by the audit and what the firm's response in the audit report should be.

At this stage the reviewer needs to consider:

- Is the impact of errors and misstatements uncovered during the audit likely to be material?
- Are there matters of principle where the auditor disagrees with the client?

The second of these questions can cause severe difficulties for the audit firm in exercising its professional judgement.

It is possible for there to be points of principle which although not material in themselves, in the current period, could lead to problems in the future, or lead to the reassessment of audit risk.

4.1 Errors discovered

ISA 450 *Evaluation of Misstatements Identified During the Audit* requires the auditor to accumulate misstatements identified during the audit unless those misstatements are trivial. The auditor must evaluate the effect of identified misstatements on the audit and evaluate the effect of uncorrected misstatements, if any, on the financial statements.

- Identified misstatements: the auditor will need to consider revising the overall plan if:
  - The misstatements identified indicate that other misstatements may exist, which when accumulated could be material, or
  - Accumulated misstatements approach the materiality level set for the audit

  Where management has corrected misstatements detected, the auditor shall perform additional procedures to determine whether misstatements remain.
- Communication and correction of misstatements:
  - The auditor shall inform management of all misstatements and request that they be corrected
  - If management refuses the auditor shall ascertain the reason and take this into account in the overall evaluation
- Examining the effect of uncorrected misstatements:
  - Reassess materiality
  - Determine whether uncorrected misstatements are material, whether individually or in aggregate

  Materiality will depend on the nature of the misstatement and its impact on the financial statements. The auditor is required to inform those charged with governance and to request that corrections be made.
- Written representations:

  The auditor shall request confirmation from management that the effect of uncorrected misstatements is immaterial
- Documentation – audit documentation shall include:
  - The amount below which misstatements are considered trivial
  - All misstatements accumulated
  - The auditor's conclusion regarding materiality of uncorrected misstatements

Certain circumstances may cause the auditor to deem misstatements material even if they are below the materiality level. These circumstances include:

- Compliance with regulatory requirements
- Masking a change in trends or affecting ratios
- Increasing management compensation
- Affecting other information in documents included with the audited financial statements

Worked example: Enron

US company Enron devised a way of hiding debt by manipulating the detailed accounting rules for dealing with subsidiaries. This led to the non-disclosure of debt in excess of $20bn. According to the Washington Post website, the initial transaction on which this technique was first used, was to artificially preserve the value of an investment of $300,000 which was immaterial in terms of the Enron audit, but the use of the technique led to misstatements which were very material indeed.

4.2 Opening balances

It may seem odd to consider opening balances at the completion stages of the audit, but the auditor needs to consider whether there is sufficient evidence to support their reliability. If the opening balances are misstated this will mean that the profits for the current year may also be misstated.

Normally where the audit engagement is continuing from previous years, this will not cause a problem, but for a new client there are questions of professional judgement about the reliability of the previous year's accounts, which in turn leads to questions about the quality of work of the previous auditors.

Where the engagement is an initial engagement (financial statements for prior period were not audited or audited by a predecessor auditor) the auditor will again have to consider the risks of unaudited figures from past periods being materially misstated.

ISA 510 *Initial Audit Engagements – Opening Balances* states that, in conducting an initial audit engagement, the objective of the auditor with respect to opening balances is to obtain sufficient appropriate audit evidence about whether:

(a) Opening balances contain misstatements that materially affect the current period's financial statements; and

(b) Appropriate accounting policies reflected in the opening balances have been consistently applied in the current period's financial statements, or changes thereto are appropriately accounted for and adequately presented and disclosed in accordance with the applicable financial reporting framework.

The auditor shall obtain sufficient appropriate audit evidence about whether the opening balances contain misstatements that materially affect the current period's financial statements by:

(a) Determining whether the prior period's closing balances have been correctly brought forward to the current period or, when appropriate, have been restated;

(b) Determining whether the opening balances reflect the application of appropriate accounting policies; and

(c) Performing one or more of the following:

   (i) Whether the prior year financial statements were audited, reviewing the predecessor auditor's working papers to obtain evidence regarding the opening balances;

   (ii) Evaluating whether audit procedures performed in the current period provide evidence relevant to the opening balances; or

   (iii) Performing specific audit procedures to obtain evidence regarding the opening balances.

Such procedures may include:

- Checking receipts from opening receivables
- Verifying opening payables in the light of payments made during the current period
- Reconciling from an inventory figure which has been audited back to the opening position
- Obtaining confirmations from relevant third parties – lenders, valuers etc

The auditor will also need to consider the comparative figures in the financial statements. ISA 710 *Comparative Information – Corresponding Figures and Comparative Financial Statements* states that the objectives of the auditor with respect to comparative information are:

- To obtain sufficient appropriate audit evidence about whether the comparative information has been presented, in all material respects, in accordance with the requirements for comparative information in the applicable financial reporting framework; and

- To report in accordance with the auditor's reporting responsibilities.

Interactive question 1: Opening balances [Difficulty level: Exam standard]

Your firm has just been appointed auditors of Cross Ltd after the previous auditors were removed following a dispute with the directors. This dispute related to certain costs capitalised by the directors, which the auditors believed should have been written off. (Last year's audit report was qualified because of the disagreement.)

State the procedures you would carry out regarding the opening balances.

See **Answer** at the end of this chapter.

4.3 Going concern

The problem

The going concern concept is fundamental to the way in which financial statements are prepared and has been so for a very long time indeed.

If you think about it carefully, you will see that it is probably a major contributor to the expectations gap which is considered at a number of places in this Study Manual.

Worked example: The way financial statements are prepared

Consider the deceptively simple example of a non-current asset such as a car. We all know that, as soon as you drive your brand new car away from the showroom it loses a disproportionate amount of its resale value and that this depreciation happens very rapidly in the early stages of the car's life, before flattening out after a couple of years or so. However, in financial statements, the depreciation charge and resultant reduction in the car's net book value is usually dealt with on a straight line basis, because, over time, it is probably truer and fairer to amortise the car's value evenly over its life – it is, after all, an asset which is 'used up' evenly over its life, whatever its resale value at any particular point in time. It is also administratively easier to calculate depreciation this way.

The reason why this treatment is acceptable is because the company has no intention of disposing of the asset at the reporting date, but will use it in the normal course of business until the appropriate time arrives for its disposal. There is, nevertheless, a very real and potentially material difference between the market value of a company's fleet of vehicles and their carrying value in the statement of financial position.

The argument used in the example also applies to a number of other assets. If the company's complete inventory had to be disposed of, or the receivables all collected in on the first day of the new year, it is highly probable that the amounts realised would be less than those shown in the statement of financial position. In addition, liabilities not reflected in the financial statements will crystallise, such as redundancy payments or lease penalty clauses.

It follows from this that, if the going concern concept is not an appropriate basis on which to prepare the financial statements, the implications will be very serious, as almost all of the normal assumptions made will be called into question.

4.3.1 Work to be done

The auditor's responsibility is to obtain sufficient appropriate audit evidence about the appropriateness of management's use of the going concern assumption. The risks of the client not being a going concern will need to be considered and planned for at the planning stage, and, at the completion stage, certain specific tasks will have to be carried out.

These will include:

- Consideration of all areas of the balance sheet to see whether there are indications that the going concern concept may be inappropriate such as:
  - Significant receivables unable to pay
  - Lines of inventory and WIP where net realisable value may be less than cost
  - Material non-current assets which are no longer usable
  - Deferred development expenditure which is irrecoverable against relevant revenues
  - Investments (in subsidiaries or other companies) which have lost value

- Review of future plans for the business including financial forecasts and projections, to ensure that it is probable that the company will be able to continue to trade for at least the forthcoming year (that is, not less than 12 months from the balance sheet date).
- Review of the company's borrowing facilities and other sources of finance to ensure that they will be adequate for the forthcoming year and that conditions and covenants imposed by lenders will not be breached.
- Review of minutes and other information such as correspondence with legal advisers, for indications of potential going concern problems.

A list of possible symptoms of going concern problems is given in ISA 570. It is reproduced here.

- **Financial indications**
  - Net liability or net current liability position
  - Fixed-term borrowings approaching maturity without realistic prospects of renewal or repayment, or excessive reliance on short-term borrowings to finance long-term assets
  - Indications of withdrawal of financial support by creditors
  - Negative operating cash flows indicated by historical or prospective financial statements
  - Adverse key financial ratios
  - Substantial operating losses or significant deterioration in the value of assets used to generate cash flows
  - Arrears or discontinuance of dividends
  - Inability to pay creditors on due dates
  - Inability to comply with terms of loan agreements
  - Change from credit to cash-on-delivery transactions with suppliers
  - Inability to obtain financing for essential new product development or other essential investments
- **Operating indications**
  - Management intentions to liquidate the entity or to cease operations
  - Loss of key management without replacement
  - Loss of a major market, key customer(s), franchise, license, or principal supplier(s)
  - Labour difficulties
  - Shortages of important supplies
  - Emergence of a highly successful competitor
- **Other indications**
  - Non-compliance with capital or other statutory requirements
  - Pending legal proceedings against the entity that may, if successful, result in claims that the entity is unlikely to be able to satisfy
  - Changes in law or regulation or government policy expected to adversely affect the entity
  - Uninsured or underinsured catastrophes when they occur

ISA 570 also says that the auditors have to discuss the going concern issue with the client's management, to test the assumptions they have made to ensure they are justified, to obtain written representations from management about the things they are intending to do in the future to ensure that the going concern basis is appropriate and to review that disclosures made in the financial statements relating to going concern are sufficient to give a true and fair view in the UK. If, in making their assessment, the directors have used a period of less than a year from the date of approval of the financial statements and have not disclosed that fact in the financial statements, the auditors should do so in the auditor's report.

4.3.2 The break-up basis

If it becomes clear that the client cannot be considered to be a going concern, the financial statements will need to disclose this and the basis for preparing them will change to the 'break-up' basis.

This means that values will have to be adjusted to the amounts expected to be realised. In practice this tends not to be a problem for the auditor, because by the time this stage is reached, the client may well have passed into the hands of the receiver or 'corporate recovery' expert.

Alternatively, when it is intended to wind-up a solvent client within the next 12 months on a voluntary basis, the values may not in the event be very different.

4.3.3 Implications for the audit report

Unfortunately, this is not the end of the story because, where there are doubts about a company's going concern status, the auditors and management are likely to reach different conclusions, and this has implications for the audit report.

If the going concern assumption is appropriate but a material uncertainty exists about the ability of an entity to continue as a going concern and the uncertainty is adequately disclosed in the financial statements, the auditor should express an unqualified opinion but modify the audit report by adding an emphasis of matter paragraph (see Chapter 13).

If the financial statements fail to give a true and fair view because it is inappropriate to use the going concern basis, the auditor should express an adverse opinion (see Chapter 13).

Interactive question 2: Gamston Burgers plc [Difficulty level: Intermediate]

You are the auditor of Gamston Burgers plc, whose principal activities are haulage and warehousing services and the repair of lorries.

During the current year the company has suffered a significant fall in revenue and gross profit, which has led to a trading loss. The company is also experiencing cash flow problems.

You have been informed by the managing director that the fall in revenue is due to:

- The loss, half way through the year, of a long-standing customer to a competitor, and
- A decline in trade in the lorry repair business.

Due to the reduction in the repairs business the company has decided to close the workshop and sell the inventory of equipment and spares.

During the year the company replaced a number of vehicles, funding them by a combination of leasing and an increased overdraft facility. The facility is to be reviewed early next year after the audited accounts are available.

The draft accounts show a loss for the current year but the forecasts indicate a return to profitability in 20X6, as the managing director is optimistic about generating additional revenue from new contracts.

Requirements

(a) Explain why an auditor attaches so much importance to considering an entity's ability to continue as a going concern.

(b) Describe the audit work you would undertake in order to ascertain whether Gamston Burgers plc is a going concern.

(c) Explain the effect on your auditors' report on the financial statements of Gamston Burgers plc if you:

(i) Agree with the director's assertion

(ii) Conclude that trading conditions will not improve

See **Answer** at the end of this chapter.

4.4 Subsequent events

If the audit report says that the financial statements give a true and fair view, but the company goes under shortly after the financial statements are published, someone is likely to question whether the auditors knew what they were talking about.

If it then emerges that there were significant receivables who failed to pay up, or material amounts of inventory which turned out not to be realisable, you might think that such questions were justified.

Clearly, therefore, a review of events after the reporting period is both a sensible thing to do and, according to ISA 560, compulsory.

ISA 560 recognises the two different types of subsequent event according to IAS 10

- Those that provide evidence of conditions that existed at the date of the financial statements ('adjusting events); and
- Those that provide evidence of conditions that arose after the date of the financial statements ('non-adjusting events)

Examples of adjusting events (that should be reflected in the financial statements):

- Resolution of a court case
- Bankruptcy of a major customer
- Evidence of the NRV of inventories
- Discovery of fraud or errors

Examples of non-adjusting events (that are not reflected in the financial statements but should be disclosed in the notes if they are material):

- Destruction of a major asset by flood or fire
- Major share transactions
- Announcement of a plant to close part of a business
- Dividends proposed/declared after the end of the reporting period

Note: if a "non-adjusting event" occurs after the reporting date that means that it is no longer appropriate to assume that the entity is a going concern then the financial statements should be restated.

ISA 560 also recognises three time periods and recommends the following responses:

Period	Audit response
Up to the date of the audit report	• Carry out audit procedures outlined in ISA 560 • Consider whether the appropriate amendments/disclosures have been made in the financial statements • Consider whether there is a need to amend the audit report
Between the date of the audit report and the date the financial statements are issued	No responsibility for further work in this period, but if the auditor becomes aware of material facts: • Discuss with management • Take appropriate action
After the financial statements are issued	No responsibility for further work in this period, but if the auditor becomes aware of material facts: • Discuss with management • Take appropriate action
	Where the relevant fact did not exist at the date of the auditors' report there are no statutory provisions for revising the financial statements: • Discuss with management whether to withdraw the financial statements • Take advice on possibility of withdrawing audit report.

4.4.1 Audit procedures up to the date of the auditors' report

Procedures testing subsequent events	
Enquiries of management	• Status of items involving **subjective judgement**/accounted for using preliminary data • Whether there are any new **commitments**, borrowings or guarantees • Whether there have been any: – **Sales** or destruction of **assets** – **Issues** of **shares/debentures** or changes in business structure – **Developments** involving **risk areas, provisions** and **contingencies** – **Unusual accounting adjustments** – **Major events** (eg going concern problems) affecting appropriateness of accounting policies for estimates
Other procedures	• **Review** management procedures for identifying subsequent events to ensure that such events are identified • **Read minutes** of general board/committee meetings and enquire about unusual items • **Review latest accounting records** and financial information and budgets and forecasts • **Obtain evidence** concerning any litigation or claims from the company's solicitors (only with client permission)

Interactive question 3: Subsequent events review **[Difficulty level: Exam standard]**

You are the auditor of Weekly Ltd, which derives half its revenue from sales to one large national company. During your audit you notice that the sales ledger balance of this customer has nearly doubled during the year, although sales to it have increased only marginally.

Note down the main elements of your subsequent events review programme relating to this receivable balance.

See **Answer** at the end of this chapter.

4.5 Management representations

You learnt about the nature and purpose of written management representations in your studies for Assurance.

According to ISA 580, the auditor is required to obtain certain written representations from management as part of its audit evidence. These representations will usually be collated and finalised at the completion stage of the audit. The representation letter should be signed by the directors (or a directors' board minute of the representation obtained) before the auditors sign the audit report – if not, the auditors have not obtained all the evidence they required to sign the audit report in the first place.

4.6 ISA 720 *The Auditor's Responsibilities Relating to Other Information in Documents Containing Audited Financial Statements*

The audited financial statements are likely to be published in the annual report, which may also include other information such as:

- The directors' or management's report
- Financial summaries or highlights
- Employment data
- Planned capital expenditures
- Financial ratios

- Names of officers and directors
- Selected quarterly data.

4.6.1 Directors' report

In the UK the auditor has a specific responsibility to give an opinion as to whether the directors' report is consistent with the financial statements. Chapter 13 illustrates how this is dealt with in the auditor's report.

4.6.2 Inconsistencies

ISA 720 also gives the auditor some limited responsibilities with regards to the other information, where there may be material inconsistencies when other information contradicts information in the audited financial statements. This could cast doubt on the credibility of the audit report.

The auditor shall read the other information and take the following action if there are inconsistencies:

AMENDMENT NECESSARY TO	AUDITOR RESPONSE IF UNCORRECTED
Audited financial statements	• Qualified or adverse opinion.
The other information	• Include an "Other Matters paragraph describing the material inconsistency; or • Take other actions, eg seek legal advice.

4.6.3 Material misstatements of fact

A material misstatement of fact in other information exists when information, not related to matters appearing in the audited financial statements, is incorrectly stated or presented.

For example the auditor may believe that there are misstatements contained in some of the employment data within the annual report.

When the auditor considers that there is an apparent misstatement of fact, he should request management to consult with a qualified third party, such as the entity's legal counsel and should consider the advice received.

If management refuses to correct the misstatement, the auditor should consider taking further action, such as notifying those charged with governance of the entity in writing or obtaining legal advice.

5 Audit completion memorandum

Section overview

- This memorandum assists the partner to draw a conclusion.

'Matters for the attention of partners' (MAPS) seems to be the most commonly used acronym for the audit completion memorandum. However, don't use this acronym in the exam without first stating what it actually is.

This procedure, if carried out effectively is the single, most effective way of ensuring that work is complete and budgets are not broken.

It will radically reduce review time.

It should:

- Be completed with care
- Be typed
- Be organised along good report writing principles
- Have space for the partner's comments

It should be completed by 'the senior' – by this we mean the person with day-to-day responsibility for completing the audit work.

The length and detail of the matters for the attention of partners will be determined by the nature and complexity of the engagement. However, the matters for attention in relation to the Companies Act audit would normally be expected to contain the following:

5.1 The business

Comments on significant changes in the client's operations during the year, and anticipated in the coming year.

5.2 The financial statements

- Particulars of any failure of the financial statements to comply with acceptable accounting policies. If difficult questions of principle or judgement arise, a summary of the relevant information and bases for the conclusion, including the results of any consultation.
- Information on significant changes in the client's accounting policies or new accounting policies.
- Matters arising from the detailed analytical procedures on the financial statements.

5.3 The audit

- Particulars of any change to the original audit plan.
- Information concerning significant audit queries or matters to be followed up that have still to be resolved.
- A summary of the aggregate effect of the estimates of likely misstatement and the overall conclusion on the implications for the audit opinion.
- Conclusion on, and explanation of, any pending litigation and other material uncertainties.

Information on any failure to comply with the requirements of the company's memorandum or with trust deeds governing loans or debentures.

5.4 The management letter

Information on key matters for inclusion in the letter.

5.5 Other

- Details of any significant cost overrun against audit budget
- Details of any opportunities for providing additional services

The partner should evidence that he has reviewed the matters for attention and record what actions need to be taken to address any unresolved or outstanding matters. Often this will involve discussing the matter with the directors of the client, to identify what additional evidence is needed to enable the auditor to conclude on a matter or to resolve a matter of judgement. The matters for attention must be updated to show how the matters have been addressed and identify the additional evidence that has been obtained.

A final conclusion must be recorded detailing the opinion to be given on the financial statements.

5.6 Why does it work?

The completion of the audit summary forces the senior to consider and explain all aspects of the assignment. All (or very nearly all) staff take a pride in their work. If they realise there is a gap somewhere, they will either close it, or realise and explain why the work is unnecessary. In preparing a logical summary of the audit, they will also ensure that the file is organised in a logical way.

It summarises the important points, so it directs the partner's attention to them.

It increases the likelihood of the file being well organised, so the partner finds the bits he or she needs to see easier to locate.

Summary and Self-test

Summary

Self-test

Answer the following questions.

1 What three questions will the partner responsible for signing the audit report seek to answer at completion?

1 ....

2 ....

3 ....

2 It is appropriate to use a checklist to determine whether the financial statements comply with the Companies Act.

☐ True

☐ False

3 Opening balances need only be checked in a new auditor situation.

☐ True

☐ False

CHAPTER 12

4 List five financial indicators that a company has going concern problems.

1 ....

2 ....

3 ....

4 ....

5 ....

5 Is the auditor responsible for discovering relevant subsequent events after the audit report has been signed?

6 List five matters that might be referred to in a MAPS.

1 ....

2 ....

3 ....

4 ....

5 ....

Exam-style questions

7 You have recently been appointed auditor of Supachill Ltd and are planning the audit for the year ending 31 December 20X5. You have obtained the following background information about the company.

The company prepares chilled foods and sells them to supermarkets under its own brand name and that of a national supermarket chain, with which it has a one year renewable contract. At present this contract represents 45% of revenue. The company is currently negotiating a substantial contract with another supermarket chain, but is reluctant to agree to the prices and 60 days' credit facility demanded.

On 1 January 20X5 the managing director, who was previously involved in property development, acquired all the shares in Supachill Ltd from Omega plc, a conglomerate, which was rationalising its operations.

Immediately following the acquisition Supachill Ltd had net assets of £2 million, after taking account of low interest loans of £5 million from Omega plc. These loans are secured on the freehold property of the company and are repayable in equal quarterly instalments over a five-year period until 31 December 20X9. Day-to-day working capital is funded by an overdraft facility of £1.5 million, secured by a fixed and floating charge on the other assets of the company. This facility is to be reviewed by the bank early in 20X6 after the audited accounts are available.

The original business plan envisaged the acquisition of an adjacent factory to enable the company to double its output, but this expansion has been postponed.

The managing director has explained that there will be a delay in preparing the draft accounts as the finance director has left and has yet to be replaced. The accountant is assisted in the day-to-day accounting function by temporary staff. There is a projected loss for the year but forecasts indicate a return to profitability in the next financial year.

Requirements

(a) From the situation outlined above, identify circumstances particular to Supachill Ltd that give you cause for concern. Explain why such factors give cause for concern. **(12 marks)**

(b) Describe the procedures that you would undertake during the course of your audit in order to satisfy yourself on the status of Supachill Ltd as a going concern. **(6 marks)**

(18 marks)

8 Your client has lost a contract with its major customer. As a result the company is in financial difficulties. The bank is threatening to foreclose on its loan.

You are concerned that the company may not be a going concern, although, looking ahead nine months from the date of approval of the financial statements, the directors inform you that there is a good future for the business.

What steps would you take to enable you to assess whether the directors' assertions are reasonable?

What impact would the nine month period referred to above have on your audit report?

(3 marks)

Now, go back to the Learning Objectives in the Introduction. If you are satisfied you have achieved these objectives, please tick them off.

Technical reference

1 Financial statements review

• Do the financial statements comply with the Companies Act 2006?	
• Other information should be consistent	ISA 720
• Do the financial statements make sense?	ISA 520
	ISA 320

2 Other matters

• Opening balances and comparatives	ISA 510 ISA 710
• Going concern	ISA 570
• Subsequent events	ISA 560
• Management representations	ISA 580

Answers to Interactive questions

Answer to Interactive question 1

Regarding all opening balances

- Check prior year closing balances have been correctly brought forward; or
- Where appropriate, restated
- Consider impact of current year work on opening balances (eg bad debts write off in current year compared to opening provision)
- Review management's working papers, accounting and internal control systems for prior year

For capitalised costs

- Agree amounts capitalised to supporting documentation (to confirm amount)
- Discuss with previous auditors reason for the qualification
- Decide whether opening balances need amendment

Answer to Interactive question 2

(a) **Importance of going concern**

(i) 'Going concern' is an accounting concept. It is presumed to apply to any financial statements, unless contrary disclosure is given.

(ii) The amount at which assets and liabilities are included in the statement of financial position may be significantly different where the company is not a going concern. For example,

- – Assets will be valued on a break-up basis
- – Additional provisions (eg for closure costs) may be required

(iii) The classification of items will differ where financial statements reflect a break-up basis. For example, non-current assets/liabilities reclassified as current.

(iv) The risk of failure is a real threat to many businesses and the failure of the auditor to give any warning may result in litigation/adverse publicity.

(b) **Audit work regarding going concern**

To ascertain whether Gamston Burgers plc can meet its debts as they fall due

(i) Obtain a written statement (management representation) from the managing director confirming his considered view that the company is a going concern.

(ii) Review management's profit and cash flow forecasts for the next financial year to ascertain, *inter alia*, the company's working capital requirements.

(iii) Confirm the appropriateness of relevant assumptions (eg average trade receivables collection period) by comparison with ratios obtained from analytical procedures.

(iv) Request a statement of borrowing facilities to be included in the bank confirmation letter.

(v) Review the day-to-day utilisation of the bank overdraft facility and its proximity to the current limit.

(vi) Obtain a loan confirmation from the leasing company and confirm that all instalments to date have been met.

(vii) Discuss with the credit controller (or financial accountant) the current pressures under which the company is being placed by larger customers who may be seeking extended credit terms.

(viii) Undertake sensitivity analysis on client's forecasts to variable factors both within the managing director's control and outside it.

(ix) Review the level of trade and other payables (including VAT and PAYE/NIC and whether any penalties are being incurred) after the balance sheet date and the extent to which they are financing short-term needs.

To ascertain whether Gamston Burgers plc can otherwise continue in business (ie return to profitable trading)

(i) Obtain a copy of tenders submitted/correspondence to date concerning any new contracts currently being negotiated and monitor all subsequent developments.

(ii) Review drivers' logs, reports on warehouse utilisation etc and discuss with management how current spare capacity will be utilised by new contracts obtained.

(iii) Review the terms of the contract with the long-standing customer which was lost and the grounds on which it was lost to a competitor.

(iv) Verify reasonableness of estimates arising from closure of workshop (eg concerning costs of external servicing of the transport vehicle fleet).

(v) Obtain written confirmation from the company's legal adviser as to whether or not there are any pending legal claims (eg in respect of inventory losses from warehouses, late deliveries, damage to goods in transit etc).

(c) **Effect on audit report**

(i) **Agree with director's assertion**

If doubt surrounding the going concern status of the company is minimal, disclosure in the financial statements would not be required in order to give a true and fair view. The audit report would therefore be unqualified.

If the branch is so material that its inability to trade could affect the going concern status of the company (unlikely), the matter should be disclosed in the financial statements. If adequate disclosure is made in the financial statements, the auditor should express an unqualified opinion but modify his report by adding an emphasis of matter paragraph that

– Highlights the existence of a material uncertainty relating to the event or condition that may cast significant doubt on the company's ability to continue as a going concern, and
– Draws attention to the note in the financial statements that discloses these matters.

(ii) **Disagree with director's assertion**

The form of audit report will depend upon the materiality of the branch and extent to which the uncertainty has been disclosed in the financial statements.

As the director appears confident about the future of this branch, it is unlikely that adequate (if any) disclosure has been made. The audit report would therefore be qualified on the grounds of disagreement due to the inadequate disclosure of the uncertainty.

Answer to Interactive question 3

- Monitor post year end customer receipts (to confirm recoverability)
- Review of customer correspondence (to ascertain problem, eg dispute)
- Calculation of trade receivables collection period, by month, after year end (to determine whether situation is deteriorating further)
- Consider likely effectiveness of any reservation of title clause/other security (to assess possible extent of recovery if customer liquidated)
- Review latest available audited accounts of customer (for indications of GC problems)
- Review level of post year end sales and orders (to determine whether situation is continuing unchecked)

Answers to Self-test

1
- Do the financial statements comply with the provisions of the Companies Act 2006?
- Do the financial statements make sense?
- Has the audit report been drafted properly?

2 True

3 False

4 From:

- Net liabilities or net current liability position
- Necessary borrowing facilities have not been agreed
- Fixed-term borrowings approaching maturity without realistic prospects of renewal or repayment, or excessive reliance on short-term borrowings
- Major debt repayment falling due where refinancing is necessary to the entity's continued existence
- Major restructuring of debt
- Indications of withdrawal of financial support by creditors
- Negative operating cash flows indicated by historical or prospective financial statements
- Adverse key financial ratios
- Substantial operating losses or significant deterioration in the value of assets used to generate cash flows
- Major losses or cash flow problems which have arisen since the balance sheet date
- Arrears or discontinuance of dividends
- Inability to pay creditors on due dates
- Inability to comply with terms of loan agreements
- Reduction in normal terms of credit by suppliers
- Change from credit to cash-on-delivery transactions with suppliers
- Inability to obtain financing for essential new product development or other essential investments
- Substantial sale of fixed assets not intended to be replaced

5 No – but he will have to take appropriate steps if made aware of them

6
1 Comments on significant changes to the business
2 Issues relating to the financial statements
3 Matters arising from the audit strategy/plan
4 Issues referred to in the management letter
5 From related issues (such as budget overruns/opportunities for other services)

CHAPTER 12

Exam-style questions

7 (a)

Circumstance	Explanation
• The client's economic dependence on its principal customer (45% of revenue on a one year renewable contract).	• The going concern assumption may not be appropriate if, for any reason, this major contract is not renewed.
• Deterioration of cash flows, due to customers demanding/taking extended periods of credit (up to 60 days).	• The risk of bad and doubtful debts is increased, and year end receivables may be materially overstated if provisions are not adequate.
• Pressure from the potential customer's demands.	• Profit margins may be adversely affected, increasing doubts about the company's continuation as a going concern.
• Sale by conglomerate on favourable terms (low interest loans).	• Omega plc may not have been optimistic about Supachill Ltd's future prospects, which therefore raises going concern doubts.
• High gearing with repayments due in near future (£250,000 per quarter).	• Any breach in loan terms (eg if instalments are not being met) may result in foreclosure. • Additional funding may be difficult to raise as security base is diminished.
• The postponement of plans for expansion (but it could be considered a mitigating factor).	• The adequacy of the working capital available, both the short and medium term must be assessed.
• The managing director's (MD) lack of knowledge of the nature of the business and the industry.	• The MD may lack the acumen to trade out of the loss-making situation, thereby increasing which it operates. Inherent risk.
• The loss of key staff (finance director).	• The reduction in supervision over the accounting functions may increase both inherent and control risk and result in – more errors arising with the increase in the accountant's workload – failure to detect and correct errors
• The delay in preparing draft accounts may increase inherent risk if the audit deadline cannot be postponed.	• Increased pressure on the audit timetable to meet a possible bank deadline late in the year could result in a material misstatement being undetected by audit procedures.
• Only temporary accounts staff are available to assist accountant.	• The risk of errors arising is increased (eg due to insufficient training/ supervision).
• The bank's reliance on audited accounts, increasing management's motive to 'inflate' profit.	• Particular attention should be given to – the accuracy of bank overdraft/ payables cut-off – the impact of potential adjustments on key ratios (eg acid test ratio)

Circumstance	Explanation
• The projected loss may cause the MD to bias the results. If, for example, the bank is already aware of (and accepts) the projection, the MD may ensure that the loss is met (eg by over-providing against asset values). Alternatively, the reported loss may be understated by understating provisions.	• Attention should be given to all matters of judgement which materially affect the income statement. In particular, the need for inventory and receivable provisions should be assessed (ie tested for overstatement) as well as their adequacy (ie tested for understatement).
• Lack of cumulative/prior knowledge from which assurance can be derived.	• Adequate planning is essential to audit efficiency to avoid over-auditing (due to increase in inherent risk) in the first year.
• The nature of the client's business.	• Chilled foods increase inherent risk as they are perishable and there may be understatement of year end inventory provisions.

CHAPTER 12

(b) **Procedures**

To ensure that the company can meet its debts as they fall due

(i) Obtain a written statement from the managing director confirming his considered view that the company is a going concern.

(ii) Review management's profit and cash flow forecasts for the next financial year (and beyond, if available) to ascertain the company's working capital requirements.

(iii) Confirm the appropriateness of relevant assumptions, eg average debt collection period, by comparison with ratios obtained through analytical procedures.

(iv) Request a statement of borrowing facilities to be included in the bank confirmation letter.

(v) Review the day-to-day utilisation of the bank overdraft facility and its proximity to the current limit.

(vi) Obtain confirmation of loan from Omega plc and that all quarterly instalments of loan repayment to date have been met.

(vii) Discuss with the credit controller (or financial accountant) the current pressures under which the company is being placed by larger customers seeking extended credit terms.

(viii) Review the MD's agreement with Omega plc for the purchase of Supachill Ltd to ascertain the circumstances under which interest rates or repayment terms could be varied.

(ix) Review the level of trade and other payables, including VAT and PAYE/NIC and whether any penalties are being incurred, and the extent to which they are financing short-term needs.

To ensure that the company can otherwise continue in business

(i) Obtain a copy of correspondence to date concerning the contract currently being negotiated, and monitor all subsequent developments.

(ii) Review production records and order books, and discuss with management how current spare capacity can accommodate substantial new contracts (as the expansion plans have been postponed).

(iii) Review the terms of the existing one-year renewable contract and correspondence with this customer, to ascertain whether there are any grounds for this contract not to be renewed.

(iv) Discuss with the MD any possible new sources of finance for the expansion.

(v) Obtain written confirmation from the company's legal advisor as to whether or not there are any pending legal claims (eg in respect of food poisoning).

(vi) Discuss with the MD and/or the company's recruitment adviser the response to any advertisement for the position of finance director.

8 **Regarding ability to continue in business**

- Discuss with directors eg
  - Likelihood of alternative sales markets
  - Advertising/marketing strategy
  - Prospects of product diversification
- Scrutinise current year's order book
- Review tenders for new contracts
- Review published trading results for industry (expanding or in decline)

Regarding ability to meet debts as fall due

- Discuss with directors eg
  - Any intention to sell surplus assets
  - Impending negotiations for new sources of finance
  - Professional advice sought from bank
  - Confirm with bank/other lenders negotiations to date

Nine month period – effect in UK

- If period used for going concern assessment < 1 year from date of approval of financial statements
- And that fact not disclosed in financial statements
- Disclose in audit report
- But do not qualify audit report regarding this

Now, go back to the Learning Objectives in the Introduction. If you are satisfied you have achieved those objectives, please tick them off.

chapter 13

Reporting

Introduction

Learning objectives

Tick off

- Understand the types of reports that assurance providers and auditors issue ☐
- Know the typical contents of a report on control weakness (management letter) ☐
- Know the standard contents of an unmodified audit report ☐
- Know when an audit report should be modified ☐

Specific syllabus references for this chapter are: 4d, e, h, i.

Syllabus links

The basic unmodified audit report was introduced in Assurance.

Examination context

This is an important area for the exam. Audit reports have featured in six of the past seven exam papers (December 2007 to June 2009) as a part or all of a 20 mark question. In the assessment, candidates may be required to:

- Draft suitable extracts for an assurance report (including any report to management issued as a part of the engagement) in relation to a specified organisation on the basis of given information, including in the extracts (where appropriate) statements of facts, their potential effects, and recommendations for action relevant to the needs and nature of the organisations being reported upon
- Advise on reports to be issued to those responsible for governance in accordance with International Standards on Auditing, legislation, regulation, codes of corporate governance
- Explain the elements (both explicit and implicit) of the auditor's report issued in accordance with the International Standards on Auditing and statutory requirements and recommend the nature of an audit opinion to be given in such a report
- Draft suitable extracts for an audit report (including any report to the management issued as part of the engagement) in relation to a specified organisation on the basis of given information, including in the extracts (where appropriate) statements of facts, their potential effects, and recommendations for action relevant to the needs and nature of the organisation being reported upon

1 Communication with those charged with governance

Section overview

- Auditors are required to report privately to those charged with governance on various matters arising from the audit.
- Relevant matters include:
  - Auditor's responsibilities in relation to the financial statement audit
  - Planned scope and timing of the audit
  - Significant findings from the audit
  - Auditor independence
- Matters may be communicated orally or in writing.
- They should be recorded in audit working papers.

Various auditing standards require auditors to report certain audit matters arising to those charged with governance. This report will be 'private' and just for the attention of those charged with governance, as opposed to the audit report, which is a published document.

The requirements in relation to this private reporting are found in the main in ISA 260 *Communication with those Charged with Governance* which deals with the auditor's responsibility to communicate with those charged with governance in an audit of financial statements.

ISA 265 *Communicating Deficiencies in Internal Control to Those Charged with Governance and Management* specifically requires the auditor to communicate any significant deficiencies in internal control encountered during the course of their audit work. Whether a deficiency is significant is a matter of professional judgement for the auditor. Matters to consider will include the likelihood of material misstatements and potential losses or fraud.

C H A P T E R 13

1.1 Appropriate persons

Definition

Those charged with governance is the term used to describe the role of persons entrusted with the supervision, control and direction of the entity. Those charged with governance ordinarily are accountable for ensuring that the entity achieves its objectives, financial reporting and reporting to interested parties. Those charged with governance include management only when it performs such functions.

In the UK and Ireland, those charged with governance include the directors (executive and non-executive) of a company or other body, the members of an audit committee where one exists, the partners, proprietors, committee of management or trustees of other forms of entity, or equivalent persons responsible for directing the entity's affairs and preparing its financial statements.

The auditors may communicate with the whole board, the supervisory board or the audit committee depending on the governance structure of the organisation. The auditor should ensure that those charged with governance are provided with a copy of the audit engagement letter on a timely basis.

To avoid misunderstandings, the engagement letter should explain that auditors will only **communicate matters** that come to their attention as a **result** of the **performance** of the audit. It should state that the auditors are **not required** to **design procedures** for the purpose of expressing an opinion on the effectiveness of the entity's internal control.

The letter may also:

- **Describe** the **form** which any **communications** on governance matters will take
- **Identify** the **appropriate persons** with whom such communications will be made
- **Identify** any **specific matters** of **governance** interest which it has agreed are to be communicated

1.2 Matters to be communicated

The scope of ISA 260 is limited to matters that come to the auditors' attention as a result of the audit; the auditors are not required to design procedures to identify matters of governance interest.

Such matters would include:

- The auditor's responsibilities in relation to the financial statement audit
- Planned scope and timing of the audit
- Significant findings from the audit
- Auditor independence (in the case of listed entities)

Under significant findings the standard lists the following:

- The auditor's views about significant qualitative aspects of the entity's accounting practices, including accounting policies, accounting estimates and financial statement disclosures.
- Significant difficulties, if any, encountered during the audit
- Significant matters, if any, arising from the audit that were discussed with management
- Written representations the auditor is requesting
- Other matters, if any, arising from the audit that, in the auditor's professional judgement, are significant to the oversight of the financial reporting process

Where the audited entity is listed, auditors shall:

- Confirm that the engagement team have complied with ethical requirements relating to independence
- Declare all relationships between the firm and the entity that may have a bearing on independence, including details of fees for non-audit services
- Detail the related safeguards that have been applied to eliminate identified threats to independence or reduce them to an acceptable level

1.2.1 Communicating deficiencies in internal control

ISA 265 does not require auditors to perform specific tests on internal control, over and above their normal audit work, but it does require them to report on deficiencies encountered during the course of that work. The specific requirements are the following:

- The auditor shall determine whether deficiencies in internal control have been identified
- Where deficiencies have been identified the auditor shall determine whether those deficiencies are significant
- Significant deficiencies shall be communicated in writing to those charged with governance
- Significant deficiencies shall be communicated in writing to management
- Other deficiencies shall be communicated to management if the auditor considers them important enough to warrant management attention
- Written communication shall include a description of the deficiencies and their potential effects, and sufficient information to understand the context of the communication

The standard gives examples of matters that the auditor may consider in determining whether deficiencies are significant. These examples include:

- The likelihood of the deficiencies leading to material misstatements
- The susceptibility to loss or fraud

- The financial statement amounts
- The volume of activity
- The importance of the controls to the financial reporting process

1.3 How?

Matters may be communicated orally or in writing, but they should be recorded in the audit working papers, however discussed. Auditors should make clear that the audit is not designed to identify all relevant matters connected with governance and they should have regard to local laws and regulations, and local guidance on confidentiality when communicating with management.

1.4 Attributes for effective communication to those charged with governance

The communication should have the following attributes:

- **Timing**: It should be sufficiently prompt to enable those charged with governance to take appropriate action, for example, items relating to the financial statements should be reported before the financial statements are approved.
- **Extent, form and frequency**: Should be appropriate. What is appropriate will depend on the size of the entity and the way in which those charged with governance operate.
- **Expectations**: It should fulfil the expectations of the auditors and those charged with governance, and therefore, the nature of the communication should be agreed early in the audit process, for example, in the letter of engagement, so that misunderstandings are minimised.
- **Management comments**: Should be included where they are relevant and will aid the understanding of those charged with governance.
- **Previous year's points**: Should be repeated if no action has been taken and the auditors believe that they are still relevant. If there are no new points to be made, the auditors should make that point
- **Disclaimer**: Should be included so that third parties do not seek to rely on the information given within the report.

Interactive question 1: Mouse and Ratty Ltd [Difficulty level: Easy]

You are currently undertaking an assurance engagement for Mouse and Ratty Ltd, a large firm of PR consultants in Leeds.

During the course of the work you have found a number of issues on which you need to report. These can be summarised as follows.

(1) You have found a total of £18,000 of unauthorised expenditure on IT equipment. Any IT expenditure in excess of £150 has to be authorised by a director.

(2) The IT expenditure for the year is 65% in excess of budget. There does not appear to have been an investment project which was not budgeted for. There seems to be little reason for the rise.

(3) Large sums for travelling expenses are not being authorised when in excess of nightly limits set. Four executives spent a total of £25,000 in excess of nightly limits throughout the year.

(4) When examining work in progress, it became clear that there were sums which have been there for more than six months without being billed. These total £56,000. There appears to be no explanation for this.

(5) When overtime forms are submitted, any amounts of more than three hours per month need to be authorised. This is rarely done. The company paid out £180,000 in unauthorised overtime.

(6) There are no controls over non-chargeable time. The proportion of non-chargeable time for individual executives varies from 5% to 34%.

Requirement

Identify

(a) The internal control weaknesses arising from the above
(b) The risks to which each identified weakness exposes the company
(c) Actions that the company should take to mitigate those risks.

See **Answers** at the end of this chapter.

2 Assurance reports

Section overview

- There is less formal requirement in relation to assurance reports generally than there is for audit reports.
- Proformas for review reports and other assurance reports are given in international standards.

As we shall see in the following sections of this chapter, audit reports are prescribed by International Standards on Auditing and also by additional guidance and legal requirements in the UK.

There is less formality surrounding more general assurance reports and these reports will often take the most appropriate form.

2.1 Reviews

Some guidance is given in international standards, notably International Standard on Assurance Engagements 3000 *Assurance Engagements other than Audits or Reviews of Historical Financial Information.*

It sets out that the assurance report should be in writing and should contain a clear expression of the practitioner's conclusion about the subject matter.

International Standard on Review Engagements (ISRE) 2400 *Engagements to Review Financial Statements* gives the following guidance about review reports. Negative assurance is given on review assignments. The ISRE says 'the review report should contain a clear written expression of **negative assurance.** The practitioner (or reporting accountant) should review and assess the conclusions drawn from the evidence obtained as the basis for the expression of negative assurance.

Based on the work performed, the practitioner should assess whether any information obtained during the review indicates that the financial statements do not give a true and fair view (or 'are not presented fairly, in all material respects,') in accordance with the identified financial reporting framework.'

If no matters have come to the attention of the practitioner, he should give a clear expression of negative assurance in his report. An example of an unqualified review report is given in the appendix to the ISRE, and it is reproduced here.

Worked example: Form of Unqualified Review Report

REVIEW REPORT TO ...

We have reviewed the accompanying balance sheet of ABC Company at December 31, 20XX, and the related statements of income and cash flows for the year then ended. These financial statements are the responsibility of the Company's management. Our responsibility is to issue a report on these financial statements based on our review.

We conducted our review in accordance with the International Standard on Review Engagement 2400 (or refer to relevant national standards or practices) applicable to review engagements. This Standard requires that we plan and perform the review to obtain moderate assurance as to whether the financial statements are free of material misstatement. A review is limited primarily to inquiries of company personnel and analytical procedures applied to financial data and thus provides less assurance than an audit. We have not performed an audit and, accordingly, we do not express an audit opinion.

Based on our review, nothing has come to our attention that causes us to believe that the accompanying financial statements do not give a true and fair view (or 'are not presented fairly, in all material respects,') in accordance with International Accounting Standards.

Date REPORTING ACCOUNTANT

Address

Notice the main components of the report:

1 Addressee

This will depend on the specific terms of the assignment. It may be addressed to the directors, or to a specified third party user such as a bank.

2 Scope and responsibilities

The first paragraph defines the scope of the work and clarifies the respective responsibilities of management and the assurance provider.

3 Nature of work and level of assurance

The second paragraph describes the nature of a review and highlights how it differs from an audit.

4 Conclusion

As was explained in Chapter 1, the conclusion is expressed in terms of negative assurance.

If matters have come to the attention of the reporting accountant, he should **describe those matters**. The matters may have the following effects.

Impact	Effect on report
Material	Express a qualification of the negative assurance provided
Pervasive	Give an adverse statement that the financial statements do not give a true and fair view

The reporting accountant may feel there has been a limitation in the scope of the work he intended to carry out for the review. If so, he should **describe the limitation.** The limitation may have the following effects.

Impact	Effect on report
Material to one area	Express a qualification of the negative assurance provided regarding the possible adjustments to the financial statements that might have been determined to be necessary if the limitation did not exist
Pervasive	Do not provide any assurance

2.2 Reviews of interim financial information

In July 2007 the APB published ISRE (UK and Ireland) 2410 *Review of interim financial information performed by the Independent auditor of the entity.* This applies the basic principles of conducting reviews and preparing review reports as set out in ISRE 2400 to one specific type of review.

2.3 Reports following examination of prospective information

Chapter 1 explained that the nature of prospective information, such as forecasts and projections, affects the level of assurance that can be given. Reports on these assignments may well contain additional 'warnings' for readers.

The IAASB standard ISAE 3400 *The Examination of Prospective Financial Information* gives the following list of components for this type of report:

(a) Title

(b) Addressee

(c) Identification of the prospective financial information

(d) A reference to the ISAE or relevant national standards

(e) A statement that management is responsible for the prospective financial information including the assumptions on which it is based

(f) When applicable, a reference to the purpose and/or restricted distribution of the prospective financial information

(g) A statement of negative assurance as to whether the assumptions provide a reasonable basis for the prospective financial information

(h) An opinion as to whether the prospective financial information is properly prepared on the basis of the assumptions and is presented in accordance with the relevant financial reporting framework

(i) Appropriate caveats concerning the achievability of the results indicated by the prospective financial information

(j) Date of the report which should be the date procedures have been completed

(k) Reporting accountant's address, and

(l) Signature

The standard also gives an extract from a report on a review of prospective financial information:

> We have examined the forecast in accordance with the International Standard on Assurance Engagements applicable to the examination of prospective financial information. Management is responsible for the forecast including the assumptions set out in Note X on which it is based.
>
> Based on our examination of the evidence supporting the assumptions, nothing has come to our attention which causes us to believe that these assumptions do not provide a reasonable basis for the forecast. Further, in our opinion the forecast is properly prepared on the basis of the assumptions and is presented in accordance with ….
>
> Actual results are likely to be different from the forecast since anticipated events frequently do not occur as expected and the variation may be material.

Notice the extra final paragraph drawing attention to the nature of prospective financial information, illustrating the type of 'caveat' referred to in (i) above.

3 Unmodified audit reports

Section overview

- The report per ISA 700 contains a number of standard elements, which can be seen in the UK audit report.
- UK auditors also report by exception on a number of legal matters.
- Some UK auditors include a 'Bannerman' paragraph in the audit report to ensure that the extent of their liability in respect of the report is understood.
- With regard to listed companies, the audit report will also refer to the review of the corporate governance statement required by the Combined Code.

The following sections will look at the types of audit reports that auditors may issue. ISA 700 and APB Bulletin 2009/2 set out standardised audit reports for auditors to use. This has the benefit of providing a degree of consistency between audit reports on financial statements and enhances their understandability.

In all cases an opinion on the financial statements will need to be included. The opinion may be:

- An unmodified **opinion**: the auditor is satisfied that the evidence obtained is sufficient and appropriate and supports the view presented in the financial statements prepared by the company's management.
- A modified **opinion**: the auditor is either not satisfied with the sufficiency or appropriateness of the evidence that has been obtained, compared with what could reasonably be expected, or has issues with the content of the financial statements.

In some cases the auditor may need to add additional paragraphs in the audit report that would only be included under certain circumstances; these do not, however, indicate that there is anything wrong with the financial statements or the audit evidence obtained. These circumstances will be discussed in detail in section 4.

When the auditor makes amendments to a standard audit report (be it due to modifying the audit opinion or adding additional paragraphs) this is referred to as a modified **audit report.**

The opinions open to the auditor are therefore to issue:

1. An unmodified audit report
2. A modified audit report with an unmodified audit opinion
3. A modified audit report with a modified audit opinion, which can be a qualified opinion (except for), an adverse opinion or disclaimer of opinion

3.1 Difficulties with the wording of the audit report

The auditing standards which deal with the wording of the audit report have a number of issues that have not yet been resolved. It is therefore difficult to give you a definitive example of the wording for audit reports in any given set of circumstances, due to the following reasons.

- The wording in common use in the UK, as these notes are being written, is different from the wording in the relevant ISA (ISA 700, *Forming an Opinion and Reporting on Financial Statements*).
- The wording of the report owes as much to the Companies Act 2006 as it does to the auditing standard.
- The IAASB has recently revised the relevant ISA as part of the Clarity project and the APB has issued Bulletin 2009/2 which applies to UK audit reports as it has not adopted ISA 700.

APB Bulletin 2009/02 *Auditor's Reports on Financial Statements in the United Kingdom* is included in your open book for this examination.

3.2 The main components of an audit report

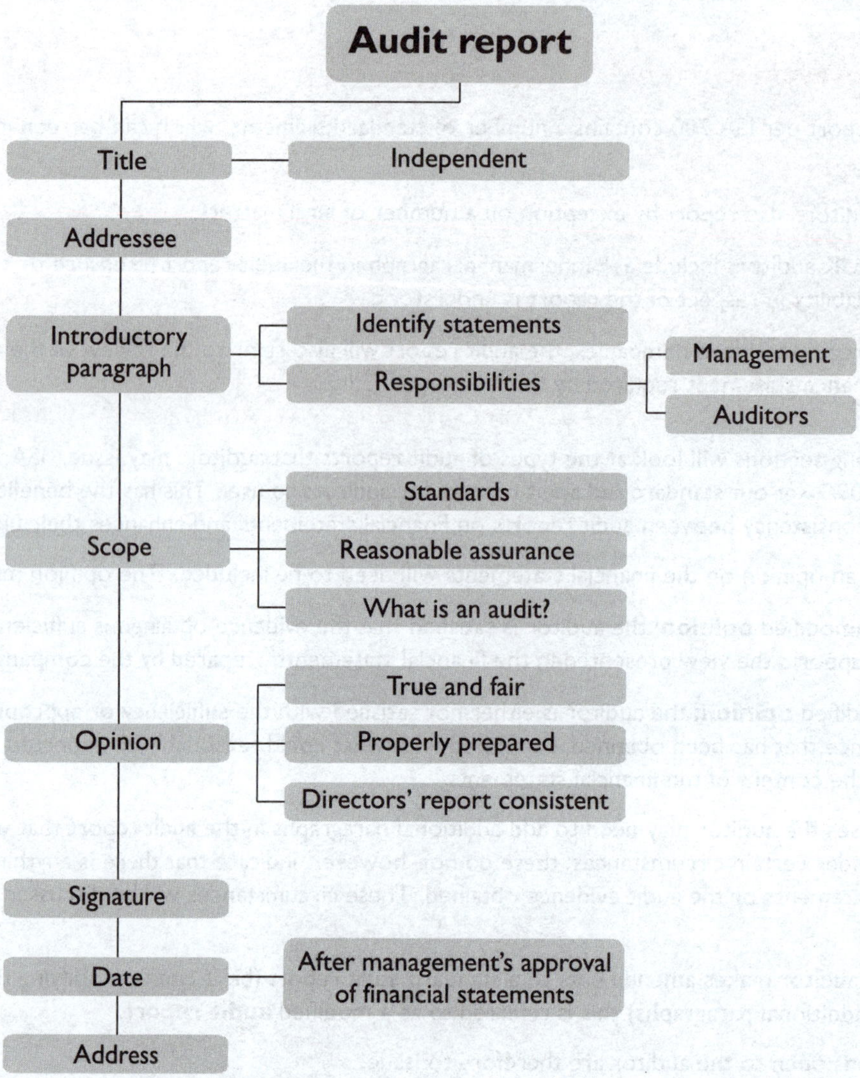

Figure 13.1: Overview: unmodified report

3.2.1 Title

The report needs an appropriate title to distinguish it from the other material included with the financial statements and to try to reduce the 'expectations gap'.

In order to do this the title will include the words '**Independent auditor**' to stress that, whilst the financial statements are management's responsibility, the audit report is the responsibility of the auditor alone.

The title usually also refers to the people to whom the report is addressed.

3.2.2 Addressee

Because in carrying out their audit work the auditors have to deal with management and work closely with the client's management team, it may be forgotten that their report is not directed towards management.

Remember the fundamental structure of an assurance engagement (Figure 13.2).

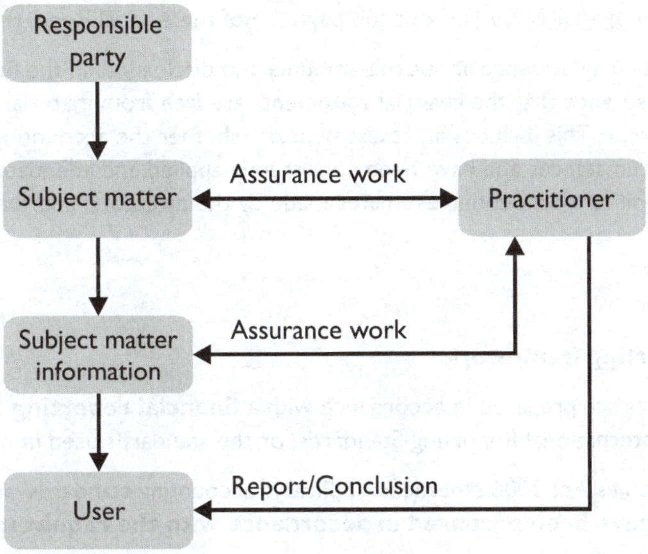

Figure 13.2: Assurance engagement

It is important to remember that the report will be addressed to the user in the tripartite relationship which exists in any assurance engagement, which for an audit in the UK means the company's shareholders.

Whilst the audit report does not represent a direct commentary on the performance of management over the period, it does state whether or not the account which management gives of its own performance is true and fair.

Understanding this relationship is important to all the parties involved, and clearly setting out the addressee of the report should also contribute to a reduction in the expectations gap.

CHAPTER 13

3.2.3 Opening or introductory paragraph

The purpose of the opening paragraph is to tell the reader what the subject of the report is.

It should therefore identify:

- The entity being audited
- The statements which have been audited
- The period subject to the audit, and
- Include a statement that preparing the financial statements is the responsibility of management.

Identifying the statements

Identifying the statements covered by the audit report has traditionally been done by referring to the relevant page numbers. However, as well as leaving scope for silly errors if the number of pages changes whilst the financial statements are being finalised, to refer to page numbers has become irrelevant if the financial statements are published as web pages, which is permitted under UK law. Best practice, therefore is to refer to the statements by name.

Respective responsibilities of directors and auditors

In the UK there is usually a statement of directors' responsibilities towards the financial statements, included either in the directors' report or as a separate statement. A cross reference is therefore made in UK audit reports.

There is also a statement of the auditors' responsibilities, emphasising that the auditors report on the truth and fairness of the financial statements.

3.2.4 Scope paragraph

It should include the following.

Either:

A description of the scope of an audit of financial statements is (provided on the APB's web-site at www.frc.org.uk/apb/scope/UKNP) / (set out (on page …) of the Annual Report): or

An audit involves obtaining evidence about the amounts and disclosures in the financial statements sufficient to give reasonable assurance that the financial statements are free from material misstatements, whether caused by fraud or error. This includes an assessment of: whether the accounting policies are appropriate to the company's circumstances and have been consistently applied and adequately disclosed; the reasonableness of significant accounting estimates made by the directors; and the overall presentation of the financial statements.

3.2.5 Opinion paragraph

The financial reporting framework

All financial statements are prepared in accordance with a **financial reporting framework**. This may be in accordance with International Reporting Standards, or the standards used in other jurisdictions.

In the UK the Companies Act 2006 embraces 'applicable accounting standards' and the framework reference is usually **'have been prepared in accordance with the requirements of the Companies Act 2006**.

The opinion itself

Under the ISA the opinion may either be:

- 'Give a true and fair view', or
- 'Present fairly in all material respects'.

The ISA stresses that the two expressions are equivalent to each other. The UK audit opinion states that the financial statements 'give a true and fair view'.

3.2.6 True and fair view

In the UK the auditors will normally express their opinion by reference to the 'true and fair view'. Whilst this term is at the heart of the audit, 'true' and 'fair' are not defined in law or audit guidance. However, for practical purposes the following definitions are generally accepted.

- **True**: Information is factual and conforms with reality, not false. In addition the information conforms with required standards and law. The accounts have been correctly extracted from the books and records.
- **Fair**: Information is free from discrimination and bias in compliance with expected standards and rules. The accounts should reflect the commercial substance of the company's underlying transactions.

3.2.7 Other responsibilities

In some jurisdictions the auditor reports on other matters as required by relevant legislation – in the Republic of Ireland, for example, the auditor's report includes a statement about the maintenance of the company's capital. In the UK, the auditor is required to express an opinion as to whether the information in the directors' report is consistent with the financial statements. UK auditors are also required to identify the matters that are required by the Companies Act 2006 to be reported on by exception.

3.2.8 Date

The date of the report should be the date when the auditor has obtained sufficient appropriate evidence to support the opinion.

It should not be earlier than the date when management approves the financial statements.

3.2.9 Auditor's signature

This may seem obvious, but it is all to do with emphasising who has responsibility for what.

Companies Act 2006 requires that where the auditor is a firm, the report must be signed by the 'senior statutory auditor' in his own name, for and on behalf of the auditor. Prior to this, reports were signed in the name of the firm. In most cases the senior statutory auditor will be the engagement partner.

The Act also gives an exemption from the requirements to name the auditor, arising from circumstances such as the protests in 2003 by animal rights extremists against Deloitte and Touche, then the auditors of Huntingdon Life Services Group plc.

The auditor's name and, where the auditor is a firm, the name of the person who signed the report as senior statutory auditor, may be omitted from:

(a) Published copies of the report, and
(b) The copy of the report delivered to the registrar of companies

If the following conditions are met:

(a) There are reasonable grounds that statement of the name would create or be likely to create a serious risk that the auditor or senior statutory auditor, or any other person, would be subject to violence or intimidation, and

(b) The company has given notice of the resolution to the Secretary of State, stating the:

   (i) Name and registered number of the company,

   (ii) Financial year of the company to which the report relates, and

   (iii) Name of the auditor and (where the auditor is a firm) the name of the person who signed the report as senior statutory auditor.

3.2.10 Address

Again this is to ensure that there is no doubt who is responsible for the report.

ISA 700 requires the report to name the location in the jurisdiction where the auditor practises.

CHAPTER 13

Worked example: UK audit report

Independent auditors' report to the shareholders of XYZ Limited

We have audited the financial statements of (name of entity) for the year ended … which comprise (specify the titles of the primary financial statements such as the Profit and Loss Account, the Balance Sheet, the Cash Flow Statement, the Statement of Total Recognised Gains and Losses, the Reconciliation of Movements in Shareholders' Funds) and the related notes. The financial reporting framework that has been applied in their preparation is applicable law and United Kingdom Accounting Standards (United Kingdom Generally Accepted Accounting Practice). Note that under IFRS primary financial statements are statements of financial position, comprehensive income, cash flow and changes in equity.

Respective responsibilities of directors and auditors

As explained more fully in the Directors' Responsibility Statement (set out on page …), the directors are responsible for the preparation of the financial statements and for being satisfied that they give a true and fair view. Our responsibility is the audit the financial statements in accordance with applicable law and International Standards on Auditing (UK and Ireland). Those standards require us to comply with the Auditing Practices Board's (APB's) Ethical Standards for Auditors.

Scope of the audit of the financial statements

An audit involves obtaining evidence about the amounts and disclosures in the financial statements sufficient to give reasonable assurance that the financial statements are free from material misstatement, whether caused by fraud or error. This includes an assessment of: whether the accounting policies are appropriate to the company's circumstances and have been consistently applied and adequately disclosed; the reasonableness of significant accounting estimates made by the directors; and the overall presentation of the financial statements.

Opinion on financial statements

In our opinion the financial statements:

- Give a true and fair view of the state of the company's affairs as at …. and of its profit [loss] for the year then ended;
- Have been properly prepared in accordance with United Kingdom Generally Accepted Accounting Practice; and
- Have been prepared in accordance with the requirements of the Companies Act 2006.

Opinion on other matter prescribed by the Companies Act 2006

In our opinion the information given in the Directors' Report for the financial year for which the financial statements are prepared is consistent with the financial statements.

Matters on which we are required to report by exception

We have nothing to report in respect of the following matters where the Companies Act 2006 requires us to report to you if, in our opinion:

- Adequate accounting records have not been kept, or returns adequate for our audit have not been received from branches not visited by us; or
- The financial statements are not in agreement with the accounting records and returns; or
- Certain disclosures of directors' remuneration specified by law are not made; or
- We have not received all the information and explanations we require for our audit.

[Signature]

John Smith (Senior Statutory Auditor) Address

For and on behalf of ABC LLP, Statutory Auditor Date

3.2.11 Bannerman

Following a Scottish legal case when it was found that the Royal Bank of Scotland was entitled to rely on the published financial statements of a company for the purposes of lending the company money, many UK auditors have introduced an extra paragraph into their audit reports. Many previous legal cases on the subject had restricted the auditors' legal duty of care to the members of the company only, but the Bannerman decision (named after the auditors in the case, Bannerman Johnstone Maclay) called this into question. The wording of the paragraph is designed to restrict the auditor's duty of care.

The wording of a 'Bannerman' paragraph is as follows:

'This report is made solely to the company's members, as a body, in accordance with Section 495 and 496 of the Companies Act 2006. Our audit work has been undertaken so that we might state to the company's members those matters we are required to state to them in an auditor's report and for no other purpose. To the fullest extent permitted by law, we do not accept or assume responsibility to anyone other than the company and the company's members as a body for our audit work, for this report, or for the opinion we have formed.'

The APB did not include such a paragraph in their standard report example.

3.2.12 Combined Code requirements

For UK listed companies, auditors are required to review a corporate governance statement that the directors are required by the Combined Code to make in the annual report.

Such reports would therefore include a paragraph like the following in the 'scope' section of the report:

'We review whether the Corporate Governance Statement reflects the company's compliance with the nine provisions of the 2003 Combined Code specified for our review by the Listing Rules of the Financial Services Authority, and we regret if it does not. We are not required to consider whether the board's statements on internal control covers all risk's and controls, or form an opinion on the effectiveness of the group's corporate governance procedures or its risk and control procedures'.

4 Modified audit reports

Section overview

- The wording of an audit report may need to be **'modified'** in certain circumstances:
  - Where the auditor wishes to highlight an issue but where the audit opinion is **not** affected – an emphasis of matter paragraph (ie modification to the **report)**
  - Where there is an impact on the audit opinion (ie modification to the **opinion**)

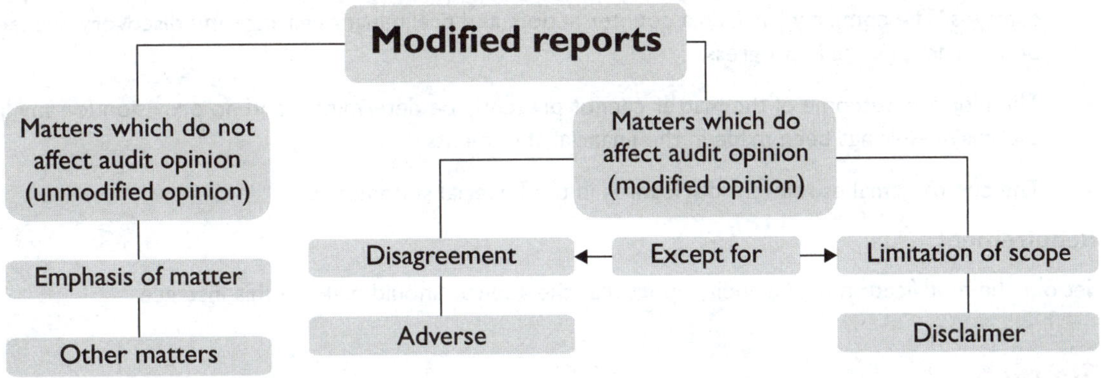

Figure 13.3: Overview: modified reports

APB Bulletin 2009/2 refers to all reports that are not unmodified as 'modified' even where the modification is an emphasis of matter paragraph, in which case the audit opinion itself is not affected. There are separate ISAs for matters in audit reports that **do not** modify the opinion (ISA 706) and those that do (ISA 705). The different terminology is unfortunately confusing; for your examination you need to be able to follow the logic of figure 13.3 above and consider the impact of scenarios given in a question on the form of the audit report and the type of audit opinion.

4.1 Emphasis of matter paragraphs and other matter paragraphs

The auditor should add an **'emphasis of matter' paragraph** to the audit report where the auditor considers it necessary to draw users' attention to a matter or matters **presented or disclosed in the financial statements** that are of such importance that they are fundamental to users' understanding of the financial statements.

The auditor should add an **'other matters' paragraph** to the audit report where the auditor considers it necessary to draw users' attention to any matter or matters other than those presented or disclosed in the financial statements that are relevant to users' understanding of the audit, the auditor's responsibilities or the auditor's report.

According to ISA 706 *Emphasis of Matter Paragraphs and Other Matter Paragraphs in the Independent Auditor's Report* the emphasis of matter paragraph should be included immediately after the opinion on the financial statements paragraph and shall:

- Use the heading 'Emphasis of Matter';
- Include a clear reference to the matter being emphasized and to where relevant disclosures can be found in the financial statements; and
- Indicate that the auditor's opinion is not modified in respect of the issue dealt with.

Similarly, an 'other matters paragraph' should be included immediately after the opinion of the financial statements paragraph and any Emphasis of Matter paragraph or elsewhere in the audit report if the content of the Other Matters paragraph is relevant to the Other Reporting Responsibilities section.

If the auditor expects to include and Emphasis of Matter or Other Matter paragraph in the audit report, the auditor shall communicate with those charged with governance regarding this expectation and the proposed wording of the paragraph.

Worked example: Modified report - unmodified opinion – emphasis of matter

A firm being audited is awaiting the outcome of a lawsuit and as a result it is not possible to quantify the effect this will have on the financial statements.

The details are as follows.

- The UK non-public company in question prepares UK GAAP financial statements.
- A lawsuit alleges that the company has infringed certain patent rights and claims royalties and punitive damages. The company has filed a counter action, and preliminary hearings and discovery proceedings on both actions are in progress.
- The ultimate outcome of the matter cannot presently be determined, and no provision for any liability that may result has been made in the financial statements.
- The company makes relevant disclosures in the financial statements.

Requirement

Set out the modification to the audit report that the auditor should make in this instance.

Solution

The auditor issues a modified auditor's **report**, ie with an emphasis of matter paragraph describing the situation giving rise to the emphasis of matter and its possible effects on the financial statements, including that the effect on the financial statements of the resolution of the uncertainty cannot be quantified. The audit **opinion** itself is an **unmodified opinion**.

In our opinion the financial statements:

- Give a true and fair view of the state of the company's affairs as at .... and of its profit (loss) for the year then ended;
- Have been properly prepared in accordance with United Kingdom Generally Accepted Accounting Practice; and
- Have been prepared in accordance with the requirements of the Companies Act 2006.

Emphasis of matter – possible outcome of a lawsuit

In the forming of our opinion on the financial statements, which is not qualified, we have considered the adequacy of the disclosures made in note x to the financial statements concerning the possible outcome of a lawsuit, alleging infringement of certain patent rights and claiming royalties and punitive damages, where the company is the defendant. The company has filed a counter action, and preliminary hearings and discovery proceedings on both actions are in progress. The ultimate outcome of the matter cannot presently be determined, and no provision for any liability that may result has been made in the financial statements.

Registered auditors *Address*

Date

4.2 Modification to the audit opinion

Circumstances that have an impact on the audit opinion are discussed in ISA 705 *Modifications to the Opinion in the Independent Auditor's Report.*

The auditor shall modify the opinion when:

(a) The auditor concludes that the financial statements as a whole are not free from material misstatement e.g.

Where there is a disagreement with management about:

(i) Accounting policies
(ii) Accounting treatment, or
(iii) Disclosure in the financial statements.

In these circumstances there are two possible outcomes:

(i) The disagreement may affect only a particular aspect of the financial statements rather than the financial statements as a whole – which will result in a 'qualified opinion' ('except for').

(ii) The disagreement with management may be so serious that the auditor concludes that the accounts do not show a true and fair view – an 'adverse opinion'.

(b) The auditor is unable to obtain sufficient appropriate audit evidence to conclude that the financial statements as a whole are free from material misstatements e.g. a limitation on the scope of the audit.

In these circumstances there are two possible outcomes:

(i) The limitation of scope may affect only a particular aspect of the financial statements rather than the financial statements as a whole – which will result in a 'qualified opinion' ('except for').

(ii) The limitation of scope may be so serious that the auditor is unable to form an opinion on the financial statements – a 'disclaimer of opinion'.

Worked example: Modified opinion – disagreement

An auditor is in disagreement with management regarding an accounting treatment. The details are as follows.

- The UK non-public traded company prepares UK GAAP financial statements.
- Included in the debtors shown on the balance sheet is an amount of £Y which is the subject of litigation and against which no provision has been made. The auditor considers that a full provision of £Y should have been made.

Requirement

Set out the opinion on the financial statements that the auditor should make in this instance.

Solution

Modified opinion on financial statements arising from disagreement about accounting treatment

Included in the debtors shown on the balance sheet is an amount of £Y due from a company which has ceased trading. XYZ Limited has no security for this debt. In our opinion the company is unlikely to receive any payment and full provision of £Y should have been made. Accordingly, debtors should be reduced by £Y, deferred tax liability should be reduced by £X and profit for the year and retained earnings should be reduced by £Z.

Except for the financial effect of not making the provision referred to in the preceding paragraph, in our opinion the financial statements:

- Give a true and fair view of the state of the company's affairs as at … and of its profit (loss) for the year then ended;
- Have been properly prepared in accordance with United Kingdom Generally Accepted Accounting Practice; and
- Have been prepared in accordance with the requirements of the Companies Act 2006.

Registered auditor *Address*

Date

Worked example: Modified opinion – limitation on scope

An auditor was unable to observe a stock count because they were not engaged by the company at the time the count took place. The details are as follows.

- The UK non-public traded company prepares UK GAAP financial statements (and therefore uses UK terminology).
- The evidence available to the auditor was limited because they did not observe the counting of the physical stock as at 31 December 20X1, since that date was prior to the time the auditor was initially engaged as auditor for the company. Owing to the nature of the company's records, the auditor was unable to satisfy themselves as to stock quantities by other audit procedures.

Requirement

Set out the audit opinion on financial statements that the auditor should make in this instance.

Solution

- The limitation in audit scope causes the auditor to issue a modified opinion – except for any adjustments that might have been found necessary had they been able to obtain sufficient evidence concerning stock.
- The limitation of scope was determined by the auditor not to be so material and pervasive as to require a disclaimer of opinion.

Modified opinion on financial statements arising from limitation in audit scope

With respect to stock having a carrying amount of £X the audit evidence available to us was limited because we did not observe the counting of the physical stock as at 31 December 20X1, since that date was prior to our appointment as auditor of the company. Owing to the nature of the company's records, we were unable to obtain sufficient appropriate audit evidence regarding the stock quantities by using other audit procedures.

Except for the financial effects of such adjustments, if any, as might have been determined to be necessary had we been able to satisfy ourselves as to stock quantities, in our opinion the financial statements:

- Give a true and fair view of the state of the company's affairs as at 31 December 20X1 and of its profit (loss) for the year then ended;
- Have been properly prepared in accordance with United Kingdom Generally Accepted Accounting Practice; and
- Have been prepared in accordance with the requirements of the Companies Act 2006.

Matters on which we are required to report by exception

In respect solely of the limitation on our work relating to stock, described above:

- We have not obtained all the information and explanations that we considered necessary for the purpose of the audit; and
- We were unable to determine whether adequate accounting records had been kept.

We have nothing to report in respect of the following matters where the Companies Act 2006 required us to report to you if, in our opinion;

- Returns adequate for our audit have not been received from branches not visited by us; or
- The financial statements are not in agreement with the accounting records and returns; or
- Certain disclosures of directors' remuneration specified by law are not made.

Registered auditors *Address*

Date

Worked example: Disclaimer of opinion

An auditor was unable to observe all physical stock and confirm trade debtors during an audit. The details are as follows.

- The UK non-public company prepares UK GAAP financial statements.
- The evidence available to the auditor was limited because the auditor was not able to observe all physical stock and confirm trade debtors due to limitations placed on the scope of the auditor's work by the directors of the company.

Requirement

Set out the opinion that the auditor should make in this instance.

Solution

The auditor has been unable to form a view on the financial statements and issues a modified opinion disclaiming the view given by the financial statements.

Opinion: disclaimer on view given by the financial statements

The audit evidence available to us was limited because we were unable to observe the counting of physical stock having a carrying amount of £X and send confirmation letters to trade debtors having a carrying amount of £Y due to limitations placed on the scope of our work by the directors of the company. As a result of this we have been unable to obtain sufficient appropriate audit evidence concerning both stock and trade debtors.

Because of the possible effect of the limitation in evidence available to us, we are unable to express an opinion as to whether the financial statements:

- Give a true and fair view of the state of the company's affairs at .... and of its profit (loss) for the year then ended;
- Have been properly prepared in accordance with United Kingdom Generally Accepted Accounting Practice; and
- Have been prepared in accordance with the requirements of the Companies Act 2006.

Matters on which we are required to report by exception

In respect solely of the limitation of our work referred to above:

- We have not obtained all the information and explanations that we considered necessary for the purpose of our audit; and
- We were unable to determine whether adequate accounting records have been kept.

We have nothing to report in respect of the following matters where the Companies Act 2006 requires us to report to you if, in our opinion:

- Returns adequate for our audit have not been received from branches not visited by us; or
- The financial statements are not in agreement with the accounting records and returns; or
- Certain disclosures of directors' remuneration specified by law are not made.

Registered auditors *Address*

Date

Worked example: Adverse opinion

A company being audited has made no provision for losses expected to arise on certain long-term contracts. The details are as follows.

- The UK non-publicly traded company prepares UK GAAP financial statements.
- No provision has been made for losses expected to arise on certain long-term contracts currently in progress, as the directors consider that such losses should be off-set against amounts recoverable on other long-term contracts.

Requirement

Set out the opinion that the auditor should make in this instance.

Solution

- In the auditor's opinion, provision should be made for foreseeable losses on individual contracts as required by (specify accounting standards).
- The auditor issues an adverse opinion due to the failure to provide losses and quantifies the impact on the profit for the year, the contract work in progress and deferred tax liability at the year end.

Adverse opinion on financial statements

As more fully explained in note x to the financial statements no provision has been made for losses expected to arise on certain long-term contracts currently in progress, as the directors consider that such losses should be off-set against amounts recoverable on other long-term contracts. In our opinion, provision should be made for foreseeable losses on individual contracts as required by (specify accounting standards). If losses had been so recognised the effect would have been to reduce the carrying amount of contract work in progress by £X, the deferred tax liability by £Y and the profit for the year and retained earnings at 31 December 20X1 by £Z.

In view of the effect of the failure to provide for the losses referred to above, in our opinion the financial statements

- Do not give a true and fair view of the state of the company's affairs as at 31 December 20X1 and of its profit (loss) for the year then ended; and
- Have not been properly prepared in accordance with United Kingdom Generally Accepted Accounting Practice.

In all other respects, in our opinion the financial statements have been prepared in accordance with the requirements of the Companies Act 2006.

Registered auditors *Address*

Date

4.3 Emphasis of matter or limitation on scope?

An emphasis of matter paragraph is used when there is a degree of uncertainty surrounding the financial statements – often to do with going concern, but possibly other significant uncertainties which have been disclosed in the financial statements. Limitation on scope arises when evidence that can reasonably be expected to be available is not available, for example:

- Appointment after the year end may mean that the inventory check may not have been attended
- The values in the accounts of an overseas subsidiary subject to an oppressive or economically unstable regime may be difficult to ascertain with sufficient reliability

4.4 Modified opinions – a summary

The available forms of **modification** to the **audit opinion** may be summarised by the following table:

	Auditor's Judgement about the Pervasiveness of the Effects or Possible Effects on the Financial Statements	
Nature of Matter Giving Rise to the Modification	**Material but Not Pervasive**	**Material and Pervasive**
Financial statements are materially misstated	Qualified opinion ('Except for')	Adverse opinion
Inability to obtain sufficient appropriate audit evidence	Qualified opinion ('Except for')	Disclaimer of opinion

Remember, that if an error or a lack of evidence is immaterial the audit opinion will not be modified at all.

Interactive question 2: Audit report [Difficulty level: Exam standard]

You are the auditor of Purity Ltd, a manufacturer of water filters for domestic use. The company headquarters are in Wapping but it also has ten regional branches to organise the sales effort in each geographical area.

Head office issued instructions for all inventories to be counted at the year end. However, due to an administrative error, the new branch in Newcastle did not receive any instructions and no physical inventory count took place. The inventories were material, estimated at £50,000 and included in the financial statements. No alternative procedures could be applied.

(a) How will your auditor's opinion be modified?

(b) What additional statement(s), if any, will need to be made in the UK audit report?

See **Answer** at the end of this chapter.

Interactive question 3: Modified audit report [Difficulty level: Exam standard]

An auditor is considering possible modification of his audit report on the financial statements of three separate companies.

(1) Watkins Ltd is being sued by a customer for material damages. Legal opinion is divided as to the outcome of the case, and all relevant information has been included in the notes.

(2) Pope Ltd suffered a flood at its head office and a significant number of accounting records have been destroyed.

(3) Tilden Ltd has included a provision of £100,000 for doubtful debts in the year end accounts. Obviously the provision cannot be estimated with complete accuracy but the reporting partner believes it should be materially higher.

Recommend, giving reasons, whether the opinion should be modified in each case.

See **Answer** at the end of this chapter.

Summary and Self-test

Summary

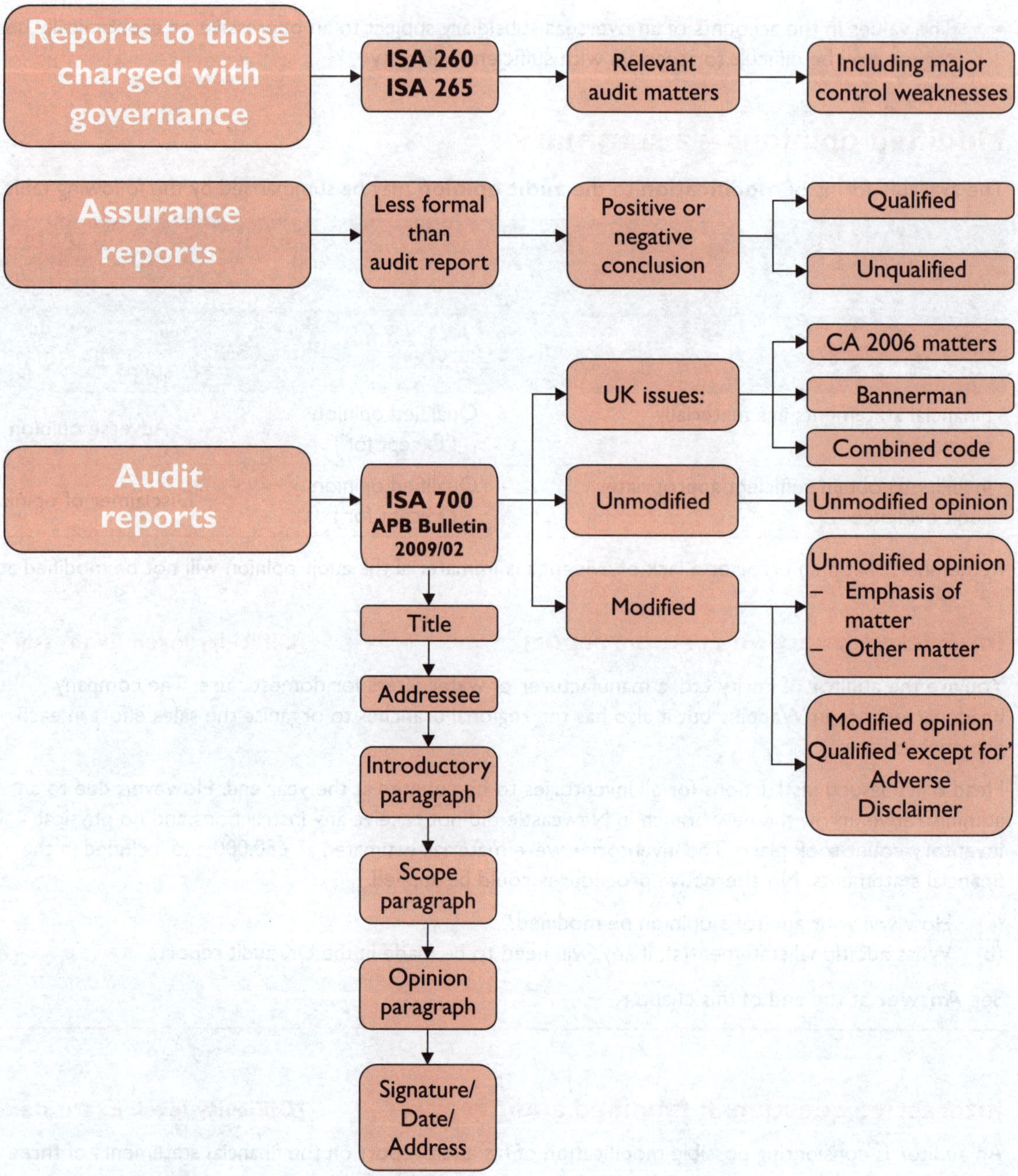

Self-test

Answer the following questions.

1 A report to those charged with governance should be in writing.

☐ True

☐ False

2 Which of the following might be included in a report to those charged with governance?

☐ The audit approach

☐ Audit adjustments

☐ The audit opinion

☐ Material control weaknesses

3 What is negative assurance?

4 When would a practitioner not give any assurance in a review engagement?

5 What three opinions are stated in a UK unmodified audit report?

1 ....

2 ....

3 ....

6 What three things does the scope paragraph include?

1 ....

2 ....

3 ....

7 What is a 'Bannerman' paragraph?

8 In what two situations should an audit opinion be modified?

1 ....

2 ....

Exam-style questions

9 Delta Ltd's sales invoices are produced by its computer system using the relevant price held as standing data on the sales master file. Selling prices are updated by the sales ledger clerk on the verbal authority of the sales director.

Requirement

Draft extracts, suitable for inclusion in the auditor's management letter, which set out the possible consequences, and the recommendations that you would make, in respect of the matters outlined above.

(4 marks)

10 You are the auditor of Mota Ltd, a distributor of automotive components, and have been provided with the following description of the sales order processing system.

Order entry

Sales orders are taken over the telephone and entered into the computer by a sales order clerk, via a terminal in the sales office, while the customer is on the line. On entry the order details are read back to the customer for confirmation. The computer checks that there are sufficient inventories to meet the order and that the customer's credit limit is not exceeded.

If the goods are unavailable, the customer is asked if he wants the order to be recorded as a 'back order' which will be fulfilled when there is sufficient inventory. Once accepted, the order is automatically given an order number which is relayed to the customer.

Orders which take a customer over his credit limit are referred to the credit controller who decides, in consultation with the chief accountant, whether or not the customer should be allowed to exceed the credit limit or have the credit limit raised. Any adjustments in respect of overrides of, or increases in, credit limits are input, via a terminal in the accounts department, by the credit controller. Printouts of these amendments are not generated and no other review of credit limits is undertaken.

New customers are referred to the credit controller who obtains credit ratings and references and, on the oral authority of the chief accountant, enters the customer account details onto the sales ledger master file via a terminal in the accounts department.

Despatch of goods

Sequentially-numbered packing notes in respect of accepted orders are printed out in the warehouse, and the goods are selected, packed and checked by warehouse staff. Confirmations of packing and any notifications of shortfalls are entered into the computer, via a terminal in the warehouse, by the warehouse supervisor. Two copies of the sequentially-numbered delivery advice are printed in the warehouse and sent with the goods to the customer who is required to sign a copy which is returned by the driver to the accounts department. All despatches are checked at the gatehouse to ensure that they are accompanied by the appropriate documentation. The packing notes are filed in numerical order in the warehouse and the sequence is checked for completeness, on a daily basis, by the warehouse supervisor.

The system does not automatically generate purchase orders with manufacturers when a customer's order cannot be fulfilled.

Computer system

All users of the system are required to log on using identification codes and individual passwords which control their level of access to the system. All passwords are changed every 90 days and when employees leave. Systems support is provided by a supplier where the service agreement provides for availability of a back-up system within 72 hours of a systems failure.

Requirements

(a) Identify the objectives of exercising internal controls over sales order processing. For each objective discuss the extent to which the procedures exercised by Mota Ltd achieve the objective.

Note: You are **not** required to consider sales invoicing or ledger processing. **(8 marks)**

(b) Set out, in a manner suitable for inclusion in a report to management, any weaknesses in the system described above. For each weakness you should include the possible consequence of the weakness and a recommendation to remedy the weakness.

Note: You are **not** required to write a covering letter. **(10 marks)**

(18 marks)

11 You attempted parts (a) and some of (b) of this sample paper question in Chapter 7. Now try the rest of part (b) about the reporting implications.

Described below are situations which have arisen in three audit clients of your firm. The year end in each case is 31 March 20X6.

Jay plc ('Jay')

The directors have included the following note to the financial statements for the year ended 31 March 20X6:

'Although the company has incurred significant trading losses and cash outflows during the last two years, the directors believe that the effects of internal restructuring and corporate disposals undertaken will bring about improved results as indicated in the detailed profit and cash flow forecasts for the period to the end of March 20X7. These forecasts indicate that the company will be able to trade within its agreed working capital facility for at least the next 12 months from the date of this report. Considerable progress has been made on the financial restructuring of the company.

On the basis of the above factors the directors consider it is appropriate that the financial statements are prepared on the going concern basis. Should the company fail to meet its forecasts, the going concern basis may prove to be inappropriate. In such circumstances adjustments are likely to have to be made to the net assets shown in these financial statements to reduce assets to their recoverable amounts, to reclassify non-current assets and payables due after more than one year to current assets and current liabilities and to provide for further liabilities that may arise.'

Finch plc ('Finch')

Finch has included the results of Wren Ltd ('Wren'), a subsidiary, in the consolidated financial statements. Wren is audited by a different firm of auditors who have modified their opinion on Wren's financial statements for the year ended 31 March 20X6 because a fire at the company's premises destroyed the physical inventory count sheets which were the only record of the year end inventory. Wren has included inventory at its estimated cost of £500,000 in the financial statements for the year ended 31 March 20X6.

The consolidated pre-tax profit of Finch is £33.4 million and the pre-tax profit of Wren is £1.2 million for the year ended 31 March 20X6.

Sparrow Ltd ('Sparrow')

On 30 April 2006, the board of directors decided to undertake a restructuring programme which would commence in June 20X6. A provision of £1.8 million in respect of the restructuring costs has been included in the financial statements for the year ended 31 March 20X6.

The pre-tax profit of Sparrow for the year ended 31 March 20X6 is £7.2 million.

Requirements

(a) Discuss what is meant by the concepts of materiality and a true and fair view. **(6 marks)**

(b) Explain why there can be difficulties for auditors regarding materiality and true and fair in relation to the three cases above: Jay, Finch and Sparrow, and state how you might modify your audit report in each case. **(14 marks)**

(20 marks)

12 Described below are three situations which have arisen in three audits. The year end in each case is 31 March 20X8.

(1) Ash Ltd uses leased motor vehicles which have been accounted for as operating leases. However, you believe that these leases are finance leases and should have been capitalised at £51,000. The current treatment does not comply with accounting standards which require finance leases, where the user takes on the risks and rewards of ownership, to be included within non-current assets and capitalised. Profit for the year would then have been reduced by £4,000.

The pre-tax profits of Ash Ltd for the year ended 31 March 20X8 were £600,000, and total assets at 31 March 20X8 were £5.4 million.

(2) A fire in the warehouse of Oak Ltd in April 20X8 destroyed the inventory sheets, which were the only record of the company's inventories at the year end. The company has included an estimated inventory figure of £780,000.

The pre-tax profits of Oak Ltd for the year ended 31 March 20X8 were £1.1 million and total assets at 31 March 20X8 were £6.5 million.

(3) Elm Ltd has included a note in the financial statements explaining that 90% of its revenue is derived from a national retailer with whom it has a three-year renewable contract. This contract is due for renewal in September 20X8. However, the directors require the audit report on the financial statements to be signed on 31 May 20X8.

Requirements

(a) Critically evaluate the use of standardised audit reports. **(5 marks)**

(b) Discuss briefly each of the situations outlined above, referring to materiality considerations. For each situation describe the effect on the audit report. **(10 marks)**

(15 marks)

Now, go back to the Learning Objectives in the Introduction. If you are satisfied that you have achieved these objectives, please tick them off.

Technical reference

1 Reporting to those charged with governance	**ISA 260 and 265**
• Relevant persons	**ISA 260**
• Relevant matters	**ISA 260**
• How?	**ISA 260**
2 Unmodified audit reports	**ISA 700**
	APB Bulletin 2009/2
3 Modified audit reports	**ISA 705 and 706**
	APB Bulletin 2009/2

Answers to Interactive questions

Answer to Interactive question 1

(a) Weakness	(b) Risks arising	(c) Action to mitigate
There has been a breakdown of controls over expenditure.	That IT expenditure is uncontrolled and investment is not always clearly for the benefit of the company.	Purchasing department to be warned that no IT expenditure should be incurred without authorisation; otherwise disciplinary action could result.
Excessive amounts are being spent on IT, adversely affecting profit.	IT expenditure is not planned properly, which means that investment may not be as beneficial as it should be.	IT expenditure must only be undertaken under the budget, unless authorised by two directors. Also, if additional investment is required the budget should be flexed.
Travelling expenses in some cases are excessive, with £25,000 being spent in excess of set limits.	Loss of profits due to excessive expenditure.	Travelling expenses should not be reimbursed when limits are exceeded, unless the prior consent of two directors has been received. The executives involved need to be informed of the problem.
Work-in-progress is not always being billed on a timely basis. This is to the extent that £56,000 has been held for more than six months.	Items involved are not being billed. This has an adverse effect on cash flow, and eventual recovery may be difficult.	Monthly billing meetings should be held at director level and within teams, where they should be told that any amounts more than two months' old must be billed.
The authorisation controls on overtime are not being exercised. This has resulted in the company paying £180,000 of excess overtime. Some may be genuine, but controls will reduce this amount.	Excessive costs, adversely affecting profits.	Overtime over one hour per week should be authorised prior to the work being undertaken, and should then be authorised once the timesheet is submitted.
There is no control over non-chargeable time. This leads to a variable amount of non-chargeable time by executives. This varies from 5% to 34%.	With some staff, an excessive amount of the time that they are spending at work is not being charged to clients, thus having an adverse effect on turnover, and hence profits.	Individual staff to be set targets for non-chargeable time, depending on their other responsibilities. Adherence to their targets must be monitored.

Answer to Interactive question 2

(a) 'Except for' limitation of scope because

- (i) Matter is material but not so pervasive
- (ii) Scope of the audit has been limited

(b) (i) State all information and explanations not received

(ii) State proper accounting records have not been kept

Answer to Interactive question 3

Recommended opinion	Reasons
(1) Unmodified opinion but modified audit report by an emphasis of matter paragraph regarding the legal case if considered significant	• Significant uncertainty, properly disclosed, does not require a modification
(2) Modified opinion – probably disclaimer	• Loss of records results in limitation of scope • 'Significant number' implies that auditors will probably be unable to form an opinion
(3) Modified opinion – disagreement 'except for'	• Audit partner disagrees with size of provision necessary • Problem limited to one area – unlikely to require adverse opinion

Answers to Self-test

1 True

2 Approach, adjustments, material control weaknesses. Although any expected modification to the audit opinion might be noted, the full audit opinion would not be given.

3 Assurance of a matter in the absence of any evidence to the contrary

4 When there was a pervasive limitation in the scope of the review or where the practitioner is of the opinion that the report being reviewed is incorrect.

5 The financial statements:

   1 Give a true and fair view
   2 Have been properly prepared in accordance with UK GAAP
   3 Have been prepared in accordance with CA 2006

6 1 A reference to appropriate accounting policies
   2 A reasonable assurance statement
   3 A summary of the nature of audit work

7 A statement limiting the liability of the auditors to the company and its members.

8 1 There has been a limitation on the auditors' work
   2 There is a disagreement with management about an item in the financial statements

Exam-style questions

9 **Consequences**

Incorrect prices resulting in undercharging of customers and loss to company or overcharging of customers and loss of customer goodwill.

Recommendations

- All price changes to be recorded on standard documentation which should be signed as authorised by sales director
- Printout of amendments obtained and checked to document authorising amendment
- Printout signed as evidence of checking
- Periodic printout of all selling prices checked on one for one basis to authorised price list held by sales director
- Standing data protected by high level password not known to sales ledger clerk
- Spot checks on invoices prior to despatch

10 (a) **Internal controls over sales order processing**

Objectives	Extent to which achieved by Mota Ltd's procedures
• To ensure that goods are available for all orders accepted.	• The availability of inventories is checked on the computer system while the customer is on the line. • This will be effective only where the system is continuously updated for new orders and deliveries of inventories.
• To ensure that existing customers are within their credit limits (including the current order being taken).	• The computer system automatically checks that the customer is within his current credit limit. • Adjustments to credit limits are carried out by the credit controller but no review of any amendments is carried out.

CHAPTER 13

Objectives	Extent to which achieved by Mota Ltd's procedures
• To ensure that new customers are creditworthy before orders are despatched.	• The credit controller carries out credit checks but details are amended on the terminal in the accounts department only after oral authority from the chief accountant, and no subsequent review of new customers is performed.
• To ensure that changes to credit limits are valid.	• As above.
• To ensure that the correct goods are despatched to each customer.	• Order details are read back to the customer to confirm their accuracy. • Packing notes are produced in the warehouse giving the details of the order. However, there is no responsibility assigned in respect of dealing with shortfalls of inventories and ensuring that the customer ultimately receives all of the goods ordered.
• To ensure that goods are despatched for all orders accepted.	• Packing notes are sequentially numbered and a completeness check is carried out on a daily basis.
• To ensure that all goods leaving the premises are in respect of valid orders	• All goods leaving the warehouse are checked at the gatehouse to ensure that they are accompanied by a valid delivery advice.
• To ensure that back orders are fulfilled when inventories become available.	• There are no procedures in place to ensure that, once goods are received by Mota Ltd, back orders are fulfilled.

(b) **Points for inclusion in a report to management**

Weakness	Consequence	Recommendation
• There is no review of amendments to credit limits once these have been processed on the system.	• Invalid amendments could be made, leading to supply of goods to non-creditworthy customers.	• An exception report should be produced on a weekly basis detailing all changes made to credit limits. This should be reviewed by the chief accountant, and evidenced by his signature, to ensure that all amendments are for valid business reasons.
• Authority to enter new customers onto the system is only given orally with no review of the credit ratings and references obtained.	• Invalid entries of new customers could be made without detection until non-payment of invoices arises.	• The chief accountant should review the credit ratings and references obtained before giving authority to accept the new customer.
• There is no responsibility assigned for dealing with shortfalls in orders when they are being selected in the warehouse.	• Delivery of part-complete orders and non-delivery of parts of orders will lead to loss of customer goodwill and subsequent loss of revenue.	• A daily printout of unprocessed orders should be produced and followed up by the warehouse supervisor.

Weakness	Consequence	Recommendation
• There are no procedures to ensure that back orders are fulfilled when the goods become available.	• Delay in fulfilling customer orders will again lead to loss of customer goodwill.	• The system should produce a daily list of items that have come into inventory for which there are current back orders. The sales ledger clerk should contact the customer to ensure that the goods are still required and then process the order in the normal manner.
• When back orders are accepted the goods which are unavailable are not immediately reordered.	• There may be significant delays in fulfilling these orders.	• The computer should automatically generate purchase requisitions on a daily basis for items which have been requested but are unavailable. A supervisor should review these purchase requisitions and raise a purchase order where the goods have not already been ordered.

Tutorial note

In (b) marks were also awarded for identification of the following.

- Credit control procedures do not take the age of the debt into consideration; this could result in goods being despatched to slow payers.
- In respect of the failure to review credit limits on a regular basis, limits may be unrealistically low for customers with a good payment history, resulting in loss of business.
- Response time in respect of systems support is too slow; this could result in delayed and lost orders.

11 Report modifications

Part of (b) only – the remainder of the answer was given in Chapter 7.

Jay

If the financial statements are prepared on the going concern basis, and the auditor agrees with this, then an unmodified audit opinion will be issued but the auditor would include an emphasis of matter paragraph to bring this fact to the attention of the members.

If the financial statements are prepared on the break-up basis, and the auditor agrees with this, then an unmodified audit opinion will be issued but the auditor would include an emphasis of matter paragraph to draw the fact that the company is not a going concern to the attention of the shareholders.

If the auditor does not agree with the basis used to prepare the accounts, eg going concern used when break-up is required, then the audit opinion will be modified, normally due to a disagreement.

Finch

If not material by nature, the audit report on the consolidated financial statements will be unmodified. If material by nature then the audit opinion will be modified (except for) on the grounds of limitation on scope. This would require modifications to the basis of opinion section and the opinion section of the audit report. It would also require the auditor to report by exception on accounting records and the availability of information.

Sparrow

As the disagreement over the accounting treatment has a material impact on the financial statements, the audit opinion will be an 'except for' modification.

12 (a) **Use of standardised audit reports**

Advantages

(i) The standard acts as a quality control mechanism, ie all audit reports contain the same level of information for the shareholders.

(ii) It enhances clarity and understanding as it is produced on a consistent basis. Shareholders know what the various forms of the audit report indicate and particularly with modified audit opinions can identify the problems immediately.

(iii) For the auditor it makes preparation easier. The auditor knows that he is satisfying his legal and professional responsibilities on the signing of this report.

Disadvantages

(i) There is a danger that readers and users of accounts become over-familiar with the report and feel that as it is not tailored to their company it is not relevant to them.

(ii) It could be seen as inflexible. There are certain situations where the audit report would provide a useful vehicle by which to pass on information to the shareholders but normally would not be used in this way, eg problem of illegal loans to directors.

(iii) It does include a certain amount of technical jargon but does not allow for the auditor to explain or expand on these terms if he feels it would be of benefit to the user. This could be particularly relevant when dealing with smaller organisations.

Conclusion

While there are arguments for and against the use of standard audit reports on balance the advantages would seem to have more weight than the disadvantages, in particular the quality control aspect which ISA 700 imposes.

(b) **Three situations**

(1) **Ash Ltd**

The accounting treatment adopted by the company does not agree with the relevant accounting standard. This should be discussed with management who should be requested to comply with the accounting standard. If they refuse to do so this should be referred to in the report to management.

Materiality

The adjustment represents 0.67% of profit and 0.94% of total assets. Based on this information it does not appear to be material to the accounts in isolation. However, the impact on liabilities and net assets should also be considered.

Impact on audit report

As the adjustment is not material, even if the directors refuse to adopt accounting standard treatment the audit opinion would be unmodified, stating that the accounts give a true and fair view.

(2) **Oak Ltd**

The issue here is one of a limitation of scope. Due to the loss of the physical inventory count records the auditor will not be able to perform normal audit procedures in this area.

The auditor will need to establish the basis for the estimated figure, eg book inventory records to determine whether it will provide a reasonable assessment of the year end balance.

Materiality

The inventory balance itself is clearly material to the accounts as it represents 70% of profit and 12% of total assets. However, in this instance the real issue is the extent to which the inventory balance quoted is incorrect. As the limitation in scope leads to uncertainty, it is not possible to quantify exactly the size of any adjustment. By its nature, however, inventory is a significant balance in the accounts and is therefore likely to be material.

Impact on audit report

Assuming that the limitation of scope is material but not so material or pervasive (as the problem is isolated to one balance in the accounts) the audit report would be affected as follows.

(i) It would refer to the fact that the audit work could not be performed fully in accordance with auditing standards.

(ii) It would state that we planned our audit so as to obtain all information necessary but the reference to performance would be dropped.

(iii) A description of the limitation would be given, ie physical inventory records destroyed including an estimate of the effect.

(iv) The opinion would be modified using the 'except for ... might' opinion.

Tutorial note

In the UK the report would also refer to the implied opinions as proper accounting records have not been maintained and all information and explanations have not been received.

(3) **Elm Ltd**

There is a significant uncertainty at the year end in respect of whether or not the company is a going concern. This is dependent upon the renewal of a contract which is significant to the viability of the company. The auditor needs to establish the likelihood of renewal. If the company is not a going concern the accounts should be prepared on a break-up basis.

Materiality

No information has been provided to quantify the adjustments necessary to prepare the accounts on a break-up basis but these are likely to be material.

Impact on audit report

Assuming the accounts are prepared on a going concern basis

(i) Provided that the auditor is satisfied that this treatment is appropriate and that disclosure of the situation is sufficient, an unmodified audit opinion will be issued. Reference to the significant uncertainty would be made by modifying the audit report using an 'emphasis of matter' paragraph, together with a statement that the opinion itself is not modified.

(ii) If the auditor disagrees with the treatment adopted (ie if he feels that it is unlikely that the contract will be renewed) or the level of disclosure is inadequate, the opinion will be modified on the grounds of disagreement.

(iii) Normally the matter is of such significance that an adverse opinion is issued (ie the accounts do not give a true and fair view).

If the accounts are prepared on a break-up basis

Provided the auditor agrees with this treatment and that the basis of preparation is fully disclosed, an unmodified audit opinion will be issued.

In this instance the most likely outcome would be modified report with reference to the significant uncertainty but an unmodified audit opinion.

Tutorial note

One other disadvantage which could have been mentioned in part (a) is that the technical distinction between different types of modifications may not be appreciated by users.

INDEX

H

I

L

REVIEW FORM – AUDIT AND ASSURANCE STUDY MANUAL

Your ratings, comments and suggestions would be appreciated on the following areas of this Study Manual.

	Very useful	Useful	Not useful
Chapter Introductions	☐	☐	☐
Examination context	☐	☐	☐
Worked examples	☐	☐	☐
Interactive questions	☐	☐	☐
Quality of explanations	☐	☐	☐
Technical references (where relevant)	☐	☐	☐
Self-test questions	☐	☐	☐
Self-test answers	☐	☐	☐
Index	☐	☐	☐

	Excellent	Good	Adequate	Poor
Overall opinion of this Study Manual	☐	☐	☐	☐

Please add further comments below:

Please return to:

The Learning Team
Learning and Professional Department
ICAEW
Metropolitan House
321 Avebury Boulevard
Milton Keynes
MK9 2FZ
ACAFeedback@icaew.com
www.icaew.com